The Definitive Guide to Catalyst

Writing Extensible, Scalable, and Maintainable Perl-Based Web Applications

■ ■ ■

Kieren Diment and Matt S Trout with
Eden Cardim, Jay Kuri, and Jess Robinson

Apress®

Lead Editor: Duncan Parkes
Technical Reviewer: Jacinta Richardson
Editorial Board: Clay Andres, Steve Anglin, Mark Beckner, Ewan Buckingham, Tony Campbell,
    Gary Cornell, Jonathan Gennick, Michelle Lowman, Matthew Moodie, Jeffrey Pepper, Frank Pohlmann,
    Ben Renow-Clarke, Dominic Shakeshaft, Matt Wade, Tom Welsh
Project Manager: Denise Santoro Lincoln
Copy Editor: Nicole Flores
Associate Production Director: Kari Brooks-Copony
Production Editor: Kelly Winquist
Compositor: Patrick Cunningham
Proofreader: April Eddy
Indexer: Carol Burbo
Artist: April Milne
Cover Designer: Kurt Krames
Manufacturing Director: Tom Debolski

Distributed to the book trade worldwide by Springer-Verlag New York, Inc., 233 Spring Street, 6th Floor, New York, NY 10013. Phone 1-800-SPRINGER, fax 201-348-4505, e-mail orders-ny@springer-sbm.com, or visit http://www.springeronline.com.

For information on translations, please e-mail info@apress.com, or visit http://www.apress.com.

Apress and friends of ED books may be purchased in bulk for academic, corporate, or promotional use. eBook versions and licenses are also available for most titles. For more information, reference our Special Bulk Sales–eBook Licensing web page at http://www.apress.com/info/bulksales.

The source code for this book is available to readers at http://www.apress.com.

For Lorna, Freya, and Hunter

Contents at a Glance

Contents

Foreword

I have been with the Catalyst framework team since the beginning. We have come a long way from our beginnings as a few guys in an IRC channel trying to hack together a better way to write web applications. Catalyst is now powering multi-million-dollar sites all over the world. It has a thriving community of developers, with thousands of people communicating via mailing lists and IRC.

That is why I'm so excited about the book you're now holding. This book gives unique insights into the process of developing web applications with cutting-edge Perl. It covers the newly released 5.8 series of Catalyst and the surrounding technologies like Moose, DBIx::Class, and Template Toolkit.

Why Catalyst?

Why do I believe Catalyst is the best way to develop web applications? I have worked with a number of other technologies over the years, ranging from the Netscape LiveWire platform early on, to Microsoft IIS, Java servlets and JSP, PHP, and, more recently, Ruby on Rails. They all provide various advantages, but for straight-out flexibility and speed of development and deployment, Catalyst is unmatched, for reasons I'll describe in the sections that follow.

Catalyst Is Flexibility

There are a couple of different reasons for this, one of which is Catalyst's supreme dispatcher. With it, you can compose any URL scheme you need to create a tight and professional web application. Catalyst also grants you flexibility in deployment, with the ability to seamlessly integrate a wide range of modern web servers and deployment configurations.

Catalyst Is CPAN

CPAN, the Comprehensive Perl Archive Network, is my number one reason for coding Perl. There is nothing quite like it elsewhere in the programming world. As I write, there are 69,096 modules distributed over 17,901 distributions made by 7,474 uploaders. Basically, if you are trying to solve a problem, there is probably a module for it on CPAN. This is why one of the Catalyst team's most important design decisions early on was to allow Catalyst to work with all of that. There are 1,526 different modules in the Catalyst and CatalystX namespaces. Most of it is code to glue Catalyst to the rest of CPAN.

Catalyst Is Community

But most of all, to me Catalyst is home. Over the years, I have gotten to know most of the active people in the Catalyst community, and I am in awe of their dedication in working to improve this framework. I believe this is Catalyst's biggest strength compared to the other Perl frameworks.

Myriad contributors are working on various aspects of the framework, from writing better tutorials and documentation, to helping newbies to get a flying start on IRC, to writing tests for edge cases in the chained dispatcher.

Perl Renaissance

At the time I started getting serious with Perl, there was a slump in popularity of the Perl language. Perl 5 was already 10 years old, and progress on Perl 6 seemed to have stalled. Many people were calling the language dead. However, a wonderful thing has happened in the last few years.

The stability of the Perl 5 platform has allowed an unparalleled level of flexibility in extending and altering the language itself. Modern object-oriented Perl hardly resembles the code people remember from the CGI scripts of the first Perl 5 surge. Thanks to Moose, Perl has an object system with flexibility only found in experimental researcher languages. Things like roles and full-featured introspection have completely changed how we write Perl applications.

This is why it was important to move Catalyst to the Moose framework. While there is still much scope for Catalyst to make even better use of Moose, the techniques you will learn in this book will be valid for a long time to come. We believe in stability and giving you the freedom to write awesome new applications, rather than spending your time rewriting your existing sites every time a new version of the framework is released.

Modern Perl

Lately there has been a flurry of activity in defining the face of modern Perl 5. The new Enlightened Perl Organisation (http://www.enlightenedperl.org/) was founded to support Perl development efforts that ensure Perl's future as an enterprise-grade development platform. Among other things, the organization has a working group to define a modern extended core of Perl modules, and it puts on the Iron Man Blogging Challenge.

There is also a modern Perl book under development and several other efforts like http://catalyzed.org/, a site dedicated to modern Perl as well as Catalyst development.

Reinventing Perl with Perl

The latest trend in this ecosystem has been reinventing Perl using Perl. Driven by underlying technologies like Devel::Declare and Variable::Magic, efforts like MooseX::Declare, which defines a new class syntax for Moose; MooseX::Lexical::Types, which is a new way to define typed variables; and TryCatch, a comprehensive exception mechanism, actually add new first-class keywords to the language. Much of this work has been inspired by the ongoing Perl 6 project.

The Future of Catalyst

I want to conclude this foreword with some thoughts on the future of Catalyst. In a large eco-system like Catalyst, developers require stability and predictability. There are a lot of add-ons that depend on the core runtime, and we have tried to keep these things as unchanged from 5.7 to 5.8 as possible. We remain dedicated to supporting this interface for the entire 5.8 Catalyst series. To put things into perspective, the 5.7 series lasted from July 7, 2006, to April 18, 2009. It's a natural progression that most of the exciting new developments happen in the edge of the dependency graph.

Still, there is a parallel run to develop the next major iteration of the framework. This effort is planned to be released under the Catalyst6 namespace, and it will likely target a lot of Perl 6 features implemented using Moose and Declare techniques on the Perl 5 platform. Much of this work is still in progress, and we're going to be taking our time with it to get it right. Even though things happen faster in the electronic world, this book is going to remain relevant for a long time to come.

Marcus Ramberg
Catalyst Release Manager
http://marcus.nordaaker.com/

About the Authors

KIEREN DIMENT is a social researcher currently doing research in health informatics in the School of Information Systems and Information Technology at the University of Wollongong, New South Wales, Australia. He was initially exposed to Unix in an artificial intelligence lab in 1994, where he learned emacs, shell, and a little bit about this thing called the World Wide Web that seemed to be catching on. He spent the next eight years ignoring computers, working in psychiatric and neurological rehabilitation instead. After reading Neal Stephenson's *Cryptonomicon* sometime in the early twenty-first century, he realized how much he enjoyed messing around with computers, and it was a short step from installing Linux on an old laptop to learning Perl. He now uses Perl every opportunity he gets in his work, mainly for doing clever things with research data. He uses Catalyst mainly for showing this off. However, seeing as web development is a small (but important) part of his work, he's had to take an interest in the documentation so that he can remember how it works—less RTFM than WTFM.

When not working, he can be found bushwalking or at the beach, where he surfs far too infrequently. A few times a year, he rides a nine-foot longboard and is goofy-footed. When the waves are heavy, or he is with his family (much more often), he bodysurfs instead.

MATT S TROUT was thrust into Perl at the tender age of 17 by a backup accident and has been happily using it for systems automation, network, web, and database development ever since. He is the second longest standing member of the Catalyst core team, the founder of the DBIx::Class ORM project, a Moose advocate since the early days of the object system, and a PAUSE administrator with a focus on helping find new maintainers for abandoned CPAN modules. Occasionally he finds time to write other CPAN modules and then inflict their maintenance on other members of the community, such as Devel::REPL, the interactive Perl shell, and Devel::Declare, the syntax extension system underlying MooseX::Declare and Method::Signatures::Simple.

Matt runs the technical team at Shadowcat Systems Limited, an open source consultancy specializing in helping clients with design, development, and deployment of Catalyst and DBIx::Class-based applications.

When occasionally not in front of his computer, he can be found playing Dungeons & Dragons, producing a blur of hair on the dance floor at goth and metal clubs, or lurking in the corner of a pub consuming copious quantities of real ale.

▪**EDEN CARDIM** has a Bachelor of Science degree in computer science and has developed in Perl since 1998. Experience with Perl applied to bioinformatics and web development has led to involvement in CPAN open source projects, Reaction as a core developer, and Catalyst, DBIx::Class, and Moose as a contributor.

▪**JAY KURI** has been working with application development and Internet systems architecture since 1994. In the 15 years since, he has worked on software for everything from portable e-book readers to 800-machine web clusters. In 2004 he founded Ionzero (http://www.ionzero.com), a software development firm dedicated to producing the best, most secure, and most maintainable software possible for its clients. Through Ionzero, Jay also stays active in the computing community in the form of contributions to open source software and community building, including the Perl and Catalyst website http://catalyzed.org/.

When Jay has free time, he enjoys spending it with his lovely (and patient) wife, Rebecca, and son, Justin. He also enjoys the occasional motorcycle trip as well as the outlet of non-code-related creativity in the form of woodworking and sketching.

▪**JESS ROBINSON** learned Perl in 2000 for personal entertainment. She likes databases for some reason and now successfully combines those two interests as the lead documentor on the DBIx::Class project. She helps out in both #catalyst and #dbix-class supporting users, and she occasionally writes her own Catalyst applications.

About the Technical Reviewer

**JACINTA RICHARDSON**, BE(Hons), BSc, is both the training coordinator of Perl Training Australia and a senior trainer. She has more than 10 years of commercial Perl and teaching experience. Jacinta is a qualified software engineer, specializing in course development, requirements analysis, and client liaison.

Jacinta is a prominent figure in the Perl community. She has been involved in organizing many community conferences including linux. conf.au 2008, the Open Source Developers' Conference (2004–2008), and the Australian System Administration Conference (2008–2009), many of which she has also presented at. Jacinta participates in a wide range of national and international computer-related user groups and regularly gives talks at Perl Monger and other meetings on her travels. One of her big passions is promoting women in IT. For her work in the Perl community, Jacinta was awarded the prestigious White Camel Award in 2008.

When away from the computer, Jacinta enjoys scuba diving, cycling, and baking.

Acknowledgments

This book was a team effort, and we're especially grateful to Jess Robinson (Chapter 6), Jay Kuri (Chapter 8), and Eden Caram and Robert "Phaylon" Seladek (both Chapter 12) for agreeing to write and do an initial review of a chapter each. Special thanks to Florian Ragwitz, who provided Kieren with much of the code in the latter part of Chapter 10 and the Mason code in Chapter 11.

Invaluable support and advice were obtained from a number of people within the Catalyst community, only some of whom are mentioned here. Apologies if I have forgotten your name in this list. Thanks to Jesse Sheidlower, Rafael Kitover, Jay Shirley, Joel Bernstein, Andrew Rodland, Tomas Doran, Kennedy Clark, Dan Dascalescu, Devin Austin, and Marcus Ramberg for help with code at timely moments. Thanks to Charley Harvey for the "out of the box" comment in the introduction. In Chapter 11, Rafael Kitover also wrote the code for the WrapCGI recipe, and Alexander Hartmeier provided code for the Email::Template recipe. Thanks also go to Jos Boumans for the Advanced Catalyst::Test recipe and to Mateu Hunter and the other MojoMojo developers for their article. Apologies to Luke Saunders for not having the time to use the material he provided on Fixtures in DBIx::Class. Also in Chapter 11, thanks go to Hideo Kumara and Cory G. Watson for fixing bugs in their software in a timely manner.

Special thanks Dave Rolsky for reviewing a portion of Chapter 2 based on his experience writing the Moose manual. I know that the section of Chapter 2 that I rewrote based on his advice will still not meet his exacting standards, but he caused it to be greatly improved.

Thanks to Dyana Wu for LolCatalyst.

Penultimately, thanks to the whole Catalyst community for making this not only the most useful of the Perl web frameworks, but also the most popular.

Finally, I would like to thank my family for tolerating me when I had to lock myself away to write enough material to meet deadlines. I couldn't have written this book without your support.

Kieren Diment

Introduction

Catalyst is a web framework written in Perl and inspired by Perl. As with its parent language, Catalyst makes the easy things easy and the hard things possible. Unlike other frameworks, it comes with very little out of the box, and in fact doesn't really come with a box. It's not designed to make the first half-day of your programming experience easy; it's designed so that the speed of development of your code is just as quick for you at the beginning of a project as it is in the middle, at the end, and some period of time later when you realize you have to return to a long-forgotten project to do maintenance programming or add new features.

In the rest of this introduction, we'll help you work out if this book is for you. While Catalyst is reasonably simple, it does require that you have some familiarity with Perl. You can learn Perl and Catalyst concurrently, and in some ways this would be a good way to learn how to program disciplined, structured, object-oriented Perl, but it will make the learning curve steep.

If you're familiar with Perl data types, references, and objects, then you can go straight to Chapter 1. If you feel that you are already a skilled web programmer and Perl programmer, then you can probably start with Chapter 3. If you're not completely confident with Perl, on the other hand, you'll want to go through this review. The rest of this introduction will help you decide if you need to read Chapter 2.

Assessing Your Perl Literacy

The following sections describe a continuum of Perl programming skills. A beginning programmer will need to go elsewhere to brush up on Perl before being able to make full use of this book. An intermediate or advanced programmer will be able to dive right in. Read on to determine your level of Perl literacy.

Beginning

A beginning Perl programmer has little or no exposure to programming in Perl but may have written very short Perl scripts. The beginner's code is likely to be procedural in style and will not make significant use of CPAN. If you are a beginner, the next thing that you need to learn about is references. The tutorials at the PerlMonks site (http://www.perlmonks.org/?node=Tutorials), and in particular the tutorials on references (http://www.perlmonks.org/?node_id=591878), are good resources for this. Despite the fact that Catalyst uses some advanced coding/programming techniques, there is really no barrier to beginning Perl programmers using Catalyst, and in fact Catalyst may have some advantages, as its structure encourages the development of good practices from a very early stage.

If you're a raw beginner, you'll probably need to go and do some more reading before you can program with Catalyst effectively.

Intermediate

An intermediate Perl programmer has started using Perl in an object-oriented manner. He or she is confident with using references (e.g., dispatch tables) and object-oriented Perl. The contents of the book *Perl Best Practices* by Damian Conway (O'Reilly, 2005) make sense to intermediate programmers, in that they are confident that they know which bits of the book's advice are sound for them and which to ignore. The next step for intermediate-level programmers is to start writing code as if it was a CPAN module and to make use of Perl's testing infrastructure.

If you're an intermediate-level Perl programmer, you can make good use of this book, but you will need to pay attention to some of the more advanced concepts. The Moose section in Chapter 2 may be of particular use to you.

Advanced

An advanced Perl programmer is familiar with all of the above and has probably written his or her own CPAN modules. The advanced programmer is familiar with the various object systems available for Perl 5 and why Moose represents a significant advance on the other Perl object systems.

If you're an advanced Perl programmer, this book will assist you in getting up to speed on Catalyst quickly and help you consolidate your knowledge and guide other, less-skilled programmers. If you are in this category, then you should at least skim Chapter 3, but you will find Chapters 4 and beyond more useful.

Catalyst and Perl

Perl has been around for a long time, so the continuum in the preceding sections reflects Perl's history. Perl started life as a procedural language. Prior to Perl version 5, object-oriented programming wasn't possible (beginner capability). However, with the release of version 5, Perl began to have object-oriented capabilities (intermediate capability). Perl's object-oriented architecture is based on its strength as a text-processing language, and it has hash-based dispatch tables at its core. Moose, the latest development in object-oriented programming in Perl 5, simultaneously simplifies and makes more powerful Perl's object-oriented capabilities (advanced capability).

Since Catalyst version 5.8, all Catalyst development is based on Moose (which, by the way, is not an acronym—it's just software named after a large herbivorous mammal, a bit of a tradition in the Unix toolchain). Moose is an all-in-one object system that really simplifies object-oriented coding in Perl, greatly easing the transition from beginner to intermediate and intermediate to advanced Perl programmer. We look at modern object-oriented Perl using Moose in Chapter 2.

Finally, we'd like to stress in this introduction that it's Catalyst's job to provide you with the tools that you need to make web programming easier. However, it's also Catalyst's job to get out of your way and let you concentrate on your programming problem. This is Catalyst's strength and what makes it such a powerful tool. Used properly, Catalyst will speed up and simplify your web development activities for a long time to come.

LATE-BREAKING NEWS

As with any good open source software, development is rapid and improvements are always happening. When we were going to press with this book, the Catalyst team had begun looking at providing binary distributions of the latest version of Catalyst to sidestep the sometimes time-consuming process of installation. At the time of this writing, a binary distribution for Windows has been prepared, but we hope to have more for all of the major operating systems in due course. Please check the Catalyst wiki at `http://dev.catalystframework.org/BinaryBuilds` to see if a binary distribution is available for your platform.

Reviewing this book we realized that we forgot to mention Catalyst::Manual::Tutorial (available in the Catalyst::Manual distribution) on CPAN. This is an excellent resource that provides much more of a worked example approach than this book—this book is designed to complement the tutorial. Finally, we've set up a page for this book on the Catalyst Wiki, which will provide community commentary (yes, that means you can contribute). The address is `http://dev.catalyst.perl.org/wiki/ApressBook`.

## CHAPTER 1

Introducing the Catalyst Web Application Framework

*W*eb application frameworks are collections of software libraries that aim to provide the programming facilities required for the creation of dynamic websites. In the early days of the Web, pretty much all websites were statically published pages of Hypertext Markup Language (HTML). Fairly early on in the history of the Web, people wanted to be able to publish dynamic information, for example, with a database store. This led to the development of Common Gateway Interface (CGI) scripts. The first CGI scripts were written in shell or C which, due to the text-centric nature of the Web, was not terribly convenient. Perl, being a language designed for data interchange and text processing, was a strong contender for CGI scripting from the early days and rapidly became popular. The CGI.pm module became part of the Perl core on the release of Perl version 5.004 in 1997.

CGI.pm contains all the basic functions for simple dynamic web scripting, including HTML-generating routines, appropriate routines for setting client-side cookies, and so on. Generally, however, the code is quite low level—one step up from writing your own CGI functionality, but with a lot of repetitive chores required to integrate such things as a database, user management, and so on. Regardless of whether your framework provides a lot of defaults for you or you are required to make choices, this saves a lot of repetitive work.

Web application frameworks generally come in two varieties. The first is one in which all the choices are made for you and you have only one way of doing things. These frameworks are suitable for a restricted range of applications, before customization, and reflect specific business rules. They can become cumbersome to fit into the framework developer's vision of how things work. The second variety is one in which you as the developer are given a large amount of choice and flexibility, so that the code you have to customize is your own, rather than the framework code itself.

Catalyst is firmly in the second camp of flexibility and choice, although it does provide sensible defaults and recommended best practices. In this chapter, we'll start by delving briefly into some background information on Catalyst before moving on to introduce the Model/View/Controller (MVC) architecture, the architectural pattern Catalyst uses. We'll then wrap up our introduction to Catalyst by quickly summarizing some of the tools that Catalyst provides to eliminate the repetitive tasks from your programming. We'll also spend some time comparing Catalyst to other web tools, particularly those for writing in Perl.

Catalyst's Usage and History

Catalyst is a very flexible web application framework written in the Perl programming language. It is suitable for high-traffic websites (e.g., Vox, http://vox.com, and the BBC iPlayer, http://www.bbc.co.uk/iplayer, which is a bandwidth-intensive site dealing with around 100 requests per second) and small-scale single-user web applications, such as the single-user text-mining tool one of the authors of this book has written (called Text Fossick) that integrates with Zotero (http://zotero.org), a Firefox extension for managing collections of documents.

The earliest web framework for Perl was CGI::Application (more on this in the "Catalyst vs. CGI::Application" section of this chapter). CGI::Application required developers to attend to a number of lower-level details, so developers began work on web application frameworks that provided more functionality. One of the first of these written in Perl was Maypole. Catalyst started life as a fork of Maypole, the first popular open source web framework. Catalyst was originally forked by Sebastian Riedel (CPAN id: SRI) in October 2004, and it was going to be a rewrite of Maypole for version 3. By the time Catalyst 5 was released in April 2005, the software had a substantial community forming around it, and it remained under heavy development. Since late 2005, the Catalyst development team has kept up a strict policy of maintaining backward compatibility between releases, achieved with a suite of around 2,000 automated tests. This means that Catalyst is reliable and has a stable development process.

In July 2006, Catalyst 5.7 was released, and since then there have been 15 minor releases, with the final one in December 2008. Catalyst version 5.8 was released in March 2009. Although version 5.8 is backward-compatible with older Catalyst applications, it has been rewritten using the Moose object system, which is rapidly becoming the recommended (best practice) object system for Perl. (We introduce Moose in Chapter 2.) Catalyst piggybacks on Moose's simple syntax, and its powerful introspective capabilities to provide a solid foundation for future development. Examples of things to come might include better encapsulation leading to development of generic application components (e.g., Catalyst::Controller::Blog, Catalyst::Controller::PhotoGallery), and the powerful introspection facility could lead to a more powerful debug screen.

In any case, the code in this book is written using Catalyst version 5.8 and so should last you many years of Catalyst development.

The Model/View/Controller Pattern

Catalyst uses the Model/View/Controller (MVC) architectural pattern. The *model* deals with application data, the *view* deals with the display, and the *controller* mediates interaction between the model and the view. From a practical standpoint, this means that Catalyst provides you with the means to minimize code duplication.

For example, say you have a website that contains a page with a list of recently added content, and you also want to provide this content as an XML feed (RSS or Atom). A proper application of the MVC architecture in this scenario would result in the same code being executed within both the model (e.g., to get a list of recently added pages) and the controller, (e.g., to customize what to obtain from the current model based on the identity of a logged-in user). The only different code being run would be in the view. In Catalyst, this would result in two separate views: one for generating HTML pages and another for generating the XML feed.

The most common types of operations in web application programming are obtaining data (model code) and applying business logic to decide what kind of data to display (controller code). The view usually consists of a template system and a way for the controller to provide data to the view. Therefore, in everyday web application programming, most programming occurs in the model and the controller—ideally in that order. The coding for the view should be restricted to writing simple templates. Controllers should also be relatively simple, although the nature of the HTTP protocol makes it desirable to break the strict separation of model and controller from time to time.

■**Note** A good rule of thumb with regard to the view is to consider whether a web designer with limited programming experience would be able to edit templates with his or her existing skill set. If not, there's too much programmatic complexity in the templates.

The MVC pattern has proved itself resilient as a conceptual approach for user interface development. In order to ease your use of this conceptualization in your own use of Catalyst, we'll cover a little of the history of the pattern (see the sidebar "A Brief History of MVC Software Design") and provide an overview of how it's normally interpreted in Catalyst applications.

A BRIEF HISTORY OF MVC SOFTWARE DESIGN

The original version of the MVC architecture was developed at Xerox PARC along with Smalltalk and the WIMP (window, icon, menu, pointer) interface. (For more information on Xerox PARC's importance in computing history, visit http://en.wikipedia.org/wiki/Xerox_Parc.) This classic MVC posited three cooperating types of components within a GUI application: the *model*, which contains program state; the *view*, responsible for rendering this state to the screen; and the *controller*, responsible for recognizing the user's input to the program and acting upon the intent so expressed by mutating the model, resulting in the view updating itself to reflect the new state of the application. The model in this formulation was very strongly a model of the user interface (UI) itself, so a model object might represent the available actions on a menu, or the underlying value of a slider, and so on. The view object was a pretty much pure rendering object that observed the values of the model, and in response to messages indicating that those values had changed would appropriately repaint parts of the screen, assuming that view object was currently attached to a chunk of screen and given authority to repaint it. In the meantime, the controller object was required to observe both model *and* view in order to understand what events were possible depending on the visible UI elements onscreen and which parts of the model were currently mutable.

A number of GUI toolkits follow a very similar paradigm—for example, the Java toolkit Spring offers components such as the GridViewModel, and provides a view in the form of a rendering engine and controller services in the form of mouse and keyboard event handlers. We can also apply this framework to Firefox, where the model is the XUL components or the HTML being displayed within the TabBrowser control, the view is the GTK+ and Gecko rendering code, and the controller is the code that dispatches events to the various JavaScript event handlers registered and, in this case, the JavaScript handlers themselves. Business and domain objects manipulated by the UI code are not considered part of the model layer here as such, but instead are referenced *by* the model and updated (or not) by the model object as its state changes.

However, this system does not map elegantly to the Web, since it is very much tied to the event-driven model of a direct user interface—the Web's statelessness and page-oriented UI leaves the view and controller existing in the browser alone, if in fact they exist anywhere. Meanwhile, the server is effectively part of the model. From here on, according to the classic MVC pattern, the HTML and the HTTP transport are a form of the Half Object Plus Protocol pattern (`http://portal.acm.org/citation.cfm?id=566122`), where parts of a single functional unit live on different sides of a transport layer. The communications between the two are an internal implementation detail. In fact, single-page JavaScript applications where communication back and forth is initiated by browser-side code and conducted via REST or XML-RPC APIs follow this pattern almost precisely.

An early attempt at adapting MVC for the Web was a variant pattern known synonymously as Web MVC or MVC2. This is where the server-side controller takes on the responsibilities formerly assigned to the model, and some of those of the view. The view works under the Template Plus Data pattern, where the controller selects a template and provides appropriate domain and UI state information to it, and the view is responsible only for rendering that template and shipping the results across the network to the browser. Under this approach, the model is now considered to consist of the business/domain objects, which are directly exposed to the controller. The controller treats HTTP requests as events with coarse granularity, handling processing and business logic required during mutation of the domain objects. This logic is used to transform data in the model into something simple enough for the dumb template to convert to HTML for display.

Early Catalyst practices resulted in a substantial amount of business logic being contained in the controller classes. For simple applications, this design works perfectly well. However, as the business logic gets more complex, the controller's dual responsibility of UI state maintenance as well as business logic leads to tangled code where functionality is difficult to factor out. Applications of this style are often referred to within the Catalyst community as *fat controller* (see Figure 1-1) and tend to be frowned upon due to the known maintenance issues. Keeping the business logic in the controller ties it to the HTTP architecture and makes it difficult to reuse code for command-line utilities, cron scripts, and other non-web clients. In addition, it is also difficult to test the business logic in isolation, forcing integration tests to attempt to cover functionality that should already be verified by unit testing.

Modern Catalyst applications make three changes to the fat controller to ameliorate these issues. First, business logic is aggressively pushed back into the model so the controller becomes entirely agnostic to the implementation. It merely checks for the validity of data received; if valid, it then asks the model if it can perform an operation, and if not valid, it sets up appropriate error/informational data for the view. This permits the controller to focus almost entirely on UI event handling and state maintenance, easing reuse of code for common situations such as forms and list views.

Second, the domain/business objects move back outside the primary hierarchy of the web application and become entirely independent of the application itself. This permits them to be reused and unit tested outside the context of the UI code. The model component of the application then becomes a thin adaptor that simply loads the external domain objects, instantiates them, and exposes them to the application. This means that a single-model class such as a Catalyst::Model::DBIC::Schema can adapt an entire database rather than requiring one model per table.

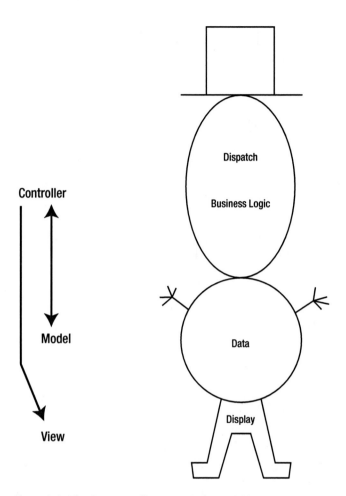

Figure 1-1. *The fat controller approach to MVC*

And finally, helper objects such as form abstractions are instantiated by the controller to represent its event requirements and mediate access to the domain. These objects are then passed to the view, where they cooperate with the template to return at least a portion of the lost intelligence to the rendering process.

This approach results in relatively minimal *thin controller* applications (see Figure 1-2), where the UI need only be tested for its properties as an interface onto the domain, and the increased flexibility available in the view simplifies issues for graphic and interaction designers. The domain objects can now be deployed separately onto back-end servers for job queue and scheduled event handling, and additional business requirements can be implemented and tested with minimal disturbance to the UI code. This approach has been successfully used in substantial applications; we've worked on systems whose primary database contains tables into the low hundreds and controller actions into the high hundreds without finding maintainability and speed of development significantly impacted as the application grew.

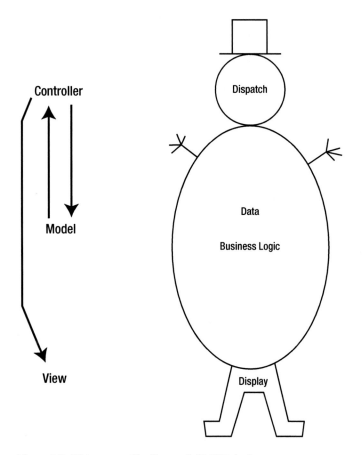

Figure 1-2. *Thin controller/fat model MVC design*

Now that we've outlined the MVC design (see the sidebar "A Brief History of MVC Software Design" for a brief technical history of MVC), in the following sections we'll discuss the components that the Catalyst framework supplies you with in order to make the development process rapid, and how it helps you avoid reinventing wheels and duplicating code through URL path dispatch logic, high-level session management, authentication and authorization, logging, templates, testing, and deployment.

URL Path Dispatch Logic

Every web application framework uses some kind of notation to trigger one or more actions when a particular URL is called. In Catalyst, this is called *URL dispatch action*. Catalyst uses labels on subroutines (called *subroutine attributes*) to provide the mapping between the URL requested by the client and the code that runs on the server. Many other web frameworks contain a central file that stores the code that is to be triggered for a particular action.

Note We introduce the dispatcher in Chapters 3 and 4, and present a detailed overview of it in Chapter 7.

High-Level Session Management

In Catalyst, extensions to the core capability are provided by *plug-ins*, separate software libraries that hook directly into the Catalyst request/response cycle. Session management for maintaining state between client and server is no exception to this. Keeping separately maintained session modules increases flexibility while providing sane defaults, making it easy to change the way that sessions are stored.

For example, you can swap server-based session storage from a file store to a database store with minimal hassle. In the default configuration, it should just be a matter of swapping the session store modules. Similarly on the client (web browser) side, it ought to be possible to swap session storage from a cookie-based mechanism to a URL session, just by changing the session state module used by the application.

■**Note** We use session management plug-ins in Chapter 8, which covers authentication and authorization.

Authentication and Authorization

Identifying the user of a privileged resource (authentication) and determining if that user has permission to perform a particular action (authorization) are core functions of a web application. Again, these are separately maintained packages in Catalyst under the Catalyst::Plugin:: Authentication and Catalyst::Authentication namespaces. Username and password details are stored in an implementation-specific authentication store—for example, they are stored in a relational database, kept in a plain text file for an Apache htpasswd-style store, or delegated to an external source as in OpenID or Lightweight Directory Access Protocol (LDAP). Configuration of authentication stores tends to be fairly involved, and so they are not as hot-swappable as session modules.

Having said this, Catalyst again emphasizes flexibility. This means that if you want to allow your users to authenticate against an OpenID store, or a local database store, or a legacy database store, you can use what the Catalyst authentication system terms *realms* to provide several independent authentication subsystems.

■**Note** We cover authentication and authorization in more detail in Chapter 8.

Logging

For many web applications, keeping server-side logging is desirable. Logging in such a way so as not to pollute the web server logs is even more desirable. Catalyst's logging interface is compatible with other Perl logging modules, notably Log::Dispatch and Log::Log4Perl for flexible, rapid setup and logging capability.

Templates

Catalyst is template language agnostic. The Perl Template Toolkit, a simplified mini-language suitable for a wide range of templating tasks, is the most popular option for Catalyst, but HTML::Mason and other template systems are also popular. It's even possible to use PHP as a templating language for Catalyst!

▌Note We use the Template Toolkit mini-language later in this chapter and then in Chapters 3, 6, and 8.

Testing

As well as providing the development server, Catalyst provides an environment for automated testing of your application using the Test Anything Protocol (TAP). This automation is particularly useful, as testing is a form of developer documentation and good test coverage makes bringing new developers on an application much easier. One reason behind the success of Catalyst and the rapid growth of its sizable developer community is the test-driven development process.

Catalyst makes it easy to write test code by including a test directory with stubs as part of the project creation. As many of the high-quality Perl modules on the Comprehensive Perl Archive Network (CPAN; http://www.cpan.org/) include extensive unit tests, as long as your application's data access layer is a thin layer around an existing CPAN module, much of your functional tests are already written for you. This leaves you to write tests that ensure that your application behaves as you expect (i.e., behavior testing). Ideally you should ensure that, as far as possible, these tests are independent of the web application.

For testing that requires interaction with the web application and for pages that are not dependent on JavaScript, you can use the Perl module HTTP::Recorder to bootstrap your behavior tests.

▌Note We cover testing in Chapters 3, 4, 5, and 9.

Deployment

Most popular web application frameworks come with a development server included, and Catalyst is no exception. A stand-alone development server greatly speeds the code to the implementation cycle by allowing you to rapidly verify the behavior of your code. However, this is not an acceptable substitute for writing proper tests.

At some stage, the application will need to be deployed to end users. Catalyst supports a wide range of deployment options, including the popular Apache-specific mod_perl and FastCGI. FastCGI runs on a variety of web servers, including Apache, IIS, lighttpd, and nginx. The test server can also be used as a stand-alone server, either as a replacement for a stand-alone web server (in conjunction with Catalyst::Engine::HTTP::Prefork) or behind a web server running as a proxy.

▓**Note** We cover deployment in Chapter 5.

Catalyst vs. CGI

CGI is an appropriate platform for building simple scripts, but for more complicated tasks, or for web applications that will get significant traffic, it quickly reaches its limit.

To illustrate this, the simplest Perl CGI script looks like the following:

```
#!/usr/bin/env perl
use warnings;
use strict;
print "Content-Type: text/plain\n\n";
print "Hello world!";
```

Constructing everything by hand like this is not ideal and is quite error-prone. Using CGI.pm, the same code looks like this:

```
#!/usr/bin/env perl
use warnings;
use strict;
use CGI;
my $cgi = CGI->new;
print $cgi->header('text/plain');
print "Hello world";
```

CGI.pm also provides a variety of routines for generating HTML, which for simple tasks is convenient (this time, we omit most of the start of the script):

```
my $cgi = CGI->new;
print $cgi->header; # defaults to text/html
print $cgi->start_html(title => 'Howdy');
print $cgi->h1('Hello World!');
```

However, this approach is somewhat limiting and mixes code with display logic. In the common situation where designers and programmers are separate people on a team, this is a problem. The most common way of separating the programming logic and the display logic is with a template system—a simplified language optimized for display of data. The most popular templating engine used with Catalyst is the Template Toolkit (http://template-toolkit.org/).

The following script is equivalent to the preceding CGI "Hello World" examples and uses the Template Toolkit instead of CGI. The Template Toolkit is not a core Perl module; it needs to be installed separately.

```
#!/usr/bin/env perl
use warnings;
use strict;
use Template;
my $template = Template->new();
```

```perl
my $stash = {
    title   => "Howdy!",
    message => "Hello World!",
};
$template->process(\*DATA, $stash);


__DATA__
Content-Type: text/html; charset=ISO-8859-1


<!DOCTYPE html
      PUBLIC "-//W3C//DTD XHTML 1.0 Transitional//EN"
       "http://www.w3.org/TR/xhtml1/DTD/xhtml1-transitional.dtd">
<html xmlns="http://www.w3.org/1999/xhtml" lang="en-US" xml:lang="en-US">
<head>
<title>[% title %]</title>
<meta http-equiv="Content-Type" content="text/html; charset=iso-8859-1" />
</head>
<body>

<h1>[%- message -%]</h1>
</body>
</html>
```

Here, the setup stage is a good bit more involved. We create the Template object in the same way we created the CGI object before, we define some data for it to display, and then we point it to a template that resides in a file. In this case, we use DATA, Perl's special internal file-handle, although the template after the __DATA__ statement in the code could reside anywhere on the filesystem. This keeps the presentation data separate from the code, and it means that the HTML template could be sent away to a designer who now doesn't need to worry about implementation details. The coder is then free to concentrate on coding and the designer to concentrate on design. Keeping presentation and business logic separate speeds development.

Let's imagine for a moment that our computer is Snow White, and one of Snow White's jobs is to greet each of the seven dwarfs when they come home from the mine. We add the following line to the Template/CGI script:

```perl
my @dwarfs = qw/Bashful Doc Dopey Grumpy Happy Sleepy Sneezy/;
```

change the $stash hash reference as follows:

```perl
my $stash = {
    dwarfs => \@dwarfs,
    title   => "Howdy!",
    message => "Hello World!",
};
```

and finally add this after the <h1> ... section of the template:

```
Hello
[%- FOREACH dwarf IN dwarfs -%]
[%- dwarf; IF dwarf != dwarfs.last %] and [% END -%]
[%- END %].
```

While this code is not much simpler than the equivalent CGI code, imagine that we had to retrieve the names of the current seven dwarfs from a database. In the case of the Template Toolkit code, we keep the business logic and the display separate as follows:

```
# code omitted for brevity
sub get_stuff_from_database {
    my @names = ....;
    return @names;
}
my @dwarfs = get_stuff_from_database();
```

The use of additional software libraries increases complexity, compile time, and the memory footprint of our script. On the one hand, software libraries do most of the heavy lifting for you and are a great way to increase programmer productivity exponentially. On the other hand, the CGI protocol itself creates substantial overhead when you require large external libraries. This is because the CGI protocol mirrors the statelessness of HTTP. Every time a CGI script is accessed from the web server, the Perl interpreter needs to compile a new copy of the script, so there is no persistence across different requests. Consequently, the overhead rapidly adds up in terms of resource usage, and allocation of processor and memory resources rapidly becomes inefficient.

While Catalyst will run under CGI, this is not recommended, because the startup for a Catalyst application is quite expensive as it is optimized to run in persistent environments. For example, here's what the startup script for a Catalyst application called MyApp looks like:

```
#!/usr/bin/perl -w
BEGIN { $ENV{CATALYST_ENGINE} ||= 'CGI' }
use strict;
use warnings;
use FindBin;
use lib "$FindBin::Bin/../lib";
use MyApp;


MyApp->run;


1;
```

In this instance, the application will have to start afresh on every request, so Myapp->run will be expensive, as it will have to call MyApp->setup every time a page from the application is requested. Note the BEGIN {} block in this code, which tells Catalyst what engine the script is running under (in this case, Catalyst::Engine::CGI). The use lib "$FindBin::Bin..." line tells the script where to find the application if it's not installed systemwide.

Because Catalyst is optimized to run in persistent environments, this startup time can be quite lengthy, so it is not recommended to run Catalyst applications under CGI.

Introducing Persistence FastCGI

FastCGI is the most popular deployment route for Catalyst applications. Deployment is simple, and reloading the script doesn't require a web server restart (unlike in mod_perl).

Here's our seven dwarfs script rewritten to use FastCGI:

```perl
#!/usr/bin/env perl
use warnings;
use strict;
use FCGI;
use Template;

# setup
my $template = Template->new();
my @dwarfs = qw/Bashful Doc Dopey Grumpy Happy Sleepy Sneezy/;
my $stash = {
    dwarfs => \@dwarfs,
    title  => "Howdy!",
    message => "Hello World!",
};


# event loop
while (FCGI::accept >= 0) {
    $template->process(\*DATA, $stash);
}
```

Here the code is divided into two sections, setup and the event loop. We set up our template variables in the setup part of the script, which persists between requests, meaning we only have to call $template->process for each request, as the remaining variables are already assigned at compile time.

Because the FastCGI event loop while (FCGI::accept = 0) { ... } is handled by Catalyst::Engine::FastCGI, the code to start up the application is nearly as simple as the CGI script. The only extra thing it needs is to read in some options for interprocess communication with the web server.

At this point, you can start to see practical gains from having a framework: you can run your web application using different server protocols, without having to change your code. The implementation-specific details are abstracted away for you.

mod_perl

The Apache extension mod_perl is an order of magnitude more powerful than FastCGI, as it embeds the Perl interpreter into the Apache web server directly. It is possible to run standard CGI scripts unaltered under mod_perl with Apache::Registry.

To add Apache::Registry support to our original seven dwarfs CGI script, we place our script in a suitable directory (say </usr/local/lib/perl/>) and add the following to our Apache configuration:

```
Alias /perl/ /usr/local/lib/perl/
PerlModule Apache::Registry
```

```
<Location /perl>
  SetHandler perl-script
  PerlHandler Apache::Registry
  Options ExecCGI
</Location>
```

For a MyApp Catalyst application, configuration is similarly simple. If MyApp's root directory is in /usr/local/apps, our configuration will look like this:

```
PerlSwitches -I/usr/local/apps/MyApp/lib
PerlModule MyApp
<Location />
  SetHandler         modperl
  PerlResponseHandler MyApp
</Location>
```

which will run our application off the server root.

Because resource usage (particularly memory) can be quite high for mod_perl applications, it's not possible to have the same application running more than once on the same server, changes in code require web server restarts, and for more complicated applications you may encounter subtle issues that are difficult to diagnose. However, for applications that need to access the web server request/response cycle directly, or for other exotic uses, mod_perl can be a useful tool.

Catalyst vs. Other Frameworks

In this section, we'll discuss Catalyst in comparison with other frameworks, starting with the design approach for URL dispatching that Catalyst takes in comparison to other frameworks. Then we'll look at Catalyst in comparison to the other two major web frameworks written in Perl: CGI::Application and Jifty.

URI Routing via External File vs. Self-Contained Controllers

One of the key differences between Catalyst and the majority of other web frameworks is the location of the information used to determine which method(s) within the application should be called to handle a request for a particular URL. The usual approach is to have some central definition of URI routing—for example, CGI::Application's dispatch specification, Jifty's MyApp::Dispatcher class, Ruby on Rails' routes file, and a Django application's urls.py. The basic principle is the same: entries are provided in the form of a URL pattern or prefix as a lookup key into a dispatch map, and the value corresponding to this key indicates what method(s) should be called when this entry is the one matched by the request.

Catalyst has no such file; instead, this information is specified as part of the definition of the methods themselves. Without digressing into the details of the dispatch specifications, the following definition in a Catalyst application's Root controller:

```
sub login_form :Path('/login') { # ...
```

indicates a handler for `http://example.com/app/base/login`. Additionally, each controller within a Catalyst application has a default path prefix, and URLs can be specified relative to this prefix (`/app/base/`, in this case). A routes-like dispatch map is built up internally from this information during application startup, but even this occurs by delegation. That is, the `register_actions` method of each controller object is called and the application is passed to it. The controller is then expected to register whatever URIs and resulting actions it needs.

This is what we mean when we say that Catalyst has "self-contained" controllers—from the code of a particular controller, you can see immediately what part that controller will take in the dispatch process without needing to check an additional external file. The Catalyst dispatcher simply works out which action in which controller has registered itself for the current URI and sends the request to it.

Catalyst's inside-out approach to dispatch map specification has a couple of important advantages. First, as an application grows to dozens or perhaps over a hundred controllers, there's no slowly growing central file that needs to be maintained and refactored along with them. The URLs handled by a piece of code are immediately apparent from the code itself. Second, parts of the dispatch specifications can be inherited from superclasses along with the functionality that those specifications describe the entry points to. This enables substantially simpler code reuse both between applications and between similar areas of functionality within a single application.

It is our experience that while Catalyst's approach is initially somewhat confusing to those used to external dispatch mappings, with a little practice it becomes much easier to work with than the alternatives for the vast majority of cases. This metainformation provides only defaults that can be overridden on a per-class, per-object, and per-deployment basis. It can be done from inside *and* outside the controller, or from inside and outside the running application. Therefore, any task that might seem easy with a centralized dispatch file can be achieved using Catalyst's approach as well.

Proof-of-concept routes-style dispatch specifications have been implemented more than once as Catalyst extensions (see `http://www.catalystframework.org/calendar/2008/11`). However, these have never seen any significant uptake.

Catalyst vs. CGI::Application

The venerable CGI::Application framework, first released in 2000, is far more minimal than Catalyst in its conception. It was designed as a thin wrapper around CGI.pm to provide basic dispatch functionality and a lightweight request cycle. It shares a philosophy with Catalyst of doing as much with plug-ins as possible. By default, CGI::Application dispatches by using a query parameter to select a *runmode*. This runmode is usually implemented as a method on the CGI::Application subclass that comprises the user's application. Plug-ins such as CGI::Application::Dispatch provide a routes-style dispatching mechanism that selects both a subapplication (also a CGI::Application subclass) and a runmode to call on.

This approach allows CGI::Application to be extremely lightweight and to load only what it needs to serve a particular request. It is therefore more suitable than Catalyst for nonpersistent environments (i.e., plain CGI). However, it also has the disadvantage that more complex dispatch strategies are difficult to implement since the core application must be able to make the decision without the assistance of the code to be dispatched to.

CGI::Application also differs from Catalyst in its approach to the request cycle. Information for a request is available in the form of a CGI object stored in $self->query, and the response is assembled from a $self->headers data structure for the HTTP headers. The response body is the return value from the runmode method call. Catalyst, on the other hand, provides a $c request context object that is passed as an argument to the controller method selected as a dispatch target, and this object has $c->request and $c->response accessors representing the respective HTTP entities in their entirety.

Next, we'll compare a CGI::Application runmode method and a Catalyst controller action method. First up is the CGI::Application version:

```
# provide $self->stream_file method
use CGI::Application::Plugin::Stream;

sub cgi_app_runmode {
    my ($self) = @_;
    my $filename = $self->query->params->{filename};
    my $file = $self->get_static_file_path($filename);
    if ( $self->stream_file( $file ) ) {
        return;
    }
    else {
        return $self->error_mode();
    }
}
```

Here is the equivalent Catalyst action:

```
  sub catalyst_controller_action :Path('image') :Args {
    my ($self, $c, @args); # controller object, request context and
                           # remaining URL parts (CGI PATH_INFO)
    my $filename = $c->request->params->{filename};

# the following line originates from Catalyst::Plugin::Static::Simple
# which is  a default plugin
    $c->serve_static_file($filename);
  }
```

Obviously, we consider the Catalyst design to be cleaner and more flexible, but CGI::Application's approach is clearly far simpler, and with a little care it can come close to Catalyst's flexibility.

CGI::Application has no equivalent to the Catalyst component loader, since other required modules are expected to be loaded on demand by the runmode. It also has no equivalent to the Catalyst dispatcher's flow control methods (forward, detach, go, visit), since there is no dispatch cycle for such functionality to exist within. However, CGI::Application's template-rendering plug-in is not dissimilar to the functionality of Catalyst's Catalyst::Action::RenderView. Its authentication and session support are both via plug-ins in much the same way that Catalyst's are (although the CGI::Application versions again reflect the preference for simplicity rather than the total pluggability of the Catalyst equivalents).

All this said, the extension-by-plug-in philosophy is a strong point of shared agreement, and while design tastes may be different, the two communities regularly share, borrow, adapt, and steal ideas from each other in the finest tradition of open source software development.

Catalyst vs. Jifty

Jifty exists at the far opposite end of the spectrum from CGI::Application. Jifty attempts to provide a standard, effective way to implement pretty much any common (and not-so-common) web application task out of the box. It emphasizes an integrated, full-stack experience over flexibility and customizability. In addition, it was also (to our knowledge) the first web framework to come with a pony (although Django, the Python web framework, now comes with one, too).

Jifty requires that you adhere to many of its design choices, in "one true way." This includes many of the details of your database layout and the approaches to form rendering and validation. It is also explicitly designed for a single application per process. This makes it unsuitable for environments such as mod_perl but allows the current request state to be stored in global variables that significantly reduce requirements to pass objects around the various methods cooperating to perform the application's dispatch cycle.

Jifty's dispatch model is interesting. It is neither a completely separate routes system nor a fully self-contained system such as Catalyst's; rather, it's a hybrid. It uses a declarative mini-language where the code for any given URL is provided directly within the specification of the URL itself. This avoids maintenance problems arising from monolithic architecture by the two techniques of allowing the core application dispatcher to include additional subdispatchers explicitly and of centering the code on collecting objects that represent either model objects for display or actions to be performed on model objects (usually forms). It also allows the view template files to contain the structural code for display decisions.

In order to enable this structural code, Jifty prefers templating systems that embed Perl. The original view of Jifty's developers was HTML::Mason, but later Template::Declare became preferred. Template::Declare is an additional mini-language in which HTML is generated by Perl code mirroring the document structure. Catalyst and CGI::Application, on the other hand, commonly use simpler templating systems. These provide, at most, a restricted mini-language that is more amenable to direct editing by UI and web design–oriented staff. Jifty adopts the attitude that it should be possible to emit HTML only as a semantic structure and to provide the design and styling purely via Cascading Style Sheets (CSS).

Summary

In this chapter, we briefly introduced Catalyst's origins and the Model/View/Controller design pattern that inspired its architecture. We looked at features that it provides for you to make web development easier and noted its emphasis on flexibility vs. "one true way." Catalyst has a learning curve optimized to be a little demanding in the early days, but this pays dividends—for example, when, six months down the road, development can still be quick rather than mired in a mesh of codependent components.

Next, we looked at the features that Catalyst provides for you at the programming and deployment levels, and we made some comparisons between Catalyst and the other (mostly Perl-based) tools available for web development.

In the next chapter, we'll describe some of the core knowledge required for Catalyst development, including using the Comprehensive Perl Archive Network (CPAN); cover what platforms Catalyst will run on (i.e., every modern server and desktop operating system as well as some mobile devices); and get Catalyst installed on your computer.

CHAPTER 2

■■■

Catalyst Setup and Background Knowledge

In this chapter, we will first describe the hardware and software prerequisites for the installation of Catalyst and then how to install Catalyst without needing root (administrator) access on your system.

In addition, to get the most out of this book, you need to know how to program and at least be somewhat familiar with programming in Perl, so we'll next cover important background knowledge in this chapter. On the server side, you need basic knowledge of the HTTP protocol, and some knowledge of HTML, CSS, and JavaScript, which is useful for the client side. As with any programmer's tool with Unix origins, you'll also need to use the command line, so skills in this area help.

Finally, this chapter also serves as an introduction to the Comprehensive Perl Archive Network (CPAN). We will describe how to use CPAN without root (administrator) access. An unprivileged installation makes maintenance and deployment of your work much easier than the traditional approach of installing all of your Perl modules at a system level.

Installing Catalyst

In this section, we'll first review some hardware and software considerations before you install Catalyst. We'll then move on to look at running Perl on various platforms, the initial setup of CPAN, and finally Catalyst installation instructions.

Choosing Hardware and Software

The best combination to work on is a dedicated developer machine where you can run a virtual machine that is as close as possible to the server(s) you eventually run your application on. That, along with using local::lib, will make things easy for you. Catalyst works with any version of Perl above 5.8.1. However, see the sidebar "A Note on Perl 5.10.0" for information about the initial release of Perl version 5.10.0.

A NOTE ON PERL 5.10.0

The earliest versions of Perl 5.10.0 have a bug in them that can cause code with a syntax error to provide entirely uninformative error messages. This bug has been fixed in many Perl 5.10.0 distributions (e.g., the Debian Perl and the Perl version 5.10 that ships with Strawberry Perl at the time of this writing), but it makes this particular distribution of Perl unsuitable for Catalyst development. To find out if your Perl version contains the bug, create an UnknownError.pm file as follows:

```
package UnknownError;
use strict;
sub MODIFY_CODE_ATTRIBUTES {}
sub  check : Blah {
$error = "please explode" ; # deliberate syntax error
   }
   1;
```

Next, run it with perl UnknownError.pm. If you get the following error message, then there's no problem:

```
Global symbol "$error" requires explicit package name at ➥
/tmp/UnknownError.pm line 5.
BEGIN not safe after errors--compilation aborted at /tmp/UnknownError.pm line 6.
Compilation failed in require.
BEGIN failed--compilation aborted.
```

However, if you get the following error, then your Perl version is unsuitable for Catalyst development (although deployment is fine), and you'll have to find a more up-to-date version of Perl 5.10 or go back to using Perl 5.8:

```
Unknown error
Compilation failed in require.
BEGIN failed--compilation aborted.
```

A Catalyst application results in the creation of a lot of source code files that interact with each other, so you should ensure you have version control software installed. The Catalyst project itself uses Subversion (SVN; http://subversion.tigris.org/), and many Catalyst developers use SVK (http://svk.bestpractical.com), which provides distributed version control functionality on top of SVN. However, plenty of alternatives are available. For example, git (http://git.or.cz/) is a popular, fast, easy-to-use, and administer-distributed version control system. Setup of git is extremely easy, as is branching and merging. Git scales well from small projects (consisting of one person) to large projects (like the Linux kernel and the entire history of the Perl interpreter source tree).

■**Note** See *Pro Git* by Scott Chacon (Apress, 2009) for more on git usage.

Catalyst also requires heavy use of CPAN. Installing Catalyst onto a clean system with nothing but core Perl modules requires around 250 modules from CPAN (plus a few more to make life as a software developer a little easier on you). These modules can take a little bit of time to install, and this is obviously something that you want to have to do as infrequently as possible. The method we use to install Catalyst and its dependencies in this chapter makes your Catalyst installation portable across different computers running the same operating system and same version of Perl with minimal work from you.

While the majority of Catalyst is written in pure Perl, some underlying libraries require a C compiler, and the whole Perl build system is based around the make utility. Therefore, you will need a C compiler and a make command.

■**Note** You need Perl version 5.8.1 or greater to run Catalyst. Use the command perl -v to check this on your machine.

Obtaining Perl

The sections that follow provide further information on obtaining and running Perl on various platforms/systems.

Linux

Most, if not all, Linux distributions come with Perl included. The sections that follow outline the specifics for individual distributions.

Debian and Ubuntu

On Debian and Ubuntu, the build-essential package needs to be installed (apt-get install build-essential). Perl is included by default on these systems.

Fedora and Red Hat

On Fedora, the command yum groupinstall "Development Tools" will install everything you need to get started with Perl development.

Some old versions of Red Hat ship with a version of Perl with the core module Scalar::Util incorrectly compiled. If you're using one of these, you may want to compile your own perl following the instructions in Appendix A; otherwise, you'll need to use the workaround that follows. To see if your version of perl is one of those affected by the Scalar::Util problem, issue the following command:

```
perl -MScalar::Util=weaken -e 'weaken \1 & warn "Your perl is OK\n"
```

If you see the output "Your perl is OK" after running that command, then you have nothing to worry about. But if you see the error "weak references not implemented in this version of perl," you will need to reinstall the Scalar::Util module as follows:

```
perl -MCPAN -e 'force("install Scalar::Util");'
```

If the weaken test line doesn't work OK after this, then you probably didn't manage to get a complete compiler toolchain, and you'll need to work back through the install build tools instructions and try again. Additionally, using local::lib on a per-user basis should help future-proof your machine against subsequent upgrades to the system Perl.

SUSE

Ensure that the make, gcc, and perl-devel packages are installed.

Mac OS X

The Mac OS X developer tools (Xcode) are included on the installation media that comes with the Mac, and you can also obtain them from the Apple website (http://developer.apple.com/technology/xcode.html). All versions of OS X 10.3 and later have a recent enough version of Perl to be able to run Catalyst. If you're using an older OS X version, you should compile your own Perl (see Appendix A).

Note that a recent Perl upgrade to OS X 10.5 resulted in problems with the system installation of the IO module. Using local::lib as described in the "Setting Up CPAN" section fixes this on a per-user basis.

Microsoft Windows

Strawberry Perl (http://strawberryperl.com/) is currently the preferred Perl distribution for Windows for Catalyst as it "works exactly the same as Perl everywhere else." Strawberry Perl works well with Catalyst, in either the Perl 5.10 or 5.8 series. Perl 5.10 has the advantage that you can move it around the system, making it suitable for use on USB thumb drives. However, note that if you're going to install CPAN modules with Strawberry Perl, you should do so in a file path that does not contain any spaces. Having said this, if you have a choice, we don't recommend using Windows for Catalyst or Perl programming because compared to the alternatives, the tools available for open source software development in Windows are much less polished.

Occasionally you see test failures for CPAN modules under Windows that do not occur in Unix. The two main culprits are signal handling and some uses of fork(), neither of which work in Windows but which are fundamental Unix tools. Catalyst doesn't require that either of these features work properly by default (although the HTTP::Prefork engine requires fork support, and so won't work under Windows). For Catalyst's dependency chain, be aware that there are occasionally test failures in modules, particularly due to Windows' lack of signal handling. However, it ought to be safe to force or notest install Catalyst's dependency chain if necessary. The real trick is to know what features to keep out of an application targeted at Windows.

BSD

In general, everything you need to get started with Catalyst (Perl, make, and a C compiler) comes preinstalled on a BSD system.

Other Unix Systems

You probably will need root or sudo access to compile perl on some Unix systems (e.g., shell accounts that universities often give out are usually on highly restricted Solaris accounts), but there's no harm trying, unless your system administrator is especially irritable.

Setting Up CPAN

The initial setup of Perl and CPAN in Unix and Windows environments differs slightly. On Windows, you have to install your own Perl, whereas nearly all Unix systems come with Perl installed by default.

Strawberry Perl comes with sensible defaults for CPAN setup, as well as a number of pre-installed modules, so there's no need to set up local::lib for Strawberry Perl. However, for Unix users you will want to set up CPAN. The most convenient thing to do when possible is use the system Perl, but store your own CPAN modules locally by installing local::lib. First, issue the following commands from the shell:

```
$ cpan
cpan[1]> install local::lib
```

Note The prompt for the CPAN shell varies slightly depending on the CPAN version you have installed on your system.

Then add the following line to your .bashrc file in your home directory:

```
eval $(perl -I$HOME/perl5/lib/perl5 -Mlocal::lib)
```

or issue the following command if you're using the C shell:

```
% perl -I$HOME/perl5/lib/perl5 -Mlocal::lib >> ~/.cshrc
```

This sets up your environment variables so that all the remaining CPAN installation should be transparent and done without root access. In fact, if you have compiled your own Perl (version 5.10 and later only) to ~/local and then installed local::lib as just shown, you can move your entire environment to another machine on the same platform simply by putting the /local and /perl5 directories into an archive, adjusting the ~/.bashrc (or equivalent file) at the other end, and expanding the archive.

Once local::lib is installed, if necessary you'll want to do the following:

```
$ cpan
<cpan[1]> o conf init urllist
# follow the prompts to pick a cpan mirror near you
<cpan[2]> o conf commit
<cpan> exit
```

It can be useful to have your own CPAN mirror, although you should update it regularly (e.g., with a daily cron job). See Appendix B for details on how to do this.

Installation

You install Catalyst from CPAN from the package Catalyst::Runtime for a production machine and Catalyst::Devel for a development machine. At this stage, things are easy:

```
$ PERL_MM_USE_DEFAULT=1 cpan
<cpan[1]> install Catalyst::Devel
```

Now go and make a cup of tea, as installation will take a little while depending on the speed of your computer. Running the test suite for each module is the most time-consuming part of the process. If you are in a hurry or on a slow computer, you can avoid running tests in the CPAN shell by issuing the command notest install Module::Name, but this is strongly discouraged. (The reason we mention it at all is that one of us routinely develops on slow hardware where tests can take a long time to run, while the other thinks we shouldn't admit that notest even exists as an option. You have been warned!)

You now have everything you need to start Catalyst development.

Catalyst Background Knowledge

In this section, we'll give an overview of the basics of the Hypertext Transfer Protocol (HTTP), which is an important but often overlooked aspect of web development. Following this, we'll talk about the revolutionary Moose object framework to provide you with the basic knowledge with which to write modern, robust object-oriented perl code. We'll finish by talking more about CPAN; specifically, we'll look at the tools available for you to make the most of CPAN, and then we'll cover some basic CPAN troubleshooting.

Hypertext Transfer Protocol

The World Wide Web was invented in 1990 by Tim Berners-Lee at CERN, the European nuclear research facility, to facilitate the electronic exchange of research documents. The protocol for transporting documents over the Web was and still is Hypertext Transfer Protocol (HTTP), a text-based stateless client/server network protocol: text-based because all of the communication between client and server happens in plain text; client/server because a client (i.e., a web browser or equivalent) requests information from a server (a web server in the case of HTTP), which then serves it; and stateless because the web server does not remember any details about the client in between requests. This makes perfect sense for a simple protocol for the interchange of static documents in a network with high levels of trust. For better or worse, the Web is now used for much more than this, and for most web applications you need to have a way of tracking client information from the server and vice versa.

A few years into the Web's history, the cookie was developed. A *cookie* is a digitally signed piece of data to be passed between client and server. While cookies can be used to maintain state between clients, this is a fairly fragile arrangement. Clients can be configured to refuse cookies, and unless alternative means of tracking state (e.g., with an identifier such as a URL query parameter and additional server-side code) are used, the protocol falls back to being completely stateless. The statelessness and fragility, although seemingly cumbersome, are a constant reminder that the Internet (the Web in particular) is a protocol built on an untrusted and unreliable foundation. Nonetheless, for the most part it seems to work.

Let's illustrate the anatomy of an HTTP request with an example. First fire up a terminal—for example, xterm on Linux, Terminal.app on Mac OS X, or cmd.exe on Windows. Next, you'll use telnet, a command-line program that starts a text-based connection to another computer, in this case a client with an address of www.example.com and a port number of 80 (a port being the networking equivalent of a PO box) to make the connection on. Now type in the following command:

```
$ telnet www.example.com 80
```

This outputs the following (you might not see this output on Windows):

```
Trying 208.77.188.166...
Connected to www.example.com.
Escape character is '^]'.
```

Following this, you are presented with a blank line. Type the following lines:

```
GET / HTTP/1.1
Host: www.example.com
```

and press Enter twice (if you're following on Windows, you might not see any output as you type).

The first line translates as a GET request (we describe different types of HTTP requests shortly) for the resource on the server root, using the HTTP protocol version 1.1. You could also replace the 1.1 with 1.0 to use the earlier version of the protocol, in which case you can omit the Host: line, which is there to handle web servers running more than one host at a time (virtual hosts). In any case, the output from this is as follows:

```
HTTP/1.1 200 OK
Date: Mon, 12 Jan 2009 12:11:43 GMT
Server: Apache/2.2.3 (CentOS)
Last-Modified: Tue, 15 Nov 2005 13:24:10 GMT
ETag: "b80f4-1b6-80bfd280"
Accept-Ranges: bytes
Content-Length: 438
Connection: close
Content-Type: text/html; charset=UTF-8


<HTML>
<HEAD>
  <TITLE>Example Web Page</TITLE>
</HEAD>
<body>
<p>You have reached this web page by typing &quot;example.com&quot;,
&quot;example.net&quot;,
  or &quot;example.org&quot; into your web browser.</p>
<p>These domain names are reserved for use in documentation and are not available
  for registration. See <a href="http://www.rfc-editor.org/rfc/rfc2606.txt">RFC
  2606</a>, Section 3.</p>
</BODY>
</HTML>
```

Note the response is divided into two sections, the header and the response body, which are separated by a blank line. The header contains details about the request and can be obtained without the body by making a HEAD request rather than a GET request, as follows:

```
$ telnet www.example.com 80
Trying 208.77.188.166...
Connected to www.example.com.
Escape character is '^]'.
```

Make a manual request here (don't forget the blank newline):

```
HEAD / HTTP/1.1
Host: www.example.com

HTTP/1.1 200 OK
Date: Mon, 12 Jan 2009 12:28:55 GMT
Server: Apache/2.2.3 (CentOS)
Last-Modified: Tue, 15 Nov 2005 13:24:10 GMT
ETag: "b80f4-1b6-80bfd280"
Accept-Ranges: bytes
Content-Length: 438
Connection: close
Content-Type: text/html; charset=UTF-8
```

This returns just the response header, without the response body. HEAD is used for various purposes, mainly to see if a resource on a server has changed between requests, for browser or intermediate proxy server caching.

As well as requesting a particular resource from the server (the root resource, or / in this case), you can also add query parameters in the GET request, which may or may not alter the way in which the web server processes your request (we'll omit the telnet command and the initial output going forward):

```
GET /?foo=bar+baz HTTP/1.1
Host: www.example.com
```

This translates as sending the request for the root resource with the additional parameter foo, which has a value of "bar baz" (literal spaces are substituted with a plus sign [+] in URL query parameters, as the HTTP protocol is sensitive to whitespace). This is equivalent to requesting http://www.example.com/?foo=bar+baz from a web browser. In this case, the response is identical, as the parameters for the request are discarded by the web server.

A POST request does the same thing but hides the query parameters in the response body. This is useful for things like longer form submissions (e.g., a text box), or if you're passing around usernames and passwords and don't particularly want to pass around URLs like http://www.example.com/?username=me&password=mysecret (also note here how additional parameters are separated by an ampersand [&]). Here's how to make a POST request manually:

```
POST / HTTP/1.1
Host: www.example.com
Content-Length: 11


foo=bar+baz
```

Note the new header in the request, Content-Length, which tells the server how many bytes to expect after the request. Get this wrong and the server may throw an error message (although the example.com web server doesn't). In this case, we've requested the URL http://www.example.com again, but this time we've put the query parameters in the body. Later on in the book we'll show how Catalyst makes a distinction between GET and POST query parameters.

■**Note** A *byte* is the length of a single ASCII character. A UTF-8 glyph, the most common encoding of non-European characters, can be between 1 and 3 bytes long.

Every web application will make use of GET requests, and almost every web application will make use of POST requests. We'll quickly mention a few other methods used to make requests to HTTP servers. OPTIONS and TRACE are used to get information from the server about what methods the server supports and information about the network, respectively (TRACE just echoes back the received request so that you can tell if it's being modified by any intermediate servers such as a proxy server). CONNECT is for setting up a secure connection under the secure HTTP protocol, HTTPS, which is beyond the scope of this short explanation.

Of more relevance to Catalyst are PUT and DELETE, which are used for the implementation of REST web services. PUT is essentially the same as a POST request, but it's supposed to be used only for the creation of resources rather than POST, which is supposed to be used for the modification of resources (in practice, most of the time outside of a REST web service POST is used for both). DELETE is used to remove resources, and it obviously requires some kind of user access control. Just for giggles, let's try and DELETE the root resource at www.example.com:

```
DELETE / HTTP/1.1
Host: www.example.com


HTTP/1.1 405 Method Not Allowed
Date: Tue, 13 Jan 2009 00:02:40 GMT
Server: Apache/2.2.3 (CentOS)
Allow: GET,HEAD,POST,OPTIONS,TRACE
Content-Length: 314
Connection: close
Content-Type: text/html; charset=iso-8859-1
```

```
<!DOCTYPE HTML PUBLIC "-//IETF//DTD HTML 2.0//EN">
<html><head>
<title>405 Method Not Allowed</title>
</head><body>
<h1>Method Not Allowed</h1>
<p>The requested method DELETE is not allowed for the URL /index.html.</p>
<hr>
<address>Apache/2.2.3 (CentOS) Server at www.example.com Port 80</address>
</body></html>
Connection closed by foreign host.
```

You can see if you make an OPTIONS request that you can't make a DELETE request because it is not supported by this server, not because you don't have permission:

```
OPTIONS / HTTP/1.1
Host: www.example.com


HTTP/1.1 200 OK
Date: Tue, 13 Jan 2009 00:04:24 GMT
Server: Apache/2.2.3 (CentOS)
Allow: GET,HEAD,POST,OPTIONS,TRACE
Content-Length: 0
Connection: close
Content-Type: text/html; charset=UTF-8


Connection closed by foreign host.
```

This concludes our whistle-stop tour of the HTTP protocol. We've included coverage of it here for any experienced web developers who have been ignoring the details of HTTP all these years, and probably shouldn't have. If you want to know more about HTTP, the specification (http://tools.ietf.org/html/rfc2616) is a good place to start. For a more general overview, the HTTP Wikipedia entry (http://en.wikipedia.org/wiki/Hypertext_Transfer_Protocol) is also useful. Finally, a (somewhat dated but still extremely useful) view of HTTP from a Perl-centric perspective appears in the freely available *Web Client Programming with Perl* book (http://oreilly.com/openbook/webclient/) in Chapters 1 and 2.

Object-Oriented Programming with Moose

The primary goal of Moose is to make object-oriented programming with Perl easier. According to the Moose::Manual, "With Moose you can concentrate on the logical structure of your classes, focusing on 'what' rather than 'how.'"

Diving right in, we'll first need to make sure that Moose is installed. If you installed Catalyst version 5.80 or later already, then you're all set. Otherwise, enter the following at the command line:

```
$ cpan Moose
```

Right now it's also handy to install the CPAN module Module::Starter:

```
$ cpan Module::Starter
```

In addition, if you haven't installed Catalyst yet, you'll also want the following module:

```
$ cpan Module::Install
```

This module will make this tutorial rather more convenient and allow us to concurrently cover test-driven development, at least in a fairly superficial way.

Installing Moose is usually pretty quick, even on a slow computer, but it does have some overhead. To that end, there's a "Moose Lite" called Mouse available. There's also another module called Squirrel that looks to see if Moose is already loaded and uses that if it is, or Mouse if it isn't. It's worth installing these modules from CPAN at this point, as for non-Catalyst purposes, using Mouse will cause your code to load quicker than Moose.

We want to get cracking with Catalyst, so this example of object-oriented programming with Moose is going to be fast-paced. The documentation perldoc Moose::Cookbook::Basics:: Recipe1 provides a classic example of an object-oriented class to provide a way of representing a point:

```
package Point;
use Moose;
has 'x' => (isa => 'Int', is => 'rw', required => 1);
has 'y' => (isa => 'Int', is => 'rw', required => 1);
sub clear {
    my $self = shift;
    $self->x(0);
    $self->y(0);
}
```

Let's get this going to see how it works. First up, we'll make a proper distribution directory so we can pass this code around to our teammates easily or upload it to CPAN. With Module::Starter installed, we can issue the following command:

```
$ module-starter --mi --module=CrashCourse::Point \
    --author="Me" --email=you@example.com
```

(Note the use of the \ character in the preceding line to break a long line of a shell command.)

Replace the name and e-mail address with your own. This command creates a set of files and directories underneath the distribution root directory, which is called CrashCourse-Point. We'll describe the structure of the files in this directory in the next chapter when we start programming Catalyst. At the moment, we care about only two files (OK, maybe three):

```
lib/CrashCourse/Point.pm
t/00-load.t
```

The third file is Makefile.PL. For the sake of completeness and of developing well-disciplined habits early, we should put the following on the line after build_requires 'Test::More';:

```
requires 'Moose';
```

This tells the build system that Moose is a dependency of this module. Now we can go into the file `lib/CrashCourse/Point.pm` and just delete everything in it and replace it with the following code:

```
package CrashCourse::Point;
use Moose;


1;
```

Note Module::Starter provides stub documentation, which can be useful because it acts as a prompt to encourage best practices. However, in this case we're using Module::Starter for the convenience of a properly structured directory tree and a decent `Makefile.PL`.

This is a Perl package file, with the name given after the `package` declaration. Moose automatically turns on `strict` and `warnings`, so we don't need to state them explicitly (no harm if we do, though). For technical reasons, a Perl package is required to return a true value. So the `1;` is equivalent to `return 1;`, which is another example of an implicit return value that you've seen previously.

Now we can just copy and paste the code from between `use Moose;` and `1;`:

```
has 'x' => (isa => 'Int', is => 'rw', required => 1);
has 'y' => (isa => 'Int', is => 'rw', required => 1);
sub clear {
    my $self = shift;
    $self->x(0);
    $self->y(0);
}
```

That's it!

Now we need to make sure it works. Open up the file `t/00-basic.t`. The first thing we'll do is remove the bit of code that says `tests => 1` and replace it with `qw/no_plan/` (the reason for this is not important at the moment; you can find out why by looking in the documentation for Test::More, `perldoc Test:More`). Also, we want to replace the top of the file where it says `#! perl -T` with `#! /usr/bin/env perl`. This switches off taint checking (a security mode). We do this because it's often useful in development to run tests under the Perl debugger with the command `perl -Ilib -d t/00-basic.t`, and taint mode won't allow us to run our script like this. However, this means that if your script inputs data from external untrusted sources, you'll have to take steps to deal with security issues yourself.

Next we'll add the following code at the end of the file:

```
my $point = CrashCourse::Point->new( x=> 1, y => 2);
print "Coordinates are ",
        $point->x , "," ,
        $point->y , "\n";
$point->clear;
print "Coordinates are ", $point->x , "," ,$point->y , "\n";
```

Let's run it. We can do this from the distribution root with the following command:

```
perl -Ilib t/00-load.t
```

and we get this output:

```
ok 1 - use CrashCourse::Point;
# Testing CrashCourse::Point , Perl 5.008008, perl
Coordinates are 1,2
Coordinates are 0,0
1..1
```

Technically, we're running this in a testing environment, which is a little different from an ordinary Perl environment. In this situation, the test module (Test::More) intercepts standard output to determine if tests pass or fail, so a plain print statement will mess this up. We can get around the issue by using the diag function provided by Test::More rather than the print statement (there's a similar function called note that may also prove useful; see the documentation for Test::More for details).

Edit your t/00-load.t file and replace the two print statements with diag instead. Now the output looks like this:

```
ok 1 - use CrashCourse::Point;
# Testing CrashCourse::Point , Perl 5.008008, perl
# Coordinates are 1,2
# Coordinates are 0,0
1..1
```

To turn this into a formal test after setting point initially, we add the following code:

```
ok ($point->x == 1, "x is 1");
```

and we get the following output:

```
ok 1 - use CrashCourse::Point;
# Testing CrashCourse::Point , Perl 5.008008, perl
ok 2 - x is 1
# Coordinates are 1,2
# Coordinates are 0,0
1..2
```

The ok function is provided by Test::More and uses the syntax ok (*[expression that evaluates to true or false], [name of the test]*). In this case, our expression is that $point->x equals 1 and the name of the test is x is 1.

A Perl script called prove is available that runs the perl interpreter in an environment more suitable for testing. To run this, we issue the command

```
prove -l t/00-load.t
```

You can run this code yourself and examine the output, which is very similar to previous output.

Moose Example: Snow White and the 57 Dwarfs

Our simple example using the Point class from the Moose documentation shows you very basic usage of Moose. You can find a wealth of other examples in the Moose Cookbook available at `http://search.cpan.org/perldoc?Moose::Cookbook`. In this section, our aim is slightly different. Most of what follows is ordinary `perl` code written as a Moose class. You'll meet a couple of really useful features of Moose on the way (type constraints and lazy_build), and you'll see how the object-oriented style keeps some fairly horrible logic encapsulated so that end users don't have to worry about implementation details. Experienced programmers who are familiar with object-oriented code can safely skip this section.

While writing this book, we spent some time thinking of compelling example code that didn't do very much that was actually useful, in order to concentrate on the code rather than the business logic underlying the code. We eventually hit upon a theme. The Disney production of *Snow White and the Seven Dwarfs* had seven dwarfs whose names were selected out of a pool of possible fifty. Our first bit of code was going to be one in which our computer, called Snow White, provided a greeting for each of our seven dwarfs. We were going to do this in an object-oriented manner using Moose.

After a couple of tries at implementation, we realized that this would become Snow White, two dwarfs, and a handful of other cartoon characters. However, this lays the groundwork and tests for a module that would actually implement the original idea—it's just that we don't have to explain it fully in the tutorial.

Initially, we'll set up the infrastructure for our module using Module::Starter as a basis, as in the last example. Then we need to think about what it is our code actually does on a slightly more abstract level than "The computer is a fairy-tale character who must greet seven creatures of short stature when they return from work, and also has to know the names of all their friends."

Let's define this with a brief specification. The software stores a list of objects that correspond to names. These names correspond to individuals that could be termed *members* (i.e., the seven dwarfs). Each of these members has a custom greeting associated with him, although other members can be greeted with his greeting in special circumstances (e.g., if Sleepy has a cold, a more appropriate greeting might be "Bless you, Sleepy!").

The software maintains a list of names that could be termed *associates*. These names are given a greeting that acknowledges their association and each associate can be greeted with a member's greeting under special circumstances.

The software will greet names that are neither members nor associates with a greeting indicating that the name is not known to the software. Unknown names cannot be greeted with members' or associates' greetings.

Let's start by beginning a new module with `module-starter` and call it Greeter:

```
$ module-starter -mi -module=Greeter -author="Me" \
      -email=you@example.com
```

Following this, we'll take a brief interlude to make sure that the module's documentation is always the README file in the distribution. Generally, a Perl module comes with a README file that provides a quick overview of usage. Since the POD documentation in the main `.pm` file should basically be this, rather than duplicating efforts, you can simply generate this file by adding the following to `Makefile.PL` in your `Greeter` directory:

```
if ($Module::Install::AUTHOR) {
    system('pod2text lib/Greeter/List.pm >README');
}
```

Now any time you, the author, run Makefile.PL, the README file will be automatically generated. However, because of the author check, when an end user (or sysadmin) runs Makefile.PL, this code will be skipped and the README you shipped in your distribution will be left untouched. Back to our implementation, we can now change to the lib/ directory and replace the file Greeter.pm with the following code and some replacement stub documentation:

```
package Greeter;
use Moose; # provides warnings and strict

1;
__END__
=head1 NAME

Greeter

=head1 SYNOPSIS

Programmer's library to store and retrieve member and guest greetings for a
group of named individuals.
```

■**Note** You can add pod documentation to the end of a package after the 1; statement. Be sure to put an __END__ token on a single line after the 1; first. Note if you put all the documentation at the end of the package like this, you should be consistent. It's also possible to put documentation inline. How you do it is a matter of preference.

Next, we need to provide an object to store each individual. Let's make a new package called Greeter::Member (create it in the file lib/Greeter/Member.pm, creating the Greeter directory on the way).

```
package Greeter::Member;
use Moose;

has 'name' => ( is => 'ro', isa => 'Str', required => 1);
has 'greeting_string' => ( is => 'ro', isa => 'Str', required => 1);
has 'greeting' => ( is => 'ro', isa => 'Str', lazy_build => 1);
```

```
sub _build_greeting {
    my ($self)   = @_;
    my $greeting = $self->greeting_string;
    my $name = $self->name
    $greeting =~ s/__NAME__/$name/e;
    return $greeting;
}
1;
```

Before we explain what all this means in the text, we'll also add some documentation.

```
END__
=head1 NAME

Greeter::Member

=head1 SYNOPSIS

Stores a name and a greeting, and provides a string to greet the individual by name.

my $member = Greeter::Member->new(

                    name => 'Sleepy',
                    greeting_string => 'Night Night __NAME__'
            );
print $member->greeting, "\n";
```

The preceding documentation shows how to instantiate our object. The name attribute stores a string containing the individual's name. The greeting_string contains the greeting. Observe that we put a placeholder in where the name is to go. This is so we can greet guests later on, and so we can deal with grammatical irregularities. The name and greeting_string attributes store static string data, as shown by the isa => 'Str' type constraint. The greeting attribute is also a string, but it has a lazy_build = 1 statement indicating that it is constructed programmatically in the _build_greeting subroutine. The lazy_build key is particularly useful for computationally expensive attributes, but in this case we're using it because it's convenient. All that the _build_greeting subroutine does is substitute the __NAME__ placeholder for the name set at object construction time.

It's also probably convenient to add a new method in here to greet someone else with the object's greeting. We'll leave the authorization checking for the Greeting module itself.

```
sub greet_guest {
    my ($self, $name) = @_;
    die "A name argument is required to greet a guest" if ! $name;
    my $greeting = $self->greeting_string;
    $greeting     =~ s/__NAME__/$name/;
    return $greeting;
}
```

We'll also have to document this method. After the print statement in the SYNOPSIS section, we can add this line:

```
print $member->greet_guest('Homer'), "\n";
```

At the end of the package, we should document the subroutine properly as well:

```
=head1 METHODS

=head2 greet_guest

Receives an argument indicating the name of the guest to greet:
$member->greet_guest('Bart').  Checking whether the member is authorized
 to greet this guest is not performed in this package.
```

Now we can make a test file that exactly reflects the previous documentation. Put this file in t/01-Member.t:

```
#!/usr/bin/env perl
use warnings;
use strict;
use Test::More tests => 6;

BEGIN {
        use_ok( 'Greeter::Member' );
}

# create a Greeter::Member object
 my $member = Greeter::Member->new(name => 'Sleepy',
                                     greeting_string => 'Night Night __NAME__'
                           );

# now test it works as advertised
 cmp_ok( ref($member), 'eq', 'Greeter::Member', "is a Greeter::Member");
 cmp_ok( $member->name, 'eq', 'Sleepy', 'correct name');
 cmp_ok( $member->greeting_string, 'eq' , 'Night Night __NAME__',
         'correct raw greeting');
 cmp_ok( $member->greeting, 'eq', 'Night Night Sleepy',
         "Correct actual greeting");
 cmp_ok( $member->greet_guest('Homer'), 'eq', 'Night Night Homer', 'Greet guest');
```

This checks that the documentation works as advertised. Note that we're using the cmp_ok method, which is documented in Test::More, instead of the ok method that we used with the Point object earlier. Doing this makes it easier to write more complex test cases that require comparison—not strictly necessary here, but a useful practice nonetheless.

We run the test with the command prove -l t/01-Member.t, and all our tests should pass:

```
$ prove -l t/01-Member.t

t/01-Member....ok
All tests successful.
Files=1, Tests=6,  0 wallclock secs ( [ ... ] )
Result: PASS
```

This concludes the implementation of the Greeter::Member class.

We can now return to the Greeter class. In here, we store the list of members and the list of valid guest names. We'll start to use Moose's type constraint facilities in a more sophisticated way. Given that we have the code portion of our class at the beginning of the file and the documentation portion at the end of the file, we add the following to the code portion before the 1;:

```
has guests  => ( is => 'rw', isa => 'ArrayRef[Str]', default => sub { [] } );
has members => ( is => 'rw', isa => 'ArrayRef[Greeter::Member]', required => 1);
has guest_greeting => ( is => 'ro', isa => 'Str',
                                        default =>
                              'Hello __NAME__, I hope you are having a nice➡
visit');
has unknown_greeting => ( is => 'ro', isa => 'Str',
                                            default =>

                              'Hello __NAME__, I don't know you, do I?');
```

And we can add the following documentation at the end of the documentation part of the file:

```
=head1 USAGE

my $member = Greeter::Member->new(name => 'Sleepy',
                          greeting_string => 'Night Night __NAME__'
                          );
my $greeter = Greeter->new(
            members => [$member],
            guests => [qw( Homer Bart Marge Maggie) ]
            guest_greeting =>
            'Hello __NAME__, I hope you are having a nice visit',
            unknown_greeting =>
             "Hello __NAME__, I don't know you, do I?"
            );
```

There are three substantial differences in the attributes of this class compared to the attributes of the Greeter::Member class. First, two of the attributes are read/write: is => 'rw'. In Greeter::Member, the attributes were 'ro' for read-only, only settable at construction time. Second, we are making a more sophisticated use of type constraints. The guest attribute is an array reference, each containing a string that should be the name of each quest. The members attribute is a store consisting of an array reference, and each entry contains an object of the type Greeter::Member. Third, we provide a default empty array reference for the guest attribute. We have to wrap it in a subroutine reference (i.e., sub { [] }). This is so that Perl creates a new one each time; otherwise, all of our objects would share the same values, which definitely isn't what we want. Before we write the classes functionality, we should probably write tests for the data storage.

■**Note** It's useful to run perl with the -c flag (for check syntax) over your class before you start writing tests in order to catch any typos that creep in. In this case, you should run perl -c lib/Greeter.pm, and if all is OK, the output you should see is as follows: lib/Greeter.pm syntax OK.

This won't catch all problems, but it will catch many obvious ones.

We should also create a test file in t/02-Greeter-store.t as follows:

```perl
#!/usr/bin/env perl
use warnings;
use strict;
use Test::More qw(no_plan);

BEGIN {
    use_ok( 'Greeter' );
}
use Greeter::Member;
my $member = Greeter::Member->new(name => 'Sleepy',
                    greeting_string => 'Night Night __NAME__'
                );
my $greeter = Greeter->new(
            members => [$member],
            guests => [qw( Homer Bart Marge Maggie) ]);


cmp_ok(ref($greeter->members->[0]), 'eq', 'Greeter::Member');
cmp_ok($greeter->guests->[0], 'eq', 'Homer');
```

Note the use of qw(no_plan) instead of the number of tests that we run. This is because we haven't finished adding functionality, and we don't know the eventual number of tests.

Now we need to add the functionality that distinguishes between members, guests, and unknowns. The most expedient way to do this is in a monolithic subroutine, with quasi-private helper routines. However, as you will see, this is not an optimal solution from either a readability or a maintenance perspective. Let's call our public subroutine greet, and this time we'll start with the documentation.

```
=head1 METHODS

=head2 greet($greeting_name, $greetee_name)

Returns an appropriate greeting for an individual of the name passed in as an
argument if only one argument is present or if the two arguments are the same
name.  Returns the greeting string for $greeting_name with the name of
$greetee_name if two arguments are present
```

There are two distinct bits of functionality here: if the greeting name and the greetee name are the same, then we'll pass the function onto the _greet_person sub, and we'll pass it to the _greet_other_person sub if the two arguments are different.

■**Note** Prepending an underscore to a subroutine indicates by convention that a sub is private and not for use outside the package, but this practice does not enforce privacy. For trivial subroutines, these methods can be minimally documented to indicate privacy. While there are ways to make truly private routines, they're generally seen as not necessary, so we won't describe them in this section.

Here's the greet subroutine:

```
sub greet {
    my ($self, $greeting_name, $greetee_name) = @_;
    my $greeting;
    # ideally we should check that we know this person before calling _greet_person
    # with their name, so this is a minor security problem.
    if (! $greetee_name || $greeting_name eq $greetee_name ) {
        $greeting = $self->_greet_person($greeting_name);
    }
    else {
        $greeting = $self->_greet_other_person($greeting_name, $greetee_name);
    }
    return $greeting;
}
```

It's not testing time yet, though, as there's still no functionality to test!

Now we're going to make use of the first subroutine provided by the Perl module List::Util, which is a core module. At the top of the file after the other use statements, place this line:

```
use List::Util qw(first);
```

Initially, we'll build the simpler of the two subroutines, _greet_person:

```
sub _greet_person {
    my ($self, $name) = @_;
    my $greeting;
# find member.
    my ($member, $guest);
    if ($member = first { $_->name eq $name } @{$self->members}) {
        $greeting = $member->greeting;
    }
    # find guest
    elsif ($guest = first { $_ eq $name} @{$self->guests} ) {
        $greeting = $self->_greet_guest($name)
    }
```

```
    # else unknown
    else {
        $greeting = $self->_greet_unknown($name)
    }
    return $greeting;
}
```

Pausing to run `prove -l t/02-Greeter-store.t` to make sure that we haven't broken anything yet, and to note that we still need to write the _greet_guest and _greet_unknown subroutines (with the leading _ to indicate they should only be for internal use), we'll move on to the more complicated subroutine, _greet_other_person. The logic in this one, while not complicated, requires a bit of interrogation of the object. The large if/elsif/else statement strongly suggests that it would be better to refactor this functionality further, and if we were to end up doing any maintenance code on this, we'd almost certainly implement a dispatch table here instead. This kind of occurrence is colloquially known as a *code smell*, and is quite common when initially implementing new programming ideas. However, we'll leave this as adequate just now.

```
sub _greet_other_person {
    my ($self, $greeter, $greetee) = @_;
    my $greeting; # return value

    # This is a bit of a shortcut we'd refactor if performance was important
    # but it improves the presentation of code right now

    my $members_greeting = first { $_->name eq $greeter } @{$self->members};
    my $member_to_greet = first { $_->name eq $greetee } @{$self->members};

    my $guests_greeting = first { $_ eq $greeter       } @{$self->guests};
    my $guest_to_greet  = first { $_ eq $greetee       } @{$self->guests};

    # greeter and greetee are both members
    if ($members_greeting && $member_to_greet) {
        $greeting =
            $members_greeting->greet_guest($member_to_greet->name);
    }
    # greeter and greetee are respectively member and guest
    elsif ($members_greeting && $guest_to_greet) {
        $greeting = $members_greeting->greet_guest($guest_to_greet);
    }
    # greeter and greetee are both guests
    elsif ($guests_greeting && $guest_to_greet) {
        $greeting = $self->_greet_guest($greetee);
    }
    # greetee is a member and greeter is a guest or unknown
    elsif ($member_to_greet) {
        $greeting = $member_to_greet->greeting;
    }
```

```
    elsif ( !($members_greeting || $guests_greeting) && $guest_to_greet ) {
        $greeting = $self->_greet_guest($guest_to_greet);
    }
    # fallback
    else {
        $greeting = $self->_greet_unknown($greetee);
    }
    return $greeting;
}
```

Recall that we also realized we had to implement the two extra private methods:

```
sub _greet_unknown {
    my ($self, $name) = @_;
    my $greeting = $self->unknown_greeting;
    $greeting =~ s/__NAME__/$name/;
    return $greeting;
}
sub _greet_guest {
    my ($self, $name) = @_;
    my $greeting = $self->guest_greeting;
    $greeting =~ s/__NAME__/$name/;
    return $greeting;
}
```

So now it's time to test the functionality. Pausing to note that it took a good while to get these tests to work because of the large and relatively opaque conditionals in _greet_other_person, which is yet another indication that we need to refactor this subroutine, we go on to write more tests in 02-Greeter-store.t.

Now that we know we will have 12 tests in total in this file, we can replace the use Test::More ... line with the following:

```
use Test::More tests => 12;
```

and then add the following tests to the file:

```
# greet guest
cmp_ok($greeter->greet('Homer'), 'eq',
        'Hello Homer, I hope you are having a nice visit',
        'greet guest');

# greet unknown
cmp_ok($greeter->greet('Papa Smurf'), 'eq',
        "Hello Papa Smurf, I don't know you, do I?",
        'greet unknown');

# greet  member
cmp_ok($greeter->greet('Sleepy'), 'eq', 'Night Night Sleepy', 'Got member');

# greet member 2 with member 1's greeting
```

```
my $member2 = Greeter::Member->new(name => 'Sneezy',
                                   greeting_string => 'Bless you __NAME__!');
$greeter->members([ $member, $member2]) ;
cmp_ok( $greeter->greet('Sneezy', 'Sleepy'), 'eq',
        "Bless you Sleepy!", 'atchoo!');

# greet guest with member's greeting
cmp_ok( $greeter->greet('Sneezy', 'Homer'), 'eq',
        "Bless you Homer!", 'atchoo! DOH!');

# try to greet member with guest's greeting
cmp_ok( $greeter->greet('Homer', 'Sneezy'), 'eq',
        'Bless you Sneezy!', 'no-op');

# try to greet guest with guest
cmp_ok( $greeter->greet('Bart', 'Homer'), 'eq',
        'Hello Homer, I hope you are having a nice visit',
        'greet guest take 2');

# try to greet guest with unknown
cmp_ok( $greeter->greet('Bart', 'Papa Smurf'), 'eq',
      "Hello Papa Smurf, I don't know you, do I?",
      'greet unknown 2');

# try to greet unknown with guest
cmp_ok( $greeter->greet('Papa Smurf', 'Bart'), 'eq',
        'Hello Bart, I hope you are having a nice visit',
      'greet guest take 3');
```

Finally, we can run the tests again with prove -l t/02-Greeter-store.t, and all 12 of them should pass.

The internal business rules of our class are nicely encapsulated. Any problems with the code originate from the author's implementation rather than from Moose, and despite slightly horrible internals, the external facing API is clear enough. Theoretically, we could prepend _ to the various greet_someone attributes to improve at least the appearance of encapsulation. As an introduction to Moose and its very basic capabilities, this gets you started.

Next, we'll talk a little about Moose's more advanced features and point to other sources where you can find more information.

More on Moose

Hopefully we've demonstrated compelling reasons to prefer Moose for your object system due to its readable syntax and the way it greatly simplifies the way that you write object-oriented code in Perl. The combination of Moose attributes for object properties (not subroutine attributes as used by the Catalyst dispatcher, which are something different) and subroutines for object methods provides a very clear syntax for basic object-oriented methods. For the built-in types, we already get basic type checking built in, and in general, everything becomes easier to read and easier to write.

In this section, we'll outline some of Moose's most compelling features to show that along with being a nice, simple syntax for object-oriented code, Moose is also extremely powerful. This power comes from the fact that it is a layer on top of a metaobject model, and thus has powerful introspective facilities.

■**Note** We've found that Moose is so simple and powerful that the kinds of data management tasks traditionally written with spaghetti code using a procedural style are greatly simplified by writing a new Moose module and doing all of the one-off data processing required for the problem at hand inside the test files. The code at https://github.com/singingfish/perl-survey-2009/tree is a good example of this approach.

Housekeeping

Making your Moose classes immutable removes much of the metaclass's ability to modify your object at runtime—once your code is made immutable, most of the object's properties (e.g., the attributes) are then set and are unable to be modified at runtime. This is usually not a problem, so you can speed up your code significantly by adding the following line just before the terminal 1; of your class:

```
__PACKAGE__->meta->make_immutable;
```

Moose provides you with its own new method, and it's generally not a terribly good idea to override this. One reason for this is that when you make your class immutable, an overridden new method will not be subject to the other optimizations. To avoid this, Moose provides BUILD and BUILDARGS subroutines that hook into object construction and allow sensible things to occur in object inheritance, while still benefiting from the performance enhancements that occur when you make your class immutable. BUILD and BUILDARGS are documented with examples in Moose::Cookbook::Basics::Recipe11.

Inheritance

Rather than use base qw/Names of Inherited Modules/, Moose has its own syntax for extending a base class. Here's a stub for an original class:

```
package My::Thing;
use Moose;
# ...
use namespace::clean -except => 'meta';
# ...
__PACKAGE__->meta->make_immutable;
1;
```

And here's our extension via inheritance:

```
package My::Other::Thing;
use Moose
extends qw/My::Thing/;
# etc ...
1;
```

There's one gotcha here. In some circumstances if you're extending a Catalyst controller using Moose, then you need to wrap your extends directive in a begin block as follows:

```
BEGIN { extends qw/My::Thing/; }
```

This is because subroutine attributes are dealt with at compile time, whereas by default Moose's extends syntax is dealt with at runtime. Placing the extends directive in a BEGIN block as just shown fixes this issue.

Note the use of namespace::autoclean in the original class to tidy up the namespace. Moose does a lot of behind-the-scenes alteration of your classes, and it's a good idea to clean these up. You should ensure that namespace::autoclean is installed from CPAN, and then place the line use namespace::autoclean in your class.

Custom Type Constraints

The preceding example shows that you aren't stuck with basic data types for Moose types. As well as the basic type constraints documented in Moose::Util::TypeConstraints, you can use straight object names, for example using has => 'URI' instead of has => 'Str' for an attribute if the attribute is to return a URI object. However, you can also provide user-defined types. Here's one convenient way of ensuring an attribute is a valid e-mail address:

```
Package MyPackage;
use Moose;
use Email::Valid;
use Moose::Util::TypeConstraints;

subtype 'MyPackage::Email'
    => as 'Str'
    => where { Email::Valid->address($_) }
    => message { "$_ is not a valid email address" };

has 'email'        => (is =>'ro' , isa => 'MyPackage::Email', required => 1 );
```

Note that rather than just calling the constraint Email, you prepend your local namespace onto it. While this is not strictly necessary, it stops you from accidentally using a namespace already taken elsewhere in your code or on CPAN.

Roles

Inheritance has some limitations. In particular, code quickly gets rather contrived; the discussion of adding custom attributes in Chapter 10 is a good example of this. Roles (sometimes also called *traits* or *mixins*) are a way of bolting functionality onto a class without having to rely on an inheritance chain to do so. Roles are unrelated to inheritance, which makes them useful for adding little discrete bits of functionality to existing objects—pick 'n' mix object creation, if you like.

The Moose Cookbook, included in the Moose distribution, is the best place to find out more about roles, with Moose::Cookbook::Roles::Recipe1, Moose::Cookbook::Roles::Recipe2, and Moose::Cookbook::Roles::Recipe3 available at the time of this writing.

Coercion

It's useful to be able to create an object from a number of sources. Here's some example code from a Moose class that creates a Config::General object from either a filehandle, a string, a filename, or a straight hash reference. It's all done in remarkably little code.

```perl
package Some::Class;
use Moose;
use Moose::Util::TypeConstraints;
use Config::General;

subtype 'ConfigGeneral' => as 'Object' => where {$_->isa('Config::General')};

 has 'some_data' => (
    is => 'ro',
    isa => 'ConfigGeneral',
    coerce =>1,
);

coerce 'ConfigGeneral'
    => from 'FileHandle'
        => via { Config::General->new( -ConfigFile => \$_) }
    => from 'ScalarRef'
        => via { # covers a literal Config::General stringConfig::General->
                    new( -String => $_)
            }

    => from 'Str'
            => via { # covers where you pass in a filename Config::General->
                        new( -ConfigFile => $_);
            }
        }
=> from 'HashRef'
            => via { Config::General->new( $_ ) };
            } ;
```

Making the Most of CPAN

Perl's most attractive feature, aside from its compact and expressive syntax, is CPAN and its associated infrastructure. The following list presents CPAN infrastructure in roughly the order in which you will encounter it in your life as a Perl programmer.

- http://search.cpan.org: This is the online source for module search and documentation. It's one of the first places you'll go in order to find if someone else has written code with the functionality you require. While there are modules to provide an HTML (web browser) interface to your locally installed modules (such as Pod::Webserver), http://search.cpan.org is the most effective way to get a quick overview of what's available for your task. Note that there's a rather nice CPAN search interface available at http://cpantools.com/ and a flashier version at http://cpantools.com/beta/.

- http://cpanratings.perl.org: CPAN Ratings provides user reviews of CPAN modules. Coverage is patchy, although this site is frequently useful. CPAN Ratings reviews are directly linked from http://search.cpan.org, so when a review is available, this site frequently contains useful information. On the other hand, if you end up using a CPAN module that you feel strongly about, it's worthwhile to provide your own review.

- http://annocpan.org: AnnoCPAN allows you to annotate the documentation for existing Perl modules. Again, this site is linked from the documentation available at http://search.cpan.org.

- *CPAN Testers Service:* The CPAN Testers infrastructure is a network of around 400 automated testing machines around the world that test CPAN modules and distributions on all of the different platforms that Perl is available for and all of the different versions of the Perl interpreter. While the CPAN Testers infrastructure is really an author's tool, examining testing results can be useful when you assess the quality and reliability of an individual Perl module. CPAN Testers reports are also available from http://search.cpan.org.

- http://rt.cpan.org: RT is an open source bug tracker written in Perl. The CPAN RT service is a bug tracker for the whole of CPAN. If you identify bugs in CPAN modules, then filing a bug report here is easy, and it is the best way to maximize the likelihood of getting a response from the author.

- http://pause.perl.org: PAUSE is the Perl Authors Upload Server. This is where you register for an account on CPAN and the location to which you upload new modules. Creating a CPAN distribution is easy if you follow the technique using module-starter outlined in this chapter.

Catalyst is designed for use with CPAN and therefore comes with little preinstalled. This means that installation of Catalyst aside, you will almost certainly use CPAN as a regular part of your Catalyst programming workflow. With this in mind, in the next sections we're going to talk briefly about the two core competencies required for effective use of CPAN: searching for modules and diagnosing problems that you may encounter.

Search Strategies for CPAN

CPAN is powerful, but it takes some getting used to when it comes to searching for modules and evaluating whether they're any good. For Catalyst-specific stuff, you can't go wrong by asking about modules via the appropriate support channels; the Catalyst mailing list (http://lists.scsys.co.uk/mailman/listinfo/catalyst) and the #catalyst IRC channel on irc.perl.org are the main ones. For material not directly related to Catalyst, the PerlMonks site (http://perlmonks.org) is a very good resource, as well as the #perl IRC channel on irc.freenode.net (but be aware that some people on this channel can be a bit hostile to novices, and it's best to try to ignore this so long as you've done some research up front).

■**Warning** It pays to be thick-skinned on IRC generally—many people don't understand the limitations of text-based communication, and this can come across as rudeness. However, if you get used to this, IRC can be an extremely useful support channel.

The home page of http://search.cpan.org provides a list of common tasks, which can be useful for finding particular functionality. However, in general you're more likely to want to use the search facility. If you're not sure of the name that a programmer might give to a module, you are referred back to the research stage.

Searching CPAN can be a bit of a black art. This is why it pays to do some brief research outside of CPAN if you're not sure what you're looking for—working out the common name for programming-related things is not always straightforward.

An illustrated example of a search strategy will be useful here. For example, say you want to look at your options for processing HTML forms in Catalyst. You can first go to http://search.cpan.org and type **catalyst form** into the search box. At the time of this writing, we get 163 results. Looking at the first page of results, you'll want to see if the name of the module returned is the top level of a distribution or if it's a smaller part of a whole distribution. In the results we received, we saw Catalyst::Plugin::Form::Processor, Catalyst::Controller::FormBuilder (along with the deprecated Catalyst::Plugin::FormBuilder), and Catalyst::Controller::HTML::FormFu right at the bottom of the first page of the search results. So at that moment, there were three main choices in Catalyst. Let's look at each of these in turn.

First, we could see that none of these modules had any reviews on CPAN Ratings (this is not uncommon), but that Form::Processor had a positive review. We noted that it was last updated in April 2008, which made it reasonably current (although a small number of modules will be very old but very stable; some modules using well-known algorithms fall into this category). However, when we looked at the Catalyst::Plugin::Form::Processor RT queue, we saw that there was a bug open on it. The bug (from one of the authors of this book) indicated that writing Catalyst::Plugins for an extension of code that belongs in the controller or the view (as form processing does) is strongly discouraged. It would appear from the discussion on the bug report that this module will be replaced with a base controller class at some point, but at the time of this writing, it doesn't exist. So we determined that we could discard this module at present.

Next, we looked at Catalyst::Controller::HTML::FormFu, which at the time of our search was last updated in December 2008. There were two open bugs, one of which had been added within the last few hours. There were also a number of closed bugs (we found these by looking at the closed bugs list), most of which had been fixed in a timely manner. It looked like this module could be of potential use to us. After doing a CPAN search on Catalyst::Controller::HTML::FormFu, we also saw that the parent distribution, HTML::FormFu, has its own manual included in the distribution (comprehensive documentation is always a good sign) and that the Catalyst Tutorial (included in the Catalyst::Manual distribution) also has a section on HTML::FormFu. This all contributes to a positive impression of this model.

Finally, we examined Catalyst::Controller::FormBuilder. At the time of this writing, the module had been last updated in 2007. A search of the Catalyst mailing list indicated that it was a popular module in the past (and was part of the Catalyst Tutorial at one point), but the number of open bugs exceeded the number of resolved bugs, which suggests a module past its prime.

Our search strategy here points at Catalyst::Controller::HTML::FormFu as our preferred module to deal with forms in Catalyst. If we want something more lightweight, we could use Form::Processor, but the current implementation of a Catalyst extension suggests that if we want to use this functionality, writing our own base controller is currently the way to go.

Basic CPAN Usage

The CPAN shell is what you get when you type **cpan** at the command line. Here's an example CPAN session:

```
$ cpan

cpan shell -- CPAN exploration and modules installation (v1.9301)
ReadLine support enabled

cpan[1]>
```

First up, you can get some help as follows:

```
cpan[1]> h
```

Let's split this information into chunks to describe each section of functionality in turn:

```
Display Information                                          (ver 1.9301)
  command  argument            description
  a,b,d,m  WORD or /REGEXP/    about authors, bundles, distributions, modules
  i        WORD or /REGEXP/    about any of the above
  ls       AUTHOR or GLOB      about files in the author's directory
     (with WORD being a module, bundle or author name or a distribution
     name of the form AUTHOR/DISTRIBUTION)
```

You'll most often use the i command, which basically searches the CPAN index in a similar way to http://search.cpan.org. In this case, however, you use regular expression syntax to search. For example, you can search for all Catalyst::Controllers that also contain the word *Form* in them with the following:

```
cpan[6]> i /Catalyst::Controller.*Form/
```

If you're unfamiliar with regular expressions, note the use of .* rather than the more common wildcard '*'. Assuming that you're connected to the Web, using http://search.cpan. org is probably more convenient than using regular expressions. Having said that, if you are familiar with regular expressions, they are very powerful and can be used to sift through CPAN with ease.

Next up are the download, examine, and install options:

```
Download, Test, Make, Install...
  get      download                 clean    make clean
  make     make (implies get)       look     open subshell in dist directory
  test     make test (implies make) readme   display these README files
  install  make install (implies test) perldoc  display POD documentation
```

When you installed Catalyst::Devel, you just used the install command. get, make, and test are performed as a part of this process. The clean command reverses the effect of make. If you encounter trouble, the look command will come in handy.

```
Upgrade
r         WORDs or /REGEXP/ or NONE    report updates for some/matching/all modules
upgrade   WORDs or /REGEXP/ or NONE    upgrade some/matching/all modules
```

The upgrade command tells you for a given search string which modules that match the string are in need of being updated. So r /Catalyst.*/ would upgrade all modules that begin with Catalyst, if newer versions exist.

```
Pragmas
force  CMD   try hard to do command  fforce CMD   try harder
notest CMD   skip testing
```

The final commands for installing modules relate to what to do when things go wrong. If you have a problem installing a module because tests fail, these commands allow you to force-install the tests or skip the tests. We cover how to deal with these sorts of issues in the next section.

Testing CPAN Modules

Quality control in CPAN is provided by social contract—it's generally voluntary, except in cases where modules are of exceptional importance to Perl's programming infrastructure. This voluntary system works remarkably well, and most CPAN modules are well covered by auto-mated testing. However, you can still end up with modules that are troublesome to install due to failing tests.

Tests can fail for various reasons, but there are four types of test failure:

- *Tests fail due to a problem with software installed on your computer.* This type of failure is a result of missing or incompatible software. Let's see what happens when we try to install DBD::mysql (the module that talks to MySQL databases) on a machine without MySQL installed:

```
cpan[2]> install DBD::mysql
```

A lot of output will scroll past, but the important output is at the end:

```
Warning: No success on command[/usr/bin/perl Makefile.PL]
  CAPTTOFU/DBD-mysql-4.010.tar.gz
  /usr/bin/perl Makefile.PL -- NOT OK
Running make test
  Make had some problems, won't test
Running make install
  Make had some problems, won't install
Failed during this command:
  CAPTTOFU/DBD-mysql-4.010.tar.gz              :
          writemakefile NO '/usr/bin/perl Makefile.PL' returned status 512
```

The Makefile.PL script failed. This usually indicates a software availability problem on the local computer, and in this case that is correct:

```
Can't exec "mysql_config": No such file or directory at Makefile.PL line 454.
```

This output tells us that the executable mysql_config is not available on this machine. To correct this problem, we need to install the MySQL client onto the computer.

- *A distribution fails to be installed due to failure to locate a dependency.* The type of message that we get in this situation indicates that a particular module can't be found in @INC. This usually means that the author forgot to mention the module as a prerequisite in the Makefile.PL. The error looks like this:

```
#     Error: Can't locate URI/Escape.pm in @INC (@INC contains: t/lib
[ output truncated ... ]
```

Generally the correct thing to do in this situation is install the module that was a missing dependency and then try to install the first module you were trying to install again (perhaps issuing the command clean Module::Name in the CPAN shell beforehand). If the author of the module that you're installing has forgotten a few dependencies, you might need to try more than once. In this situation it's always worth filing a bug report on http://rt.cpan.org.

- *A distribution fails tests.* This is the case where there's either a problem with the distribution or, more likely, a problem with the way the distribution's tests have been laid out. The final line of the test will mention the number of tests that were scheduled and the number of tests that failed, for example:

```
80 tests and 211 subtests skipped.
Failed 1/318 test scripts. 1/13206 subtests failed.
Files=318, Tests=13206, 601 wallclock secs ([...])
Failed 1/318 test programs. 1/13206 subtests failed.
```

To resolve this issue, you'll have to dig into the failing tests and decide whether it's a bug that you're concerned about or not.

- *One of the module's dependencies fails tests.* CPAN automatically installs dependencies, so if a module you're trying to install depends on fails, the same message will occur as in the previous example. The only difference is that there is a lot more output to sift through.

If you think that a test failure is innocuous, you can just install it from the CPAN shell with the force or notest pragmas. Most of the time, test failures are innocuous but irritating. It's usually worth filing a bug report with the author via http://rt.cpan.org if you know that the problem is not caused by your system. The real skill to learn, though, is how to detect what's failing for important reasons and what's a minor annoyance that needs further attention.

The first thing to do is look in the directory that the module has been unpacked in. Then you can run the tests yourself with the command prove -l t. From here, you can easily identify which tests are failing and use the source code for the tests to identify why that may be the case. This sounds more complex than it is, especially when you consider that on the rare occasion that this type of problem happens, it's usually innocuous or easily fixed.

Here's an example CPAN session that contains a failing test:

```
cpan[2]> install Template::Magic
```

We'll just show the output at the end of the installation:

```
make: *** [test_dynamic] Error 255
  MARKOV/OODoc-1.04.tar.gz
  /usr/bin/make test -- NOT OK
//hint// to see the cpan-testers results for installing this module, try:
  reports MARKOV/OODoc-1.04.tar.gz
Running make install
  make test had returned bad status, won't install without force
Failed during this command:
 DOMIZIO/Template-Magic-1.39.tar.gz          : make_test NO
 MARKOV/OODoc-1.04.tar.gz                    : make_test NO
```

This output shows that tests failed for the dependency Template::Magic. Next, we look in the distribution:

```
cpan[2]> look Template::Magic
Running look for module 'Template::Magic'

Trying to open a subshell in the build directory...
Working directory is /Users/kd/.cpan/build/Template-Magic-1.39-90J5Qx
```

Which leaves us able to run through a manual installation of the module, so we can examine each step:

```
$ perl Makefile.PL
 Writing Makefile for Template::Magic
$ make
[output removed ]
```

This worked, so we can test it:

```
kd@fenchurch>/.cpan/build/Template-Magic-1.39-90J5Qx$ make test
PERL_DL_NONLAZY=1 /usr/bin/perl "-MExtUtils::Command::MM"
"-e" "test_harness(0, 'blib/lib', 'blib/arch')" t/*.t t/01_template_inclu-
sion.........ok

[ remaining passing tests cut for space ]


t/27_FillInForm................1/2
#   Failed test at t/27_FillInForm.t line 65.
# <form>[ removed some html from output ]
# </form>
```

```
# Looks like you failed 2 tests of 2.
t/27_FillInForm................. Dubious, test returned 2 (wstat 512, 0x200)
 Failed 2/2 subtests
t/28_memory_leaking.............ok


[ more passing tests omitted from output ]


Test Summary Report
-------------------
t/27_FillInForm                (Wstat: 512 Tests: 2 Failed: 2)
  Failed tests:  1-2
  Non-zero exit status: 2
Files=33, Tests=53,  2 wallclock secs ( [ ... ])
Result: FAIL
Failed 1/33 test programs. 2/53 subtests failed.
make: *** [test_dynamic] Error 255
kd@fenchurch>~/.cpan/build/Template-Magic-1.39-90J5Qx$
```

We can run the failing test file manually with Perl directly (mainly because it's inconvenient to sift through so much output, and we want to focus on the failing test only):

```
kd@fenchurch>~/.cpan/build/Template-Magic-1.39-90J5Qx$ perl -Ilib t/27_FillInForm.t
1..2
not ok 1
#   Failed test at t/27_FillInForm.t line 65.
#          got: '
# <form>
# <input name="fieldA" type="text">
# <input value="B" name="fieldB" type="text">
# <input name="fieldC" type="text">
# </form>
#
# '
#     expected: '
# <form>
# <input name="fieldA" type="text">
# <input value="B" name="fieldB" type="text">
# <input name="fieldC" type="text">
# </form>
# '
not ok 2
#   Failed test at t/27_FillInForm.t line 69.
#          got: '
```

```
# <form>
# <input value="A" name="fieldA" type="text">
# <input value="B" name="fieldB" type="text">
# <input value="C" name="fieldC" type="text">
# </form>
#
# '
#     expected: '
# <form>
# <input value="A" name="fieldA" type="text">
# <input value="B" name="fieldB" type="text">
# <input value="C" name="fieldC" type="text">
# </form>
# '
# Looks like you failed 2 tests of 2.
kd@fenchurch>~/.cpan/build/Template-Magic-1.39-9oJ5Qx$
```

Our conclusion is that this is a poorly formed test. It should be testing against the Html::Parser data structure rather than a text serialization of the same, as the test is failing on whitespace differences. We can force-install the module (or just run make install in the shell), and then go back and try to install OODoc again.

```
cpan[4]> install OODoc
[copious output snipped]
  MARKOV/OODoc-1.04.tar.gz
  /usr/bin/make install  -- OK
```

Summary

In this chapter, we covered setting up Catalyst and the some of the fundamental knowledge that you need to be able to use Catalyst effectively. During the setup, we covered hardware, operating system, and software requirements, and the Perl versions you need for Catalyst development. Finally, we went through the basics of the Moose object-oriented framework and finished with a discussion of CPAN.

In the next chapter, we'll program a simple Catalyst application that will get you started programming your first application. This will provide you with the basis to get through the rest of the book.

## CHAPTER 3

Your First Catalyst Application

Now that you have Perl and Catalyst installed, you're ready to build your first web application. In this chapter, we'll show you how to build a simple application with a single model, two views, and some simple URL action dispatch logic.

At this point, the preparation you did to install Catalyst and its dependencies properly starts paying off very quickly. One of the things that Catalyst::Devel does is install the script `catalyst.pl` into your $PATH. This script provides you with the files to get your application started. So without further ado, let's start your first application, called LolCatalyst::Lite, by issuing the following command from the prompt:

```
$ catalyst.pl LolCatalyst::Lite
```

This results in a couple of pages of output to the terminal, which tell you about the files and directory structure that Catalyst::Helper creates to get your application started. Catalyst uses Module::Install to create the same directory structure that would be created by any other Perl *distribution* (i.e., a Perl module, script, or batch of related modules). In other words, when you create a Catalyst application, you create a Perl module. You can then, if you so choose, upload the module to CPAN and install it to your system (or you can just choose to run it from a local directory, which is what most people do).

In the next section, we'll get started by outlining the sample application.

Sample Application Overview

These are the functions we want this chapter's sample application to perform:

- We get a web form when requesting the root page.

- When we make a POST request to /translate, we get a kitty pidgin translation of our form contents in HTML.

- When we make a POST request to /translate_service, we get a kitty pidgin translation of our form contents in JSON format.

▪Tip To understand what kitty pidgin (also known as LOLspeak) is, see `http://en.wikipedia.org/wiki/Lolcat`.

That's not much, but in the process we'll provide a fair bit of background to help you understand what Catalyst is doing for you.

Once we've done the initial implementation, we will add HTTP basic authentication for the web service portion of the application with a Catalyst Helper module.

Files and Directories

When you start up your application, you can see that Catalyst::Devel has created the directory `LolCatalyst-Lite`, which includes a number of files and directories. We'll examine these on a directory-by-directory basis in the sections that follow.

Top-Level Directory

The top-level directory is also called the application's root directory. This is not the same as the `root` directory described in the upcoming "root Directory" section. It contains the following files:

- Changes
- Makefile.PL
- README
- lolcatalyst_lite.conf

The Changes and README files start as boilerplate files that you should keep up to date. The Changes file contains a human-readable history of changes for the release of your module, as the convention is to list new features and bug fixes for each release of a module. We'll make sure to update this after we've made the application do something.

The README file tells us how to test the application:

```
Run script/lolcatalyst_lite_server.pl to test the application.
```

We might want to add to this a description of what the application does and provide other instructions. There's nothing stopping you from making any other kind of file or directory here (an INSTALL file comes to mind, especially if your application depends on modules that don't come from CPAN).

The Makefile.PL file is the first thing that we will discuss when we start building the application. This file contains important information about the modules that your application depends on. It is also used internally by Catalyst and therefore it should *never* be deleted.

The lolcataylst_lite.conf file is for per-deployment configuration. It contains the kind of information that might change for each installed instance of the application—for example, database connection information, the default language for the application (for an internationalized application), or web service authentication keys. This is so that system administrators and other nonprogrammers are able to modify the configuration of the application without having to modify code.

In older versions of Catalyst, YAML was the default configuration file format, but this was seen as a problem for two reasons. First, YAML uses whitespace to define different variables, so as a result it is difficult for nonprogrammers to use. Second, POD (the Perl documentation format) also uses whitespace to convey meaning (literal blocks of text such as code and configuration data structures are padded with leading spaces on the left side), but this is not treated consistently by different POD formatters (e.g., pod2html, pod to Unix man page), so for an inexperienced programmer, it's very difficult to see what the correct usage of YAML is because the two formats have whitespace dependency that interact to impair usability. On the other hand, Config::General, the newer default format, does not suffer from this problem. Having said that, Catalyst supports a number of configuration formats, including YAML and Config::General, so you are free to choose from a range of formats.

▨**Tip** See the Config::Any documentation for a complete list of supported configuration formats.

---

lib Directory

The lib/ directory contains all the Perl code for our application. Initially, Catalyst::Helper creates the Model, View, and Controller directories for us, the LolCatalyst::Lite module, and the LolCatalyst::Lite::Controller::Root module. The LolCatalyst::Lite module can contain application-level configuration and global methods for use by the application. It is good practice to put only configuration that does not need to be changed per deployment in this file. The configuration file (lolcatalyst-lite.conf, in this case) is for deployment-specific information (e.g., database connection information).

The LolCatalyst::Lite::Controller::Root module is for top-level dispatch actions—for example, what to do when the application's base is requested. In the case of the development server, this will be http://localhost:3000 unless you specify another port in the development server startup.

root Directory

The root/ directory is where we will put the templates. The root/static/ directory will include static files, such as style sheets, images, and JavaScript files. Where access control is not required, this directory might also be a suitable location for files uploaded by the user. Catalyst::Helper provides a number of images by default.

script Directory

The script/ directory contains scripts to run helpers to create models, views, and controllers (lolcatalyst_lite_create.pl); the script to run as a CGI script (lolcatalyst_lite_cgi.pl); the FastCGI script (lolcatalyst_lite_fastcgi.pl); a script to test individual URLs (lolcatalyst_lite_test.pl); and last and most important, the development server script (lolcatalyst_lite_server.pl).

If we run the script/lolcatalyst_lite_server.pl script now, we get a lot of useful debug information in the terminal it was run from, and we can visit http://localhost:3000 to get a nice welcome screen.

You should always use the built-in server for development, unless there's a very good technical reason not to do so (and we can't think of any right now). Occasionally we encounter people on the #catalyst@irc.perl.org IRC channel who are trying to do development using a FastCGI server, or worse, mod_perl. Live web server deployment issues should be the last things you deal with in your development cycle, and almost always there won't be any issues moving from the development server to production.

Using the development server is a quick and convenient way to get your application up and running for development. Under some circumstances, the development server is a suitable target for deployment itself. See Chapter 5 for details.

t Directory

The t/ directory is where scripts for automated testing of your application go. For now, if we run the command prove -l t in the application root directory to run the automatically generated tests over the automatically generated source code, we get the following output:

```
$ prove -l t
t/01app...........1/2 [debug] Debug messages enabled
[debug] Statistics enabled
[debug] Loaded plugins:
.-------------------------------------------------------------------------.
| Catalyst::Plugin::ConfigLoader  0.21                                    |
| Catalyst::Plugin::Static::Simple  0.20                                  |
'-------------------------------------------------------------------------'


[debug] Loaded dispatcher "Catalyst::Dispatcher"
[debug] Loaded engine "Catalyst::Engine::CGI"
[we remove the rest of the debug output from the Catalyst test server]
t/01app...........ok
t/02pod...........skipped: set TEST_POD to enable this test
t/03podcoverage....skipped: Test::Pod::Coverage 1.04 required
All tests successful.
Files=3, Tests=2,  7 wallclock secs ( [ ... ])
Result: PASS
```

The preceding output means that we run the command prove, which is a wrapper around the Perl interpreter optimized for automated testing. We came across this in Chapter 2, but it's worth explaining what's going on a little bit here. The -l flag tells prove to add the library ./lib directory to the module search path (@INC), and t is the directory that contains the tests. If we wanted to just run one test file, we could issue the command prove -l t/01-app.t instead. To avoid all the debug output in the test harness, we have two choices. We can remove the -Debug line from the use Catalyst qw/ ... / statement in LolCatalyst::Lite, or we can run the command CATALYST_DEBUG=0 prove -l t. If we remove the -Debug flag from LolCatalyst::Lite, we can force debug mode to be switched back on by setting the CATALYST_DEBUG environment variable to 1 or by running the test server with the -d flag (although in tests, you have to use the environment variable as there is no test server to start).

Getting Started Writing Our Application

The Makefile.PL file contains important information to enable applications to run, and it should *never* be deleted. As well as telling the Perl build system (Module::Install) where to find the application files, Makefile.PL also keeps information about an application's dependencies (i.e., CPAN modules required for it to run). Let's have a look at the contents of the default Makefile.PL (the inline comments differ slightly):

```
# IMPORTANT: if you delete this file your app will not work as
# expected.  You have been warned.
use inc::Module::Install;

name LolCatalyst';
all_from 'lib/LolCatalyst.pm';

requires 'Catalyst::Runtime' => '5.7014';
requires 'Catalyst::Plugin::ConfigLoader';
requires 'Catalyst::Plugin::Static::Simple';
requires 'Catalyst::Action::RenderView';
requires 'parent';
# The next line should reflect the config file format you've chosen
# See Catalyst::Plugin::ConfigLoader for supported formats
requires 'Config::General';

catalyst;

install_script glob('script/*.pl');
auto_install;
WriteAll;
```

Apart from the comment not to delete this file (notice how we stress this—it is really very important!), the next line tells the Perl build system which build module to use. In this case, we want to use Module::Install, with the option to use modules local to the distribution residing in the inc/ directory if available (this is only added if you run perl Makefile.PL).

The name and all_from directives concern metadata about the application. The first is straightforward, while the second obtains information about the module author, the module abstract (a summary of what it does), the software license the code is issued under, the Perl version the code requires (which for a Catalyst application will be version 5.8001 at a minimum), and the version number of the distribution (which defaults to version 0.01 for a new Catalyst application). The catalyst line tells the build system to use Module::Install::Catalyst, which contains some convenience functions we will use later. The install_script directive tells Module::Install that if the Catalyst application is installed, then all the files in the script directory will need to be installed into the user's PATH (usually into /usr/local/bin on a Unix system). The auto_install directive instructs Module::Install to try to install all the CPAN prerequisites indicated in Makefile.PL, and WriteAll is the instruction to proceed with writing Makefile.PL and some other files required for the build process.

The next section of MakeFile.PL contains information about our application's dependencies. Our application will translate sentences into kitty pidgin with the Perl module Acme::LOLCAT, so we add the line requires 'Acme::LOLCAT' to this section of Makefile.PL.

We are going to want to make our application available both as a standard web page and as a very simple web service, so we need to install a suitable view for each. The TT (Template Toolkit) view is the usual choice for rendering HTML for Catalyst applications. For the web service view, we will use a JavaScript Object Notation (JSON; a data serialization language that is similar to YAML but easier to write by hand). We might want Unicode strings to be dealt with transparently, which means that our application should have no problems accepting characters like 김치 in our input, so we will make use of Catalyst::Plugin::Unicode. The whole set of modifications to this part of the Makefile.PL file is as follows:

```
requires 'Acme::LOLCAT';
requires 'Catalyst::View::TT';
requires 'Catalyst::View::JSON';
requires 'Catalyst::Plugin::Unicode';
```

Next, we install these dependencies. Rather than entering a CPAN shell, we can call perl Makefile.PL from the shell, which results in the following (truncated) output:

```
$ perl Makefile.PL
include /Users/fj/LolCatalyst-Lite/inc/Module/Install.pm
[snip]
*** Checking for Perl dependencies...
[Core Features]
- Catalyst::Runtime              ...loaded. (5.8000 >= 5.8000)
- Catalyst::Plugin::ConfigLoader   ...loaded. (0.20)
- Catalyst::Plugin::Static::Simple ...loaded. (0.20)
- Catalyst::Action::RenderView     ...loaded. (0.08)
- parent                         ...loaded. (0.221)
- Config::General                ...missing.
- Catalyst::View::TT             ...missing.
- Catalyst::View::JSON           ...missing.
- Catalyst::Plugin::Unicode      ...missing.
- Acme::LOLCAT                   ...missing.
==> Auto-install the 5 mandatory module(s) from CPAN? [y] y
CPAN: File::HomeDir loaded ok (v0.80)
*** Dependencies will be installed the next time you type 'make'.
    (You may need to do that as the 'root' user.)
*** Module::AutoInstall configuration finished.
[snip]
Warning: prerequisite Acme::LOLCAT 0 not found.
Warning: prerequisite Catalyst::Plugin::Unicode 0 not found.
Warning: prerequisite Catalyst::View::JSON 0 not found.
Warning: prerequisite Catalyst::View::TT 0 not found.
Warning: prerequisite Config::General 0 not found.
Writing Makefile for LolCatalyst::Lite
```

You can see from the preceding output that we need to install a number of modules. Next we type **make**, which results in a lot of output that we won't show here, but we should end up with all of the dependencies for the application being installed.

```
> *** Module::AutoInstall installation finished.
```

If you have trouble with this process, most likely due to failing tests, see Appendix C. Note that even though you have Catalyst::Devel installed, this process will still end up installing a lot of other modules from CPAN. This is because Catalyst doesn't make any assumptions about the various components (e.g., templating view, business logic model, etc.). By the end of this chapter, we will have installed the majority of the CPAN modules required for this book. Note that sometimes this can be time consuming, particularly on slow hardware or on Windows-based systems (including Cygwin).

Writing the Application

Now that we have installed all the dependencies we're going to need, we can get started with the application. Initially, our front page should display a form in which to enter some text. The root controller is responsible for handling the logic of the top-level namespace in your application. That is, if you request http://localhost:3000 with the development server running, Catalyst will by default call code in LolCatalyst::Lite::Controller::Root. So we open up the file lib/LolCatalyst/Lite/Controller/Root.pm. For the rest of this section, we'll look at the code generated by the catalyst.pl script.

```
package LolCatalyst::Lite::Controller::Root;
use strict;
use warnings;
use parent 'Catalyst::Controller';
__PACKAGE__->config->{namespace} = '';
```

The first part of the module is just the standard setup for a Catalyst::Controller. Catalyst is just Perl code, and a Catalyst::Controller is just a Perl module.

```
sub index :Path :Args(0) {
    my ( $self, $c ) = @_;
    # Hello World
    $c->response->body( $c->welcome_message );
}
```

Note In this chapter, we usually refer to a particular file by its package name, so LolCatalyst::Lite:: Controller::Root is contained in the file lib/LolCatalyst/Lite/Controller/Root.pm. This can be a bit confusing, as occasionally we would want to add code to LolCatalyst::Lite (i.e., the file lib/LolCatalyst/ Lite.pm) itself. This is not a controller class, but it's easy for beginners to mistake it for one. So if we think there's potential for confusion, we'll refer to the package name and the filename (relative to the application root directory); otherwise, we'll just stick to the package name and let you infer the filename.

The name of the subroutine, in this case index, is arbitrary (although good programming practice would suggest that you name it something meaningful). The :Path attribute means that this subroutine will run when the Catalyst dispatcher receives a request for a particular path or range of paths. The :Args(0) attribute configures the conditions of this path—in this case, the path that the controller is configured for with no subsequent arguments. That is, if an application is configured to run from http://example.com/ (the application root), then this index subroutine will run when the application root is requested with nothing else after the URL path. Note that code generated with older versions of Catalyst::Helper will have sub index :Private instead. This was a stylistic change introduced in Catalyst::Devel version 1.08 that simply improves readability and consistency.

The second subroutine in the code is the default :Path subroutine. This is configured to be called if no other URL in the entire application is callable—compared to index :Path :Args(0), default :Path is called if no other URL in the application matches. This makes it ideal for the "Page not found" action, which is what it's almost always used for. Note that before Catalyst::Devel version 1.08, this was generated as sub default :Private as well.

```
sub default :Path {
    my ( $self, $c ) = @_;
    $c->response->body( 'Page not found' );
    $c->response->status(404);
}
1;
```

The final subroutine is the call to end, which dispatches the completed request to the relevant view.

```
sub end : ActionClass('RenderView') {}
```

This is the code that runs after all of the other controller code. We can provide postprocessing logic in this subroutine, but even if we have no additional logic, the empty subroutine is necessary. An example of adding some postprocessing code is as follows. This code adds the Last-Modified HTTP header to each page requested from the application:

```
sub end : ActionClass('RenderView') {
    my ($self, $c) = @_;
    $c->response->headers->header(
        'Last-Modified' => localtime(),
    );
}
```

This code might be useful if rather than using localtime, we obtained a timestamp from a database, or from a file's last modification time. Later on we'll show how to process application errors with a simple error-handling mechanism using the end action.

A Brief Explanation of Views

There are essentially three different kinds of views:

- The first view is a simple web page. Typically these use a templating mini-language to provide an interface between Perl and an HTML (+ CSS + JavaScript) web page. We went through the basics of this in Chapter 1 when we examined CGI scripting in some detail. Later on in this chapter, we'll look at how to plug Catalyst into the Template Toolkit view.

- The second kind of view is typically used to provide data for a program using your application as a web service. Here the usual requirement is to send and to receive data in a web-friendly (i.e., text-based), computer-readable format. Common formats are JSON, XML, and YAML. The following example Perl script shows a simple example of these three formats:

```perl
#!/usr/bin/env perl;

use warnings;
 use strict;

 my @list = qw/Fred Wilma Barney Betty Dino Pebbles/;

 use YAML;

 print Dump \@list, "\n";

 # Output
 # ---
 # - Fred
 # - Wilma
 # - Barney
 # - Betty
 # - Dino
 # - Pebbles
 # ---

 use JSON;
 print to_json(\@list), "\n";

 # Output:
 # ["Fred","Wilma","Barney","Betty","Dino","Pebbles"]

 use XML::Simple;
```

```
    my $xs = XML::Simple->new;
    # note arg to XMLout needs to be a hashref;
    print $xs->XMLout({flintstones => \@list });  # Output:
    # <opt>
    #   <flintstones>Fred</flintstones>
    #   <flintstones>Wilma</flintstones>
    #   <flintstones>Barney</flintstones>
    #   <flintstones>Betty</flintstones>
    #   <flintstones>Dino</flintstones>
    #   <flintstones>Pebbles</flintstones>
    # </opt>
```

Note that the XML, as generated by XML::Simple, is going to be harder to parse than the other two formats. Where XML needs to be read from or written to an existing schema, usually the Perl module XML::LibXML should be used. However, in simple cases, XML is generally an overcomplicated data transfer format. JSON is usually a good default, as it is supported natively by JavaScript and can be easily used for client-side scripting.

• The third kind of view involves serving non-HTML files (e.g., spreadsheets, CSV, and streaming media). Usually this code is sufficiently simple so as not to require a special view. The following code will serve a string as a text file called data.txt in a Catalyst controller action:

```
    # make sure the $txt variable  contains your plain text data
    $c->res->content_type('text/text-plain');
    $c->res->header('Content-Disposition', qq/attachment; filename="data.txt"/);
    $c->res->body($txt);
```

Our First Template

First we need to create the view. We can do this with the Catalyst::View::TT helper (called, slightly confusingly, Catalyst::Helper::View::TT) with the following command from the application root directory:

```
script/lolcatalyst_lite_create.pl view Web TT
```

This command allows you to use the powerful Template Toolkit templating language within Catalyst. Template Toolkit is used in Catalyst::Helper, so it will always be on a machine that has already had Catalyst::Devel installed. In this case, we have created a view called LolCatalyst::Lite::View::Web.

We are going to change the index action in LolCatalyst::Lite::Controller::Root to display a form. This requires that we delete most of the code in the subroutine.

```
sub index :Path :Args(0) {
    my ( $self, $c ) = @_;
}
```

Note that Catalyst will automatically look for a template with the same name as the sub-routine (with the configuration variable TEMPLATE_EXTENSION appended; by default, this is .tt), so for the index sub, Catalyst::View::TT will look for the same template name as the subroutine it was called from if $c->stash->{template} is not explicitly set. This also prepends the namespace, so an action like the following in a hypothetical Controller::Test:

```
sub add : Local { }
```

will automatically try to render the template in root/test/add.tt.

Next, we change directory to root/ and make a quick and basic HTML page with the following command:

```
perl -MCGI=:standard -e 'print start_html("[% title %]"),end_html;' > page.tt
```

This uses the module CGI (included in Perl's core) to generate a stub web page and uses the CGI module's procedural interface to do so. We want to place a form as follows in the page, just after the <body> tag:

```
[% content %]
```

Now, in the same directory, we create a file called index.tt and put the following inside it:

```
[% WRAPPER page.tt title = c.config.name ; END %]
<form name="translate" method=POST action="translate">
  <input type="text" name="lol" value="" title="enter text to translate">
  <input type="submit" value="Translate">
</form>
```

The WRAPPER directive tells the Template Toolkit to use page.tt as a wrapper and to include the content of index.tt in the [% content %] portion of the wrapper page. This is a simple way of providing consistent headers, footers, and other layout elements across a site without having to repeat yourself. Later on, we will show how to use the WRAPPER configuration directive in the TT view to avoid having to specify it in every template.

We can now test our application by running the server from the application root with this command:

```
script/lolcatalyst_lite_server.pl
```

We will see a lot of debug output. For now, we can visit the web page http://localhost: 3000 and we'll see a text box with a button next to it labeled Translate. We can enter some text into the text box and submit the form, and sure enough we get the text "Page not found" and the 404 response status. The form submits to the page "/translate", so we want to write an action that will be called when this page is requested. We have some choices to make here. For simple applications like this one, we can use :Local as an attribute so that sub translate :Local will be run when we make a request to /translate from our action. The terminal part of the request path is the name of the subroutine that will be called. Note that the :Local attribute is a simplified interface to the Catalyst dispatcher, and it is only really suitable for simple applications that will not have a long maintenance cycle. Also note the comments in the code that show how to deal with GET and POST parameters separately, or together. Again in LolCatalyst::Lite::Controller::Root, we add the following:

```
sub translate :Local {
    my ($self, $c) = @_;
    my $lol = $c->req->body_params->{lol}; # only for a POST request
        # $c->req->params->>{lol} would catch GET or POST
        # $c->req->query_params would catch GET params only
    $c->stash(
      lol => $lol,
      result => $c->model('Translate')->translate($lol),
      template => 'index.tt',
    );
}
```

Unlike the `index` action, here we explicitly set the template. You can see from the call to `$c->model` that it's nearly time to write our first Catalyst::Model. But first to check that the code we've just written compiles, we'll need to restart the server: `script/lolcatalyst_lite_server.pl`. Although the development server compiles and runs at this stage, and POST data can be sent to `http://localhost:3000`, as soon as this action is requested we get the following error:

```
"Caught exception in LolCatalyst::Lite::Controller::Root->translate
"Can't call method "translate" on an undefined value at
/Users/kd/LolCatalyst-Lite/script/../lib/LolCatalyst/Lite/Controller/Root.pm
line 24."
```

We should handle this error more elegantly for the end user, so we modify the `end :` `ActionClass('RenderView')` action to the following:

```
sub end : ActionClass('RenderView') {
    my ($self, $c) = @_;
    my $errors = scalar @{$c->error};
    if ($errors) {
        $c->res->status(500);
        $c->res->body('internal server error');
        $c->clear_errors;
    }
}
```

We then restart the server and check the website. This returns an HTTP status code of 500 as well as the text "internal server error" for use by the web client.

Note the syntax `my $errors = scalar @{$c->error}`. If you have trouble understanding what this means, you will have to improve your understanding of Perl references to be able to make use of this book. The code `$c->error` is an array reference as defined by Catalyst. `@{$c->error}` returns the array that the reference points to. Calling the scalar function on this array returns the number of elements in the array. If there are no elements in the array, this value is 0 and so evaluates to false. So the HTTP status code and returned text are set only if there are any errors in the array. Note that it's possible to do many things in this action, including setting the stash and the template to provide a "pretty" error page.

A Brief Introduction to Catalyst Models

A best practice for a Catalyst model is for it to be a thin wrapper to provide access to data-related functionality. It's generally good to make your modules entirely self-contained wherever possible, and then plug them into Catalyst after the business logic for the model data is complete. We'll see how to do that in Chapter 4. Sometimes we will need to write our own module, like a database schema that lives outside the Catalyst application's namespace that is then used by the Catalyst::Model.

The model connector (which inherits from Catalyst::Model) is what Catalyst uses to communicate to the business logic model(s). It provides a means to access the model from the controller while maintaining clear separation of concerns. Having said that, here we're going to shove all our business logic into the Catalyst model.

In this case our model is pretty simple. We can get it started with another Catalyst helper:

```
script/lolcatalyst_lite_create.pl model Translate
```

which will create the Translate.pm file in the directory lib/LolCatalyst/Lite/Model/.

This file is nearly empty, containing just some documentation and the following:

```
package LolCatalyst::Lite::Model::Translate;


use strict;
use warnings;
use parent 'Catalyst::Model';


1;
```

We want to add our external model here, with the following code:

```
use Acme::LOLCAT ();

sub translate {
  my ($self, $text) = @_;
  return Acme::LOLCAT::translate($text);
}
```

Back in LolCatalyst::Lite::Controller::Root, our code in the translate subroutine is basically complete. Next we can add the following line to root/index.tt just above the form:

```
[% IF result %]<p>[% lol _ ": " _ result %]</p> [% END %]
```

There are a couple of subtleties to note here. First, Catalyst::View::TT will allow you to refer to variables in the stash as c.stash.variable or simply as variable, which is the style we've used in the preceding code. Second, while we can refer to other things that are present in the $c object in our templates, this is not terribly good practice—in general, it is best to explicitly set the stash with things that you want to use in the template, so we end up using lol (aliased from c.stash.lol) rather than c.req.params.lol in our code. When we restart our server (script/lolcatalyst_lite_server.pl) and reload our page, we are now able to translate text into LOLspeak.

Adding a Different View

Let's say we want to make a simple web service. The translate action provides us with a web page with the translation. We will also provide a translate_service action that does the translation but provides a JSON data structure for processing by external software.

Note This section is very short, but it is crucial to get the rest of this chapter's application running properly. Make sure you don't miss out. If you have failing tests later on in this chapter, the most likely reason is that you've forgotten to add the Service view.

First we have to add the JSON view to the application. We'll give it the name Service to indicate that it's the view for the web service.

```
script/lolcatalyst_lite_create.pl view Service JSON
```

Now we should adjust the application configuration to set a default view, which is called by default in your application. In this case, it will be the HTML view. We add the following to lolcatalyst_lite.conf in the root directory of the application:

```
default_view Web
```

This indicates that unless $c->stash->{current_view} is set to something else, the web view will be used to render requests. (Actually, there are other circumstances in which the default view won't get called, but this is the most common one.)

The code to add to LolCatalyst::Lite::Controller::Root to provide the web service is very simple:

```
sub translate_service : Local {
    my ($self, $c) = @_;
    $c->forward('translate');
    $c->stash->{current_view} = 'Service';
}
```

We'll defer trying this out to the next section, where we discuss testing.

ADDING MULTILANGUAGE SUPPORT

While Acme::LOLCAT really only deals with translating from English to kitty pidgin, there may be circumstances in which we want to include Unicode characters such as 김치 in our translations. So we modify LolCatalyst::Lite (lib/LolCatalyst/Lite.pm) to include the Unicode plug-in:

```
use Catalyst qw/-Debug
                ConfigLoader
                Static::Simple
                Unicode/;
```

This should transparently deal with all the encoding and decoding of user input for us. Trying it out is deferred to the "Testing" section. You won't actually see any difference in most cases, but using the Unicode plug-in will ensure that Unicode input from the Web will be treated correctly automatically.

Testing

As mentioned previously, the built-in server is an essential tool. Being able to quickly test how the application works during the development cycle is very important. In this case, we can now start the development server and verify that the application works manually with the following procedure.

1. Start the development server:

   ```
   $ script/lolcatalyst_lite_server.pl
   ```

   and then go to the provided web server (e.g., http://localhost:3000).

2. Enter some text ("Can I have a cheese burger?") into the text box and click the Translate button.

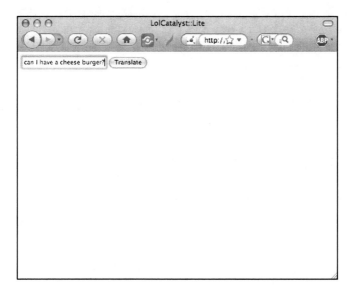

3. Verify the returned text is a correct translation ("I CAN HAZ CHEEZ BURGR" or similar; remember that Acme::LOLCAT is nondeterminant).

■**Note** You can use the CPAN module HTTP::Recorder along with Test::WWW::Mechanize::Catalyst to quickly rig up automated tests for your application (although if your application is JavaScript dependent, HTTP::Recorder won't work very well). We don't use Test::WWW::Mechanize::Catalyst in the automated testing section for many applications in this book, but it is a useful choice.

The script/lolcatalyst_lite_test.pl script will test individual pages of our application from the command line. Because our application shows only interesting behavior on a successful POST request, this is of limited use to us for the time being. However, it is worth noting that issuing the following command:

```
script/lolcatalyst_lite_test.pl /
```

will print out the HTML for the form we just wrote, as well as the debug information.

Tip If you're on a Unix system and have the Lynx text mode web browser installed, try `script/`
`lolcatalyst_lite_test.pl / | lynx -dump -stdin | less` for a simple text rendering of your page.
You may also want to set the environment variable `CATALYST_DEBUG` to 0 (`CATALYST_DEBUG=0 script/`
`lolcatalyst_lite_test.pl / | ...`) to suppress debug messages.

If we run the following:

```
script/lolcatalyst_lite_test.pl /translate
```

we get the same output, as we are unable to use this test script to perform an appropriate
POST request.

In the sections that follow, we'll cover automated testing of our application. We'll use the
Perl debugger to step into the application's code to fix an issue with the web service portion of
the application. Finally, we'll add and test an authentication layer to our application.

Automated Testing

If we look in the t directory of our application, the various helpers have already generated a
few tests for us:

```
01app.t            03podcoverage.t    view_Service.t
02pod.t            model_Translate.t view_Web.t
```

We can run these tests already with the command `prove -l t` from the application root,
which finishes with the following output:

```
All tests successful.
Files=6, Tests=5,  4 wallclock secs ( [ ...])
Result: PASS
```

All this tells us at this stage is that all our modules compile OK. We want to test the three
things that our application does. To reiterate, these are

- We get the web form when requesting the root page.

- When we make a POST request to `/translate`, we get a kitty pidgin translation of our
  form contents in HTML.

- When we make a POST request to `/translate_service`, we get a kitty pidgin translation
  of our form contents in JSON format.

We can replace the code generated by `catalyst.pl` in `t/01app.t` with the following.
This code performs a request for the front page and then makes a POST request to both the
`/translate` and `/translate_service` actions, and checks the content type, response status,
and returned content for both requests. Note that `http://localhost` is a "pretend" domain.
Catalyst::Test translates this internally with no web server involved (although if the `CATALYST_`
`SERVER` environment variable is set, Catalyst::Test can be used to test against a running server).

```perl
use strict;

use warnings;
use Test::More qw(no_plan);

BEGIN { use_ok 'Catalyst::Test', 'LolCatalyst::Lite' }
use HTTP::Headers;
use HTTP::Request::Common;

# GET request

my $request = GET('http://localhost');
my $response = request($request);
ok( $response = request($request), 'Basic request to start page');
ok( $response->is_success, 'Start page request successful 2xx' );
is( $response->content_type, 'text/html', 'HTML Content-Type' );
like( $response->content, qr/Translate/, "Contains the word Translate");
# test request to translate
$request = POST(
        'http://localhost/translate',
        'Content-Type' => 'form-data',
        'Content'      => [
            'lol' => 'Can i have a cheese burger?',
        ]);
$response = undef;
ok( $response = request($request), 'Request to return translation');
ok( $response->is_success, 'Translation request successful 2xx' );
is( $response->content_type, 'text/html', 'HTML content type' );
like( $response->content, qr/CHEEZ/, "Contains a correct translation snippet");
# test request to translate_service
$request = POST(
        'http://localhost/translate_service',
        'Content-Type' => 'form-data',
        'Content'      => [
            'lol' => 'Can i have a cheese burger?',
        ]);
$response = undef;
ok($response = request($request), 'Request to return JSON');
ok( $response->is_success, 'Translation request successful 2xx' );
is( $response->content_type, 'application/json', 'JSON content type' );
like( $response->content, qr/CHEEZ/, "contains translated string");
```

■**Note** Recall the is, ok, and like functions from our discussion of Moose in Chapter 2.

Note that with the exception of the last test, we don't really need to test the full text of the translation, as that should already have been taken care of in the Acme::LOLCAT test suite. In the case of the request that returns JSON, we have taken a shortcut—we probably ought to have deserialized the JSON data into a Perl data structure and then tested that as Perl data. However, for our current purposes, this is simpler and works. Having said that, we may need to change this test when we extend the application.

Fixing the Plan

Note at the beginning of the test we have the following line:

```
use Test::More qw/no_plan/;
```

Once a full test plan has been developed, it's a good idea to explicitly state the number of tests that are going to be performed. The output of the command CATALYST_DEBUG=0 prove -l t/01app.t results in the following output:

```
t/01app....ok
All tests successful.
Files=1, Tests=13, 12 wallclock secs ( 0.04 usr  0.01 sys +  1.36 cusr
 0.40 csys =  1.81 CPU)
Result: PASS
```

We can see from Tests=13 that there are a total of 13 tests in this file, so we can replace qw/no_plan/ with tests => 13, as follows:

```
use Test::More tests => 13;
```

If we add a couple more tests to the test file without altering the plan, with the following code:

```
ok(1, 'true');
ok(0, 'false');
```

this results in the following output:

```
#   Failed test 'false'
#   at t/01app.t line 46.
# Looks like you planned 13 tests but ran 2 extra.
# Looks like you failed 1 test of 15 run.
t/01app.... Dubious, test returned 1 (wstat 256, 0x100)
 All 13 subtests passed

Test Summary Report
-------------------
t/01app (Wstat: 256 Tests: 15 Failed: 2)
  Failed tests:  14-15
  Non-zero exit status: 1
  Parse errors: Bad plan.  You planned 13 tests but ran 15.
Files=1, Tests=15,  5 wallclock secs ( 0.04 usr  0.02 sys +  1.27 cusr
 0.27 csys =  1.60 CPU)
Result: FAIL
```

This output indicates that there were two more tests than expected, and that one of these extra tests passed and the other failed. If you don't understand why ok(1) passes and ok(0) fails at this point, you probably need to read the documentation for Test::More with the command perldoc Test::More. In general, having a plan with an explicit number of tests is a good idea, because it makes it easier to keep track of development activity. Remove those final two tests now.

Checking and Fixing the JSON Request

Using automated testing also allows us to keep track of what is happening with data in our application more readily. We can use the Perl debugger to have a look at the content of our JSON response. Initially, we need to run the test script. The quickest way to do this under the Perl debugger is by issuing the command CATALYST_DEBUG=0 perl -Ilib -d t/01app.t (again with server debugging turned off to suppress Catalyst's debug output). Note the annotations in the following transcript:

```
Loading DB routines from perl5db.pl version 1.28
Editor support available.


Enter h or `h h' for help, or `man perldebug' for more help.



1..13
ok 1 - use Catalyst::Test;
main::(t/01app.t:14):    my $request = GET('http://localhost');
```

Here we instruct the debugger to break at line 51, which is where we want to examine the JSON request.

```
DB<1> b 51
```

Immediately after specifying the break point, we want to continue execution of the test script.

```
DB<2> c
ok 2 - Basic request to start page
ok 3 - Start page request successful 2xx
ok 4 - HTML Content-Type
ok 5 - Contains the word Translate
ok 6 - Request to return translation
ok 7 - Translation request successful 2xx
ok 8 - HTML content type
ok 9 - Contains a correct translation snippet
ok 10 - Request to return JSON
main::(t/01app.t:51):    ok( $response->is_success, 'Translation request success
ful 2xx' );
```

This is the point in the script where we want to look at the JSON response to see what it looks like.

```
  DB<2> p $response->content
  {"current_view":"Service","template":"index.tt","lol":"Can i have a cheese➥
burger?","result":"I CAN HAZ CHEEZ BURGR?"}
  DB<3> c
ok 11 - Translation request successful 2xx
ok 12 - JSON content type
ok 13 - contains translated string
Debugged program terminated.  Use q to quit or R to restart,
  use O inhibit_exit to avoid stopping after program termination,
  h q, h R or h O to get additional info.


  DB<3>q
```

Tip You can programmatically add debugger break points into your Catalyst application by adding the code $DB::single=1; to where you want the debugger to stop. If you then run your tests using perl -Ilib -d t/test_file.t, execution will stop in the middle of your request so that you can inspect the data for debugging purposes.

Note that in the preceding JSON output, we found a problem with our application. While we're only interested in the output from the translation at the moment, we're also getting information about the template for the HTML view and the name of the current view (i.e., all the presentation-specific information in the stash). As it happens, all we're interested in is the data in the stash, so we need to configure LolCatalyst::Lite::View::Service so that we receive only data from a JSON request. The simplest way to fix this is to allow only the lol item from the stash to be delivered by the JSON view. To this end, we add the following line to LolCatalyst:: Lite::View::Service (just before the final line containing 1; and nothing else) in the file:

```
__PACKAGE__->config({ expose_stash => [ qw/lol result/ ] });
```

The special keyword __PACKAGE__ is a Perl shortcut for the current package name (in this case, LolCatalyst::Lite::View::Service). The expose_stash configuration variable tells the JSON view that only the stash keys lol and result should be rendered by the JSON view. With the updated configuration, we can then run the debug session again, and the JSON data structure looks like this:

```
{"lol":"Can i have a cheese burger?","result":"I CAN HAZ CHEEZ BURGR?"}
```

The JSON response contains only relevant data, and not information required by Catalyst's presentation layer.

Having demonstrated how to make a simple web page and web service–based application with no code duplication, the next task we will take on is a common one in web development: adding an authentication layer to our application. In this case, we have decided that we want web service calls only from authenticated users. The next section describes how to add this.

Adding Authentication for the Web Portion of Our Application

Aside from accepting and receiving data, the next most important part of writing web applications is authentication. Here we will use a Catalyst::Helper module from CPAN to set up authentication for us. Following that, we will demonstrate how to require authentication for different parts of the application.

In this case, our authentication scheme (username/password with no fine-grained access control) is simple enough that we can use the module Catalyst::Helper::AuthDBIC to generate all the code required to provide authentication. Note that if you don't have DBIx::Class installed, it could take some time while CPAN deals with the prerequisites. By default, this helper can generate all the code and templates required for web-based or HTTP (basic) authentication. In this case, we are going to use HTTP authentication for two reasons: first because it is simpler than web page/cookie-based authentication with fewer "moving parts," and second because HTTP authentication is often used for web services.

To start, we need to install the Catalyst helper from CPAN:

```
cpan Catalyst::Helper::AuthDBIC
```

This installs a script, auth_bootstrap.pl, into the system path. This script is a helper that adds authentication code to the application by creating a SQLite database and a DBIx::Class::Schema model to go with it, and modifies the application's root package (LolCatalyst::Lite, in this case). After we make sure we're in the application root directory for LolCatalyst::Lite, we issue the following command:

```
auth_bootstrap.pl -credential http
```

which produces the following output:

```
created "db"
Dumping manual schema for LolCatalyst::Lite::Auth::Schema to directory lib ...
Schema dump completed.
 exists "/Users/kd/LolCatalyst-Lite-auth/script/
   ../lib/LolCatalyst/Lite/Model"
 exists "/Users/kd/LolCatalyst-Lite-auth/script/../t"
created "/Users/kd/LolCatalyst-Lite-auth/script/
   ../lib/LolCatalyst/Lite/Model/Auth.pm"
created "/Users/kd/LolCatalyst-Lite-auth/script/
   ../t/model_Auth.t"
Configuring http credential
created "script/lolcatalyst_lite_auth_admin.pl"
```

This helper provides the application with the capability to use HTTP (basic) authentication using a SQLite database to store the username and password information, with a SHA-1 encrypted password stored in the database. Behind the scenes, the module does the following:

- Adds the authentication dependencies into LolCatalyst::Lite's Makefile.PL

- Adds the authentication plug-ins and configuration into lib/LolCatalyst/Lite.pm

- Creates a SQLite database in db/auth.db

- Creates DBIx::Class schemas associated with the SQLite database in LolCatalyst:: Lite::Auth::Schema

- Adds a `lolcatalyst_lite_auth_admin.pl` script to add users from the command line

Adding a New User

We can add a new user to the database by issuing the following command from the application root directory:

```
script/lolcatalyst_lite_auth_admin.pl -user fred -password wilma
```

This command should succeed with no output. We can confirm that the username and password were entered into the database by entering the SQLite database used for storage and checking the users table as follows:

```
$ sqlite3 db/auth.db
SQLite version 3.1.3
Enter ".help" for instructions
sqlite> select * from user;
1|fred||9f468ec766842079d75a616826eeeb01cd877a1d|||
sqlite>
```

Note that we've stored the password as a (hex-encoded) SHA-1 hash using the CPAN module Digest::SHA1 (although this is dealt with transparently by DBIx::Class::Encodedcolumn). The use of a one-way encryption algorithm such as SHA-1 improves security (if a hacker obtains the database, the passwords are not recoverable). A downside, however, is that the password is not recoverable, so if a user forgets her password, she will need to have a new one set.

Requiring Authentication in the Application

In this section, we'll demonstrate how to require authentication in two parts of the application. First, we'll show how to require that only requests to the web service require authentication. Following this, we'll show how to require that all requests need to be authenticated.

Requiring Authentication for Web Services Requests Only

This approach requires that we add a single line of code to the `translate_service` in LolCatalyst:: Lite::Controller::Root by inserting a call to `$c->authenticate` right after `$self` and `$c` are defined, as follows:

```
sub translate_service : Local {
    my ($self, $c) = @_;
    $c->authenticate;
    $c->forward('translate');
    $c->stash->{current_view} = 'Service';
}
```

We can check that this worked by running the application test suite. Previously all tests passed; now the service test should fail. Again, we will switch off debugging to reduce the amount of output the test produces.

```
$ CATALYST_DEBUG=0 prove -l t/01app.t
t/01app.t .. 2/13
#   Failed test 'Translation request successful 2xx'
#   at t/01app.t line 51.

#   Failed test 'JSON content type'
#   at t/01app.t line 52.
#          got: 'text/plain'
#     expected: 'application/json'

#   Failed test 'contains translated string'
#   at t/01app.t line 53.
#                    'Authorization required.'
#     doesn't match '(?-xism:CHEEZ)'
# Looks like you failed 3 tests of 13.
t/01app.t .. Dubious, test returned 3 (wstat 768, 0x300)
Failed 3/13 subtests

Test Summary Report
-------------------
t/01app.t (Wstat: 768 Tests: 13 Failed: 3)
  Failed tests:   11-13
  Non-zero exit status: 3
Files=1, Tests=13,  9 wallclock secs ( 0.15 usr  0.04 sys + 1.88 cusr  0.80 csy
s = 2.87 CPU)
Result: FAIL
```

Now that we have a failing test, it's clearly unacceptable to leave our application in this state. However, some data is needed for testing, and it's not acceptable to keep that data in our production database. To fix this, we'll have to change our application setup and some configuration.

By convention, code, data, and configuration information required for testing lives in a t/lib directory. So we will make a t/lib/db directory and copy the db/auth.db file into that directory:

```
$ mkdir -p t/lib/db
$ cp db/auth.db t/lib/db/
```

We can also delete the user information from the production database:

```
$ sqlite3 db/auth.db
SQLite version 3.1.3
Enter ".help" for instructions
sqlite> delete from user;
sqlite> exit
```

Next, we copy the file lolcatalyst_lite.conf to t/lib/lolcatalyst_lite_testing.conf and modify the line in our new file from this:

```
connect_info dbi:SQLite:__path_to('db/auth.db)__
```

to this:

```
connect_info dbi:SQLite:__path_to(t/lib/db/auth.db)__
```

The final part of modifying the application code requires that we change LolCatalyst::Lite to set up the testing environment if the testing environment variable is set. We replace the line __PACKAGE__->config(name => 'LolCatalyst::Lite'); with the following:

```
if ($ENV{APP_TEST} ) {
    __PACKAGE__->config( 'Plugin::ConfigLoader' =>
                        {file => __PACKAGE__->path_to
                            ('t/lib/lolcatalyst_lite_testing.conf')}
                   );
}
__PACKAGE__->config( name => 'LolCatalyst::Lite' );
```

See the "Advanced Usage of Catalyst::Test" section in Chapter 11 for a better approach to test data.

Now that the configuration is complete, we need to modify t/01app.t to authenticate for the call to the translate_service action so that the request can succeed. To do this, we need to add some code after this line:

```
$request = POST(
    'http://localhost/translate_service',
    'Content-Type' => 'form-data',
    'Content'      => [
        'lol' => 'Can i have a cheese burger?',
    ]);
```

as follows:

```
$request->headers->authorization_basic('fred', 'wilma');
```

Now we are ready to run the test. At this stage, we need to let our application know that we want to use the testing database, so instead of running CATALYST_DEBUG=0 prove -l t/01app.t, we have to set the APP_TEST environment variable, so we run the script as follows:

```
$ CATALYST_DEBUG=0 APP_TEST=1 prove -l t/01app.t
```

However, there is a final problem. If we forget the APP_TEST variable, the tests will fail. Therefore, we need to modify our testing code to enclose everything in a SKIP block. After the line use HTTP::Request::Common in t/01app.t, we add the following code:

```
diag <<EOF


***********************************WARNING****************************
The APP_TEST environment variable is not set.  Please run this test
script with the APP_TEST variable set to one (e.g. APP_TEST=1 prove -l  $0 ) to
ensure that the authentication component of the application is tested
properly.
EOF
if !$ENV{APP_TEST};
```

Then before the line

```
# test request to translate_service
```

we add the following code:

```
SKIP: {
    skip "Set APP_TEST for the tests to run fully",
        4 if !$ENV{APP_TEST};
```

and add a single closing curly brace (}) at the end of the test script.

The diag command is from Test::More and is for printing out diagnostic messages during testing. This is because Test::More monitors STDIN and STDOUT, so a warn statement may not be displayed (depending on the test environment) and a print statement will cause failing tests. The skip function takes two arguments: the first is a textual reason for skipping the test (used in automated reporting), and the second is of the form $number_of_tests condition. In this case, we want to skip four tests if the environment variable APP_TEST is false.

Now if we run the command CATALYST_DEBUG=0 APP_TEST=1 prove -l t/01app.t, all tests pass with the following output:

```
t/01app....ok
All tests successful.
Files=1, Tests=10,  6 wallclock secs ( [ ...])
Result: PASS
```

However, if we omit the APP_TEST environment variable, we get the following output:

```
t/01app....1/10 #
# *******WARNING*********
# The APP_TEST environment variable is not set.  Please run this test
# script with the APP_TEST variable set to one (e.g., APP_TEST=1 t/01app.t ) to
# ensure that the authentication component of the application is tested
# properly
t/01app....ok
All tests successful.
Files=1, Tests=10,  3 wallclock secs ( [ ...])
Result: PASS
```

The reason that the skipped tests pass is because SKIP tests need to pass in an unattended testing environment.

Requiring Authentication for the Whole Application

This approach is also simple, but rather than one line of code, we need to add a new action. First, we remove the $c->authenticate line we added to LolCatalyst::Lite::Controller::Root earlier. Then we add the following code instead, after the translate_service subroutine:

```
sub auto : Private {
    my ($self, $c) = @_;
    $c->authenticate;
}
```

If we then add the code for authorization, $request->headers->authorization_ basic('fred', 'wilma'), after each time we set the value of $request in the test file, all tests will pass again.

Summary

This chapter has been a whirlwind tour of a small number of Catalyst's capabilities. We have built an application that translates snippets of text to kitty pidgin, providing an HTML (web page) view and a JSON (web service) view. We then built HTTP (basic) authentication on top of this, and we demonstrated how to require authentication for either the web service portion only or application wide.

Note that we've emphasized automated testing of the application during this chapter. This is for two reasons: first, it's a convenient way to ensure that the web service is working correctly, and second, one of the strengths of Catalyst is that it makes automated testing of your application easy, so it's good practice to write new tests as you implement parts of your application.

LolCatalyst::Lite does not use the Catalyst dispatcher to its full extent, so its extensibility is limited. In the next chapter, we'll refactor LolCatalyst::Lite to use more advanced features of the dispatcher, and we'll demonstrate how this makes the application easier to extend (e.g., by allowing for multiple language translators).

CHAPTER 4

■ ■ ■

Extending LolCatalyst-Lite

In this chapter, we're going to take the application we built in the last chapter, clean it up, and then extend it. The overall idea here is to show you not only how to refactor an application, but also what a real-world development rhythm is like: the think, code, test, think, code, test cycle we'll use is pretty much exactly what we follow in our production applications. Note that we're not going to do test-driven development as such, since the tests are generally written after the code is blocked out. Instead, we're following a more relaxed rule that in our opinion is the most important part of that practice.

Another thing we're going to do is show each change as it exists in a commit, and the git repository so created will be available online with the rest of the code in the book (you can download the code from the Source Code area of the Apress website, `http://www.apress.com`). If a section of code is in bold, that means that it was newly added; if a section is grayed out, that means that it was removed as part of the commit. The idea here is that you can see what we had before and what we have after, and hopefully understand the thought process that went into making the change and why it was useful and important.

■**Note** In this chapter we're not only describing the architecture of a Catalyst application, but also trying to illustrate the design process and the programmer's thought process. A programmer should make upfront design decisions that allow her to change his mind later; in this chapter, we do just that a handful of times. Keep an eye out for the "Interlude" sections of this chapter. They deal with programmers' thought processes and the "little discoveries" that we make while writing the code, rather than the actual business of writing and shipping our applications.

First Comes the Model

One recurring theme in this book from here on is that the vast majority of the business logic driving your code is essentially independent of the web-based view. The most important part of your code is the model code that reflects the business logic. Therefore, you should always start with the model: the *M* of MVC.

This section outlines the development process which allows us to focus on this model logic. We describe a development process that allows us to achieve clean separation of concerns (a pragmatic version of test-driven development) and begin refactoring the existing LolCatalyst-Lite code so that it will allow LolCatalyst-Lite to handle an arbitrary number of translators and not just LOLCAT. In other words, this section lays the groundwork for the rest of this chapter.

New Model Capabilities

A key tenet of best-practice Catalyst application design is that while you need to have some idea how the user interface (UI) looks before you can start on development, the first thing you should solidify for any given feature should always be the business/domain logic required to support the feature. By correctly modeling the domain before the UI is built, you avoid the risk of UI details coloring your view of the domain, which can easily make later refactoring to provide alternative interfaces very difficult. An extreme example of this would be the many "funny" examples online of stored procedures returning HTML—it does us good to remember that such things are humorous only until we have to maintain the code in question.

Application As Pure UI

The best way to understand what should live in your application's primary files (i.e., MyApp.pm, MyApp/(Model|View|Controller)/*.pm) is to ask the simple question, Is this code specific to this web application? Or to put it more clearly, Is this code specific to the UI workflow for this particular web interface onto my data?

In larger projects, a good pattern is to use MyApp::Web for the Catalyst application and put everything else in the MyApp:: namespace. This makes it easy later to split the web interface off so the domain classes can be deployed on batch servers or similar without requiring a Catalyst installation.

By keeping the application as pure UI, you enable cron jobs, command-line tools, and job queue systems to be built around the same data model with relative ease, and you enable people working on UI changes to focus on the UI without considering the domain model implementation.

Measure Twice, Code Once

While you shouldn't try to design an entire application in one attempt, when working on the design for a particular piece of code it's often worth thinking a few moves ahead. Our normal approach is as follows:

1. We consider the feature we're about to add in isolation and add to the design only those things that are strictly required for the feature.

2. We look at the next few features we expect to add to this area of the application (or think we might add, if the plan isn't that clear yet) and ask how easy they would be to implement given the design we just came up with.

   a. If the answer is that we'd have to rewrite everything, we go back to the drawing board entirely.

   b. If we don't have to rewrite everything, we decide whether it's worth going back to step 1 or if that amount of refactoring will be acceptable at that point.

   c. If there isn't any refactoring required in our guessing about the next feature after this one, or the quantity is acceptable, we move on to step 3.

3. We start sketching out the implementation.

While we're building/modifying the two or three classes that will form the core of the feature, we tend to do so without writing tests as yet. This is because we'll look over the design as we go and often find that in doing so, we need to go back to an earlier stage briefly and change the way the code is coupled together. However, even before you get as far as writing the first line of code, you should be thinking about how you *will* test the code. This helps shake out tight couplings that shouldn't be there, and it forms a rough test plan by the time you have code that compiles, which helps with the next stage.

Always Run the First Code from a Test

The single thing that we find most effective in terms of producing tests without feeling like we're slowing down development is to always make sure the first time a piece of code is run is from a t/ file. Even if it's only a warn [something] at the bottom of a file with no actual tests in it yet, we can then wait until that produces the correct output and trivially record that expected output as a test by changing the warn to is([something], "string", "explanation") or similar. As the first tests for a piece of code are written, we check to see if, again, the design needs to be tweaked, and keep writing until we are reasonably confident the code is correct. If we manage to break something, we can write a test for that and then go and fix the relevant code. While we are not test-driven development addicts, we are great fans of *test-driven debugging*.

Over the course of this chapter, we will rework the LolCatalyst::Lite application from Chapter 3 to create a domain model, refactor the application to use it, and then extend the application, presenting the addition of both code and tests in the order we would do them during development of a real-world application.

Extracting the Model

Before trying to extend the application code, our first project is to factor domain logic out of the web application itself in order to get to the MVC setup we'd normally try to start with. In order to do that, we need to create a domain class that exists on its own outside of the web application, begin making tests for it that can be expanded later as we add functionality, and then refactor the application to make the external classes available via $c->model again.

PRESENTATION OF CODE IN THIS CHAPTER

All of the code in this chapter is available in a git repository downloadable from the Source Code area of the Apress website (http://www.apress.com). Each piece of code in the chapter is presented in an adaptation of the unified diff format. Each section of code starts with a commit message and the filename relative to the application root in the first two lines as follows:

```
# commitmsg: initial external translator object and test
  # lib/LolCatalyst/Lite/Translator.pm
```

When we write completely new code, it looks like all the other code presented in this book. However, if we modify existing code, the line starts with a plus sign (+) if it's a new line, or it starts with a minus sign (-) if it's code to be deleted from the existing code. New lines of code are also presented in bold, and lines for deletion are grayed out to clarify this, so that a block of modified code will look like this within this chapter:

```
# commitmsg: move Translate to be Translator
# lib/LolCatalyst/Lite/Controller/Root.pm
-        result => $c->model('Translate')->translate($lol),
+        result => $c->model('Translator')->translate($lol),
```

Moving the Model Logic into an Application-Independent Class

Looking at LolCatalyst::Lite::Model::Translate, you can see that it currently provides only a single method: translate(). So the stand-alone version is pretty trivial, but there's one important thing to think about before you create it: what should it be called? Originally, we called it translate because that seemed like a simple and obvious name, but it's time to think a bit more about this. translate is a good *method* name, in that $obj->translate($string) means "Object, please translate this string." But if we try to replace "object" with its name we get "Translate, please translate this string," which is clearly nonsense. On the other hand, "Translator, please translate this string" is perfectly parsable as a human sentence, and saying "This model is a translator" reads fine, as does $translator->translate($string).

That established, we create our new lib/LolCatalyst/Lite/Translator.pm file with code that should seem pretty familiar:

```
# commitmsg: initial external translator object and test
# lib/LolCatalyst/Lite/Translator.pm
package LolCatalyst::Lite::Translator;

use Moose;
use Acme::LOLCAT ();
use namespace::clean -except => 'meta';

sub translate {
  my ($self, $text) = @_;
  return Acme::LOLCAT::translate($text);
}
```

```
__PACKAGE__->meta->make_immutable;

1;
```

The use Moose line sets us up as a class with a superclass of Moose::Object, so there's still no need for a new() method. Loading Acme::LOLCAT with () prevents the translate sub from being imported into our namespaces, which we need in order not to clash with the translate method we're going to write. Then we ask namespace::clean to remove everything that's currently in our namespace except for meta when we get to the end of the file. That means that the Moose directives like has, before, and so forth that have been shoved into our namespace will be removed without the requirement for an explicit no Moose call. If we later need to import other directives (e.g., if we have a MooseX::Types-based library of types per project that we import type symbols from), they will also be automatically cleaned out for us, provided we use the other libraries before the namespace::clean line.

Note We use namespace::clean in this example. Elsewhere in the book we use namespace::autoclean, which takes care of all of the straightforward use-cases for this module while requiring less thought from the developer.

Then we need to call make_immutable on the metaclass (which meta is an accessor for; this is why we asked namespace::clean to leave that one in place for us) to tell Moose that we're done declaring this class and it can optimize various things (notably it creates a new() method that's substantially faster than the default because it already knows what slots in the object hashref are valid). A quick

```
perl -Ilib lib/LolCatalyst/Lite/Translator.pm
```

later, we now know that our code builds fine.

Note that using -c for a class file is not a sufficient check, since it tests only that the Perl module compiles, whereas this way we see that the class construction completes as well—as happens, for example, when we use Foo; from a script. This is why perl -c myscript.pl would check both compilation and construction of lib/Foo.pm. Unfortunately, the perl -Ilib approach just gives no output at all when it works, rather than a message saying everything's OK, but if you don't get an error, it compiled and ran fine. Alternatively, you can use the Unix construct:

```
perl -Ilib lib/LolCatalyst/Lite/Translator.pm && echo compiles ok
```

which will output compiles ok if everything works.

Next, it's time to write a rudimentary test for our code:

```
# t/translator/simple.t
use strict;
use warnings;
use Test::More qw(no_plan);
use LolCatalyst::Lite::Translator;
```

```
ok(
  (my $tr = LolCatalyst::Lite::Translator->new),
  'Constructed translator object ok'
);

like(
  $tr->translate('Can i have a cheese burger?'),
  qr/CHEEZ/,
  'String translated ok'
);
```

Notice that we've created a directory for tests for the translator class, so if we want more than one test script later on, we can run them conveniently as a group. We're about to do this for a group currently consisting of one:

```
$ prove -lv t/translator
t/translator/simple......
ok 1 - Constructed translator object ok
ok 2 - String translated ok
1..2
ok
All tests successful.
Files=1, Tests=2,  0 wallclock secs ( [...] )
Result: PASS
```

Having established that works, we can commit and move on to refactor the application to use our new class. Going back to why we called our Catalyst-independent domain model Translator rather than Translate, we should ask ourselves why the copy in the class is called ::Model::Translate but our new class is called ::Translator. Well, a class is what an object *is*, so class names should generally be nouns or at least something nounlike. On the other hand, methods that do things (rather than attribute accessors) should generally be named as verbs, so translate() is correct as a method name, but Translator works better for the class. So we rename LolCatalyst/Lite/Model/Translate.pm to LolCatalyst/Lite/Model/Translator.pm, fix up the package line, and then we change the code in Controller/Root.pm:

```
# commitmsg: move Translate to be Translator
# lib/LolCatalyst/Lite/Controller/Root.pm
-        result => $c->model('Translate')->translate($lol),
+        result => $c->model('Translator')->translate($lol),
```

After a quick prove -lv t/ to make sure the application still passes all tests, we commit.

Now we can switch the Model::Translator class over to using the external object:

```
# commitmsg: hook external translator model back up to the app
# lib/LolCatalyst/Lite/Model/Translator.pm
package LolCatalyst::Lite::Model::Translator;

use strict;
use warnings;
use parent 'Catalyst::Model::Adaptor';
```

```
__PACKAGE__->config(
  class => 'LolCatalyst::Lite::Translator',
  args => {},
);
```

```
1;
```

Catalyst::Model::Adaptor is a (fairly) simple superclass that adopts in an external class and returns an instance of that instead of an instance of itself when Catalyst asks it to create an object. For example, when Catalyst says to the LolCatalyst::Lite::Model::Translator class, "Can I please have your component object for $c->model?" it loads LolCatalyst::Lite::Translator and returns the following:

```
LolCatalyst::Lite::Translator->new({})
```

where the curly brackets {} come from the args configuration key.

So, having replaced our original Model::Translator code with code that should return an identically functioning object, we call prove -lv t/ again. Lo and behold, it passes—LolCatalyst::Lite is now relying on the independent ::Translator object for all its LOLcatting needs.

Extending the Model

Now that we have an extracted model, it's time to start adding features. The first one is to provide multiple different translation types. In order to do that, we need a way to make and use multiple drivers, one for each translation type. We could just add a method per translation type like so:

```
sub _translate_to_lolcat {
  ...
}
```

```
sub translate_to {
  my ($self, $type, $text) = @_;
  my $method_name = '_translate_to_'.$type;
  $self->$method_name($text);
}
```

However, while the LOLCAT translator is relatively simple, we might need to do something more complex later. The second translator we have in mind needs a lot more code, and there's a third or a fourth translator on the horizon that might want to do something even more complex (e.g., talking to a web service to do the translation). So it's probably going to be less hassle to have a class per translation target up front, and it's certainly a better illustration of the techniques involved for the purposes of this text.

In the sections that follow we take our refactored model and write code that will perform generic translation across any number of specified translators. We use techniques used by Catalyst itself to achieve this, while ensuring that our translation modules remain independent of Catalyst.

A Driver Model for Generic Translation

The idea behind a *driver model* is that you have multiple classes that all implement the same interface, one per back end, and provide a uniform calling convention across disparate back ends. The classic example of this in Perl is DBI, where each DBD::SomeDatabase abstracts away the details of how database and statement handle objects have to be implemented for different databases and hides them behind a standard, common API that has proven remarkably resilient over time.

In our case, of course, the driver interface will (at least initially) be a single method.

```
$translator->translate($method)
```

If we open up LolCatalyst/Lite/Translator.pm and change the package line to LolCatalyst::Lite::Translator::LOLCAT, we now have an in-file translator, and we can go on to add code defining the new, driver-using LolCatalyst::Lite::Translator class at the top.

```
# commitmsg: refactor translator to driver-based system
# lib/LolCatalyst/Lite/Translator.pm
package LolCatalyst::Lite::Translator;

use Moose;
use namespace::clean -except => 'meta';
```

We've been here before. Moving on, we need to store a default translation target so $translator->translate can continue to work:

```
has 'default_target' => (
  is => 'ro', isa => 'Str', required => 1, default => 'LOLCAT'
);
```

This Moose definition says that default_target must be either defaulted or supplied from the constructor; it is read-only after the object has been created (it's a good practice to make attributes read-only by default and change them to be read-write only when you find a specific use case for it), and it must be a string. The default has to be LOLCAT, of course, to maintain current behavior.

```
has 'translators' => (
  is => 'ro', isa => 'HashRef', lazy_build => 1
);
```

We'll keep a read-only hashref of translators keyed by the type which, for simplicity, we're going to make the last component of the package name. Note that ro can't actually stop the user from setting and deleting keys of the referenced hash, but anybody who does that gets to keep both halves when the code breaks. The lazy_build key, which we encountered in Chapter 2, says that this attribute should be marked required, that it gets its default by calling _build_$name, and that the default should be called only when somebody actually asks for the value. Of course, we don't mind if it happens sooner than that in this case, but for expensive operations that may not be needed, the laziness is extremely handy.

```
sub _build_translators {
  my ($self) =@_;
  return { LOLCAT => LolCatalyst::Lite::Translator::LOLCAT->new };
}
```

Since we currently have only a single translator, we can hard-code the hashref construction to get started.

```
sub translate {
  my ($self, $text) = @_;
  $self->translate_to($self->default_target, $text);
}
```

```
sub translate_to {
  my ($self, $target, $text) = @_;
  $self->translators->{$target}->translate($text);
}
```

The meat of the code uses a driver-selecting translate_to() method along the lines of the one from the method-based spec and provides a translate() method that just uses the default in order to maintain interface compatibility. Additionally, having a method that uses the default is going to continue to be useful later anyway.

A quick prove -lv t/ later and we have proof this refactor works so far.

Fixing Up the Makefile.PL

Except that, actually, we ran make test out of reflex and got very confused when the t/translator/ tests didn't get run. Which reminds us that our Makefile.PL hasn't had some love in a while, and we should really correct that.

First, we need to remove the bogus requires line for Acme::Bleach and add in the two genuine dependencies we've added so far:

```
# commitmsg: remove bogus requires, add Moose and n::c, add tests_recursive
# Makefile.PL
-requires 'Acme::Bleach'; # test
+requires 'Moose';
+requires 'namespace::clean';
```

Second, we need to add tests_recursive() to tell Module::Install to do a search of subdirectories under t/. We usually add it just above WriteAll, although it works anywhere in the Makefile.PL file. Having done that, we check that make test now tests everything it's supposed to be testing, and we move on to figure out what to do next.

The first thing is to move the LolCatalyst::Lite::Translator::LOLCAT code into its own lib/LolCatalyst/Lite/Translator/LOLCAT.pm file. Having more than one package in a single file is occasionally handy, but it's really not something you should be doing long term. Then we add the following:

```
# commitmsg: factor LOLCAT translator out into its own file
# lib/LolCatalyst/Lite/Translator.pm
use LolCatalyst::Lite::Translator::LOLCAT;
```

to `Translator.pm` and rerun the `make test` to check that everything's still happy.

Of course, writing Translator plug-ins is not going to be fun if we have to remember to go back and add a `use` line and modify the `_build_translators` method every time we add a new driver, and it's not going to make it remotely elegant to provide additional optional drivers either. But hang on—doesn't Catalyst already have a solution to this for models, views, and controllers? Yes, indeed it does: that solution is written using Module::Pluggable, and there's no reason we can't use it. So we update ::Translator to use Module::Pluggable::Object (a less intrusive OO interface to the same functionality, which is also what Catalyst uses) and refactor `_build_translators`:

```
# commitmsg: refactor translator to use Module::Pluggable to find child classes
# lib/LolCatalyst/Lite/Translator.pm
-use LolCatalyst::Lite::Translator::LOLCAT;
+use Module::Pluggable::Object;

 sub _build_translators {
   my ($self) = @_;
-  return { LOLCAT => LolCatalyst::Lite::Translator::LOLCAT->new };
+  my $base = __PACKAGE__;
```

We're using `__PACKAGE__` as the base here because we want to search for things under LolCatalyst::Lite::Translator:: even if we're actually in a subclass of the translator object.

```
+  my $mp = Module::Pluggable::Object->new(
+    search_path => [ $base ]
+  );
+  my @classes = $mp->plugins;
```

Then we can create the Module::Pluggable::Object object, telling it to search only that namespace, and ask it for the list of available plug-ins. This goes away and searches @INC (which in a checkout will include `lib/`) for all `.pm` files whose package names should match the search path. Currently, the only one it's going to pick up is `LOLCAT.pm`, but as we add additional drivers it will find those as well.

```
+  my %translators;
+  foreach my $class (@classes) {
+    Class::MOP::load_class($class);
```

Class::MOP is the core metaobject protocol that Moose is built on top of. It also provides some low-level but extremely handy utility functions. `load_class` will work out what to `require()` to get the class loaded.

```
+    (my $name = $class) =~ s/^\Q${base}::\E//;
```

Then we copy the class to $name and strip the base off the front of the copy in $name. The \Q...\E says that if any regular expression special characters appear in the stuff between them, those characters should be ignored (it uses perldoc -f quotemeta on the delimited chunk, basically). This leaves $name containing LOLCAT for a $class value of LolCatalyst::Lite::Translator::LOLCAT.

```
+     $translators{$name} = $class->new;
+   }
+   return \%translators;
  }
```

Finally, we instantiate an object of the driver class and store it under the name we just generated in the hash that we'll return for the value of the $obj->translators attribute.

And one make test later it appears to work. However, looking at Translator.pm again, it strikes us that "translators" isn't actually something you should ever be looking at from outside the object, so we rename it to _translators, update the calls to it to use the new name, and rename the builder method to _build_translators, again following the _build_$name pattern that lazy_build expects (commitmsg: switch translator hashref from public to protected). Notice that this means that the method name contains a double underscore, which is easy to miss, but since there's nothing stopping you from having both a foo and a _foo attribute, it's the only way to avoid clashes and still make it easy to work out what the method name should be for a given attribute.

This being Perl, the underscore isn't special, but it's a common convention that the character means "You're allowed to subclass this, but don't call it from outside of the class"—approximately a "protected" method in C++ parlance. For a truly private method, you would usually write the following:

```
my $_frobnicate = sub { my ($self, ...) = @_; ... };
...
  $self->$_frobnicate($some, $arguments);
...
```

which makes the method scoped to the block it was defined in, or the file if it's not within braces.

Infrastructure in place, now we can add an extra translator plug-in. Since it has the honor of being used in the only Catalyst::Plugin::Acme:: module other than ::LOLCAT, we're going to implement an in-word scrambler. We're shamelessly stealing both the idea and the code from Catalyst::Plugin::Acme::Scramble on CPAN. We'd prefer to use just a module, but this plug-in has its scrambling code built in, so theft is the only available option.

The idea of a scrambler is that the human brain can still read words, no matter how badly misspelled, so long as the first and last letters are correct and all the right ones are in the middle. So for eamxlpe tihs snetcene souhld siltl be ptrtey redalbe (at least to some extent).

Now we will add the stolen code to a new file, above the namespace::clean line. Putting it there means that code in the file afterward will see the subroutine definition and be able to use it, but at the end of the file the subroutine will be removed just like has, extends, and so forth are. Thus, we don't pollute the method namespace of the final object.

```
# commitmsg: add scramble translator plug-in and tests
# lib/LolCatalyst/Lite/Translator/Scramble.pm
package LolCatalyst::Lite::Translator::Scramble;
```

```perl
use Moose;

# stolen from Catalyst::Plugin::Acme::Scramble under the Artistic License

sub shuffle {
    for ( my $i = @_; --$i; ) {
        my $j = int(rand($i+1));
        @_[$i,$j] = @_[$j,$i];
    }
}

sub _scramble_word {
    my $word = shift || return '';
    my @piece = split //, $word;
    shuffle(@piece[1..$#piece-1])
        if @piece > 2;
    join('', @piece);
}

sub _scramble_block {
    my $text = shift;

    ${$text} =~ s{
                ( (?:(?<=[^[:alpha:]])|(?<=\A))
                  (?<!&)(?-x)(?<!&#)(?x)
                  (?:
                    ['[:alpha:]]+ | (?<!-)-(?!-)
                  )+
                  (?=[^[:alpha:]]|\z)
                )
              }
              {_scramble_word($1)}gex;
}

use namespace::clean -except => 'meta';
```

Below that, we can call _scramble_block exactly as if it had been imported from an external module.

```perl
sub translate {
  my ($self, $text) = @_;
  _scramble_block(\$text);
  return $text;
}

1;
```

Note that the _scramble_block routine modifies its argument in-place, hence wanting a scalarref as the argument (of course, it's possible to do in-place modification without that, but the explicit calling convention is nice). We also need a test for this translator:

```
# t/translator/scramble.t
use strict;
use warnings;
use Test::More qw(no_plan);
use LolCatalyst::Lite::Translator;

ok(
  (my $tr = LolCatalyst::Lite::Translator->new),
  'Constructed translator object ok'
);

my $input = 'hello world';
my $scrambled = $tr->translate_to('Scramble', $input);

like($scrambled, qr/h...o w...d/, 'text matches first/last');
isnt($scrambled, $input, 'text altered');
```

Since the scrambling is randomized and therefore not predictable, all we can do is check the invariants: the first and last letters of each word will remain the same, and the characters in between are randomized. Notice also that we implicitly test the plug-in loading by using the translate_to method rather than testing the Scramble class directly. If you are really keen on unit testing, you might be concerned about this. We consider it a reasonable trade-off to check the loader, and we don't see much advantage to separately testing the two pieces of code.

Looking over the code again, it occurs to us that the subclass of LolCatalyst::Lite:: Translator probably wants to live in its subnamespaces and that perhaps our choice of driver class name wasn't ideal. Since we've been talking about them as translation drivers all through this, LolCatalyst::Lite::Translator::Driver:: seems like a better namespace. So we move the files and adjust their package lines, and change ::Translator to match:

```
# commitmsg: move drivers to better namespace
# lib/LolCatalyst/Lite/Translator.pm
-  my $base = __PACKAGE__;
+  my $base = __PACKAGE__.'::Driver';
```

Enforcing the Interface Using a Role

Finally, since we now have more than one driver package, we should enforce the interface a little to make for easier checking of new code. Happily, Moose provides for this purpose. First, we create a role that indicates the requirement for a translate method:

```
# commitmsg: provide interface definition role and update translator to ➥
check for it
# lib/LolCatalyst/Lite/Interface/TranslationDriver.pm
package LolCatalyst::Lite::Interface::TranslationDriver;
```

```
use Moose::Role;
use namespace::clean -except => 'meta';


requires 'translate';


1;
```

A role is basically a form of mixin/interface on steroids—in this case, we're creating an interface only. When this role is applied to a class, it will verify that a translate method exists and throw an exception if not. Next, we add use aliased at the top of Translator.pm (you'll need to install aliased from CPAN) to load the role and alias it as TranslationDriver so we don't have to type the full package name:

```
# lib/LolCatalyst/Lite/Translator.pm
 use Moose;
+use aliased 'LolCatalyst::Lite::Interface::TranslationDriver';
 use namespace::clean -except => 'meta';
```

Then we add code to the plug-in loading loop to ensure that each class that has declared it does this role:

```
foreach my $class (@classes) {
  Class::MOP::load_class($class);
  unless ($class->does(TranslationDriver)) {
    confess "Class ${class} in ${base}:: namespace does not implement ➥
Translation Driver interface";
  }
  (my $name = $class) =~ s/^\Q${base}::\E//;
  $translators{$name} = $class->new;
}
```

Before we fix the classes to declare they implement the interface, we should run prove -lv t/translate and watch it explode. This proves that the checking is actually doing something. (Another useful rule of thumb is if you're testing a refactor or bug fix, the test should almost always fail on the previous revision of the code but pass on the one you're about to commit.) Then we add the following line to both drivers:

```
with 'LolCatalyst::Lite::Interface::TranslationDriver';
```

to ask Moose to load and apply the role to our class, and run the tests again to verify that everything's working again. And with that, it's time to move on to exposing this new functionality through the application.

Interlude: LolCatalyst::Lite::Model::SnippetStore

In order to illustrate controller refactoring, we're also going to use a simple in-memory store to persist the snippets for the life of the stand-alone server. We'll support the following methods:

```
$store->create({ text => $text });
$store->find($snippet_id);
$store->all;
```

This store will exist for the lifetime of a LolCatalyst::Lite process. The create() method constructs an object from the provided hashref, gives it an ID, and stores it; find() retrieves an object from the store by numeric ID; and all returns all objects in the store. In Chapter 6 (which covers using databases with DBIx::Class), you'll see that this is basically a subset of the ResultSet API, so the code we create here that uses this could be switched to database-backed storage with only the $c->model call name needing to change.

The implementation isn't particularly interesting, but we'll expand it later, so for reference here's the code we're starting with:

```perl
# commitmsg: simple in-memory snippet store
# lib/LolCatalyst/Lite/SnippetStore.pm
package LolCatalyst::Lite::SnippetStore;


use Moose;
use namespace::clean -except => 'meta';

has '_snippets' => (is => 'ro', default => sub { [] });

sub find {
  my ($self, $id) = @_;
  return $self->_snippets->[$id - 1];
}

sub all {
  my ($self) = @_;
  return @{$self->_snippets};
}

sub create {
  my ($self, $new) = @_;
  $new->{id} = @{$self->_snippets} + 1;
  push(@{$self->_snippets}, $new);
  return $new;
}

__PACKAGE__->meta->make_immutable;

1;
```

And here are the tests:

```perl
# t/snippet_store/basic.t
use strict;
use warnings;
use Test::More qw(no_plan);
```

```
use_ok "LolCatalyst::Lite::SnippetStore";

my $store = LolCatalyst::Lite::SnippetStore->new;

my $num_snips = 3;

ok(
  (my @snip = map $store->create({ text => "snippet $_" }), 1 .. $num_snips),
  'Creates ok'
);

cmp_ok(scalar(@snip), '==', $num_snips, "$num_snips created");

is_deeply(\@snip, [ $store->all ], 'deep snippet check');

foreach my $snip (@snip) {
  my $id = $snip->{id};
  is($snip->{text}, $store->find($id)->{text}, "find by id $id ok");
}
```

Another Interlude: Spotting Business Logic Errors

As an interesting aside, when we ran the test suite after writing this, the tests for Scramble
failed. The reason for this turned out to be that we'd written the test as an *ne* check, and the
scrambling process, being random, can actually end up producing something that's identical
to the original input (in fact, "the eel ate the feed" would always do so). This means the test is
wrong, and we should remove it:

```
  # commitmsg: remove test for "is text changed" for scramble since it ➥
can be a no-op
  # t/translator/scramble.t
  like($scrambled, qr/h...o w...d/, 'text matches first/last');
 -isnt($scrambled, $input, 'text altered');
```

Anyway, onward.

Extending the Application

Returning to the meat of the application, it's now time to take advantage of the additional
model code we have to add features to the user-visible part of the application. The reason for
the preceding "Interlude" was that if you have multiple translation types, it's much more fun
if you can submit a piece of text once and then translate it multiple times to different things.
Plus the API of the snippet store is similar to that of DBIx::Class—or it will be when we're done
tweaking it—so the pattern we're about to use is quite similar to how you'd do this for a particular item type/table in a "real" application.

In the sections that follow, we finish up writing our application by bolting the dispatch logic on top of everything else that we've written in this chapter. The design process we've outlined, along with the dispatch logic provided by Catalyst's dispatcher, makes this seem almost like it's an afterthought. While not exactly an afterthought, the fact that the "web part" of this chapter is so short should demonstrate that by taking care of the business logic in a systematic and web application–independent way, it becomes very easy to deal with the logic with which the user interacts with the application.

First New Features

If we're going to have multiple translation types, we're going to need additional URLs, so the first thing to do is to think about the URL space. This is always important for any application that's going to be, well, used by anybody, really, since links and bookmarks can live forever. So if we make a mistake in the URL design, we can clean it up later, but we then have to worry about maintaining redirects (302 permanent redirects preferably, so Google knows to transfer the link rankings). A bit of thought is in order.

/translate/ will still be the main entry point, and it will be the URL to create a snippet. We'll also need a URL for each snippet. Using the numeric ID is fine for us since we don't mind whether the URLs are guessable or they reveal the number of records we have (otherwise we'd use Encode::Base32::Crockford or something similar to obfuscate them), so the remaining question is whether we need to put a path part in front of the ID:

```
/translate/123
    vs.
/translate/id/123 (or the Google style /translate/-/123)
```

In most applications, we would tend to say yes by default to ensure maximum flexibility, but here we think the number of other actions we'll want in this URI space is pretty low, so the prettiness factor of having no extra path part wins.

Next, we need to decide what to use for specific translation types. Since those are names rather than numbers and *could* clash, these do want an extra path part. After a bunch of thinking, we realized that "translate this snippet to LOLCAT" sounded like a good description of what we wanted.

```
/translate/123/to/LOLCAT
```

The preceding line provides reasonable brevity, safety, and prettiness—and room to have an edit action or similar if we add users to the site later.

A Chained Controller

We have our URL map, so now it's time to work out how that decomposes. The steps required to create a new snippet are as follows:

1. Get the snippet store object.

2. Call the ->create method.

3. View the new snippet.

The steps required to view a snippet are as follows:

1. Get the snippet store object.

2. Call the ->find method.

3. View the retrieved snippet.

There are four distinct steps here: get the snippet store, call create to make new object, call find to get an existing object, and set up the view for the snippet object. The logical approach is to write four controller methods that each handle one of these steps. Starting with a blank file lib/LolCatalyst/Lite/Controller/Translate.pm, we write code that attaches /translate/ to an action that loads the snippet store:

```
# commitmsg: chained translator with store
# lib/LolCatalyst/Lite/Controller/Translate.pm
package LolCatalyst::Lite::Controller::Translate;

use strict;
use warnings;
use parent qw(Catalyst::Controller);

sub base :Chained('/') :PathPart('translate') :CaptureArgs(0) {
    my ($self, $c) = @_;
    $c->stash(collection => $c->model('SnippetStore'));
}
```

Here, Chained('/') indicates to the dispatcher that this is the root of a chain (i.e., it comes at the start of the part of the URL that's owned by the application). :PathPart specifies that we want to handle 'translate' rather than it defaulting to the subroutine name 'base'. CaptureArgs(0) serves two purposes: first, it indicates that we have no variable URL parts for this action, and second, the very presence of CaptureArgs tells Catalyst that this action isn't an endpoint in and of itself, and that it should keep looking for further chain parts before it can consider the result dispatchable.

Next, we create the method to do snippet creation:

```
sub create :Chained('base') :PathPart('') :Args(0) {
    my ($self, $c) = @_;
    my $req = $c->req;
    if ($req->method eq 'POST' && (my $lol = $req->body_params->{lol})) {
        my $snippet = $c->stash->{collection}->create({ text => $lol });
        $c->stash(object => $snippet);
        $c->detach('view');
    }
}
```

Here we set Chained to 'base' to say "chain off the base action in the same controller," then set PathPart to '' in order to still be matching /translate/, and provide Args(0) to indicate that we're an endpoint action (i.e., dispatchable, but there are no variable path parts on the end). So now for /translate/ Catalyst will call $controller->base($c) and then $controller->create($c).

Notice that if the request is a GET, we don't do anything at all. The create form can be rendered without further interference from the controller.

If it is a POST request, we also test to see if the lol was filled out, and then we create the snippet and stash it. Obviously in a more serious application, we'd want to do more complex verification, but for our purposes "Did they send us any string at all?" is fine. Having created the object, we put it in the stash under object (the generic key name rather than lol or similar enables code reuse between controller superclasses).

Finally, we detach to the view action (which we're going to write next). This calls that action (as forward() would) as part of the Catalyst request flow control, and then ends processing of this dispatch phase so Catalyst skips straight to calling the end() action in Controller::Root that will render the template.

The idea here is that the view action can set up the things that are common between show existing and show newly created, which in this case would be the translated text:

```
sub view :Chained('object') :PathPart('') :Args(0) {
  my ($self, $c) = @_;
  my $object = $c->stash->{object};
  $c->stash(
    result => $c->model('Translator')
                ->translate($object->{text})
  );
}
```

And to close the loop so the view action actually works on its own, we need to provide a simple object midchain part:

```
sub object :Chained('base') :PathPart('') :CaptureArgs(1) {
  my ($self, $c, $id) = @_;
  my $object = $c->stash->{collection}->find($id);
  $c->detach('/error_404') unless $object;
  $c->stash(object => $object);
}
```

The one interesting thing here is the detach to an /error_404 action. The / indicates that we want an error_404 action in Controller::Root, and doing a detach under :Chained aborts the entire chain call, so view is never called (which is important given it requires the not-going-to-be-present object stash key).

Note In the process of making the main code work, we completely forgot to add the error_404 action. Fortunately, as you'll see in the next section, a test managed to pick that up for us before the end of development and we were able to fix it then.

Adding Templates

With the controller done, it's time to write some templates. First up is a simple view template:

```
# root/translate/view.tt
<p>[% object.text _ ": " _ result %]</p>
```

Our object is currently actually a hash reference, but since Template Toolkit treats . as "method on an object, key lookup on a hashref," this will work now and will continue to work fine later if (when) we change up to a full object.

We also need a create template that needs to remember that it gets called after a successful creation as well, so it needs to call the view template in that case. We test this by seeing if result has been supplied so as to minimize coupling in the code:

```
# root/translate/create.tt
[% IF result; INCLUDE translate/view.tt; END %]
<form name="translate" method="POST" action="translate">
    <input type="text" name="lol" value="" title="enter text to translate">
    <input type="submit" value="Translate">
</form>
```

Next, we need to create a Model/ file for the SnippetStore. Since we don't need anything clever, this can be an empty class that returns a new SnippetStore object from its COMPONENT method (which is what Catalyst calls on classes that provide one to get the runtime component. Catalyst::Model and friends provide a basic one for you, but we don't even need that):

```
# lib/LolCatalyst/Lite/Model/SnippetStore.pm
package LolCatalyst::Lite::Model::SnippetStore;

use strict;
use warnings;
use aliased 'LolCatalyst::Lite::SnippetStore';

sub COMPONENT { SnippetStore->new }

1;
```

Finally, we need to modify Controller/Root.pm so that its translate action isn't bound to /translate/ anymore, since we want our new code to handle it instead:

```
# lib/LolCatalyst/Lite/Controller/Root.pm
-sub translate :Local {
+sub translate :Private {
```

We change the action to be :Private rather than deleting it entirely because the translate_ service action still needs to forward to it in order to operate. :Private is the standard signifier in Catalyst for "This is just an action and nothing else, don't let it be bound to a URL." Note that this means you can't add any other attributes to a :Private action, so as a result our end action has the :ActionClass attribute but not :Private.

Back to the Test Cycle

The next step, as always, is to run the tests, and they pass, so we know that at least the /translate/ create functionality still translates. Then we clean up the tests a bit so they accurately reflect which controller they're testing. The new test file looks like this:

```
# commitmsg: extract translate controller tests
# t/controller_Translate.t
use strict;
use warnings;
use Test::More qw/no_plan/;

BEGIN { use_ok 'Catalyst::Test', 'LolCatalyst::Lite' }

use HTTP::Request::Common;

my ($request, $response);

$request = POST(
        'http://localhost/translate',
        'Content-Type' => 'form-data',
        'Content'      => [
            'lol' => 'Can i have a cheese burger?',
        ]);

ok( $response = request($request), 'Request');
ok( $response->is_success, 'Response Successful 2xx' );
is( $response->content_type, 'text/html', 'Response Content-Type' );
like( $response->content, qr/CHEEZ/, "contains translated string");
```

Notice that rather than specifying the number of tests up front, in this case we use the no_ plan option to Test::More. This is safe provided our test doesn't exit 0 halfway through (highly unlikely), since an uncaught die() will cause a nonzero exit from the interpreter. Specifying the number of tests for the entire file doesn't really gain anything; if you have a specific set of tests in a loop, you should explicitly test that the loop ran the expected number of iterations as we did in the snippet store tests. Experience shows that on large projects that branches heavily to achieve effective parallel development, a top-level test number specification causes merge conflicts and messy version control logs, and can easily break the build through a mistaken merge resolution of the test number.

Interlude: Converting the Snippets to Be Object Based

For the next refactoring, we need our snippets to be objects rather than hash references. We'll explain what this means as we write the code.

For context for the stuff that *is* relevant, here's the diff:

```
# lib/LolCatalyst/Lite/Snippet.pm
package LolCatalyst::Lite::Snippet;
use Moose;
use namespace::clean -except => 'meta';
has 'id' => (is => 'ro', required => 1);
has 'text' => (is => 'ro', required => 1);
__PACKAGE__->meta->make_immutable;

1;
```

```
# lib/LolCatalyst/Lite/SnippetStore.pm
 use Moose;
+use aliased 'LolCatalyst::Lite::Snippet';
 use namespace::clean -except => 'meta';


 sub create {
   my ($self, $new) = @_;
-  $new->{id} = @{$self->_snippets} + 1;
-  push(@{$self->_snippets}, $new);
-  $new;
+  my $snippet = Snippet->new(
+    %$new,
+    id => (@{$self->_snippets} + 1),
+  );
+  push(@{$self->_snippets}, $snippet);
+  return $snippet;
 }
```

Thin Controller, Smart Model

Looking at our controller code, it seems relatively clean, but one piece of code in particular violates the rule that the controller should contain only UI workflow code:

```
# lib/LolCatalyst/Lite/Controller/Translate.pm
my $object = $c->stash->{object};
$c->stash(
  result => $c->model('Translator')
               ->translate($object->{text})
);
```

In order to get the translated text, we need to not only know where to grab the source from, but also pass it to the translator. Well, why can't a snippet know how to translate itself?

So what we're aiming for instead is to say this:

```
# commitmsg: add translation functionality into snippets
# lib/LolCatalyst/Lite/Controller/Translate.pm
my $object = $c->stash->{object};
$c->stash(
  result => $object->translated
);
```

In order to do this, first we need to add a ->translated method to our snippet object and an attribute to keep a reference to the translator in:

```
# lib/LolCatalyst/Lite/Snippet.pm
has '_translator' => (
  is => 'ro', required => 1, init_arg => 'translator',
);


sub translated {
  my ($self) = @_;
  $self->_translator->translate($self->text);
}
```

Notice that we pass init_arg here to make the key to pass to new() translator rather than _translator. While the _translator attribute, once provided, is internal only, the new() argument forms part of the public interface.

We also need to modify the snippet store to hold a reference to a translator so it can pass it to the snippets when they're constructed:

```
# lib/LolCatalyst/Lite/SnippetStore.pm
has '_translator' => (
  is => 'ro',
  required => 1,
  init_arg => 'translator'
);
```

and we make sure it actually passes the translator object along:

```
    my $snippet = Snippet->new(
      %$new,
      id => (@{$self->_snippets} + 1),
+     translator => $self->_translator
    );
```

Next, we add a test to ensure that the fact that the translator object is required is enforced:

```
# commitmsg: test snippetstore translator requirement, improve debugging, fix app
# t/snippet_store/basic.t
+use Test::Exception;

  use_ok "LolCatalyst::Lite::SnippetStore";
```

```
-my $store = LolCatalyst::Lite::SnippetStore->new;
+dies_ok {
+    LolCatalyst::Lite::SnippetStore->new;
+} 'Create without translator object fails';
+
+my $store = LolCatalyst::Lite::SnippetStore->new(translator => 'DUMMY');
```

Notice that because we didn't set a type on the translator attribute, we can supply any value and it passes. Maybe we should restrict it, but this is easy to test and probably good enough.

However, when we run the application tests, it all falls to pieces—huge amounts of output and lots of fails. First, we need to stop debugging being on by default so the output is a little less verbose:

```
# lib/LolCatalyst/Lite.pm
-use Catalyst qw/-Debug
-                 ConfigLoader
+use Catalyst qw/ConfigLoader
```

Note You almost always want to remove -Debug a short way into the development of your application. To turn debugging on, you can set the LOLCATALYST_LITE_DEBUG environment variable (substitute your application name as appropriate) or the CATALYST_DEBUG environment variable to affect all applications, or pass the -d option when you start lolcatalyst_lite_server.pl.

For an alternative approach for dealing with Catalyst's debug output, see Chapter 11.

Second, because we handle the error, we don't actually see the exception, which means we don't know what went wrong yet. In order to fix that, we need to change the error-handling code so that we output the errors to the log:

```
# lib/LolCatalyst/Lite/Controller/Root.pm
    if ($errors) {
+        $c->log->error("Errors in ${\$c->action}:");
+        $c->log->error($_) for @{$c->error};
        $c->res->status(500);
        $c->res->body('internal server error');
```

At this point, we can see the exception, which is the exact same one caught in our dies_ok block because we forgot to update Model::SnippetStore to pass a translator object.

```
# lib/LolCatalyst/Lite/Model/SnippetStore.pm

+use aliased 'LolCatalyst::Lite::Translator';
```

```
-sub COMPONENT { SnippetStore->new }
+sub COMPONENT {
+   SnippetStore->new(translator => Translator->new);
+}
```

Now everything works again. It's always the tiny things you forget that blow up the entire application.

Adding Tests for the New View Functionality

The next step is to add more integration tests, since while we've verified that we didn't break any existing functionality yet, we don't actually have tests for the new view functionality:

```
# commitmsg: tests for view and 404 action
# t/controller_Translate.t
ok(
  $response = request(GET 'http://localhost/translate/1'),
  'Request for default translation type'
);

ok( $response->is_success, 'Response Successful 2xx' );

like( $response->content, qr/CHEEZ/, "contains translated string");

ok(
  $response = request(GET 'http://localhost/translate/100'),
  'Request for default translation type on non-existent object'
);

cmp_ok( $response->code, '==', 404, '404 error returned');
```

The first one passes perfectly. The second one . . . doesn't. This is because the error_404 action is missing.

So we fix that and switch our default action over to use it:

```
# lib/LolCatalyst/Lite/Controller/Root.pm
sub default :Path {
    my ( $self, $c ) = @_;
    $c->detach('/error_404');
}

sub error_404 :Private {
    my ( $self, $c ) = @_;
    $c->response->status(404);
    $c->response->body( 'Page not found' );
}
```

Now, having done this, we go back to the original feature: exposing multiple translation types through the interface. This is now, happily, relatively trivial. This is the point at which shifting logic into the model starts to pay dividends in terms of ease of development. We want to support translate/$id/to/$type, so we chain off object again to reuse the translate/$id logic for free:

```
# commitmsg: 'to' action and tests
# lib/LolCatalyst/Lite/Controller/Translate.pm
sub translate_to :Chained('object') :PathPart('to') :Args(1) {
  my ($self, $c, $to) = @_;
  my $object = $c->stash->{object};
  $c->stash(
    result => $object->translated_to($to)
  );
  $c->stash(template => 'translate/view.tt');
}
```

Notice that since to is purely an endpoint, we can use :Args to indicate the single variable part at the end of the URL. We already have a translate_to method in Translator.pm, so now all we need to do is hook it up:

```
# lib/LolCatalyst/Lite/Snippet.pm
sub translated_to {
  my ($self, $to) = @_;
  $self->_translator->translate_to($to, $self->text);
}
```

It's time to write some tests. Here we'll test that the snippets are being stored and that they do indeed contain the correct text.

```
# t/controller_Translate.t
ok(
  $response = request(GET 'http://localhost/translate/1/to/LOLCAT'),
  'Request for specific translation type'
);

ok( $response->is_success, 'Response Successful 2xx' );

like( $response->content, qr/CHEEZ/, "contains translated string");
```

These tests do indeed pass. Finally, we need to handle the "What if we get an invalid translator?" case, so in a concession to test-driven development, we add more tests first to define the behavior we want in this case:

```
ok(
  $response = request(GET 'http://localhost/translate/1/to/NONEXISTENT'),
  'Request for non-existent translation type'
);

cmp_ok( $response->code, '==', 404, '404 error returned');
```

Of course, currently this code generates an exception from within the translator, so we need to add a guard clause to our translate_to controller. But at this point, we have no way to tell whether a given translation type is available, so the first step is to make that facility available in the translator object:

```
# commitmsg: 404 handling for unknown translation types
# lib/LolCatalyst/Lite/Translator.pm
sub can_translate_to {
  my ($self, $target) = @_;
  return exists $self->_translators->{$target};
}
```

All we need to do is an exists check since we're guaranteed by the way the rest of our code's written that any key is a valid translator. Then, since the controller doesn't know about the translator object, we need to make sure it can ask the snippet object for the information:

```
# lib/LolCatalyst/Lite/Snippet.pm
  has '_translator' => (
    is => 'ro', required => 1, init_arg => 'translator',
+   handles => [ 'can_translate_to' ],
  );
```

What handles says to Moose is "Create a method called can_translate_to, that when called on this object is passed on to the object in the attribute." It's basically equivalent to writing the following:

```
# no file
sub can_translate_to {
  my $self = shift; $self->_translator->can_translate_to(@_);
}
```

except rather shorter. Finally, we hook it up to the controller:

```
# lib/LolCatalyst/Lite/Controller/Translate.pm
  sub translate_to :Chained('object') :PathPart('to') :Args(1) {
    my ($self, $c, $to) = @_;
    my $object = $c->stash->{object};
+   unless ($object->can_translate_to($to)) {
+     $c->detach('/error_404');
+   }
```

We write a test to verify we got it right:

```
# t/controller_Translate.t
+
+ok(
+ $response = request(GET 'http://localhost/translate/1/to/NONEXISTENT'),
+ 'Request for non-existent translation type'
+);
+
+cmp_ok( $response->code, '==', 404, '404 error returned');
```

and one full run of prove -l t later, we have a confirmed working feature.

Notice that once we got the controller and model refactored elegantly, adding the feature was a matter of some upfront thinking about what responsibilities belonged where and then adding a small amount of code each to a number of files. Then we wrote a couple more tests to verify we got it right. This sort of clean and elegant addition of features is what you should strive for in your Catalyst development and what we've been trying to illustrate over the course of this chapter.

You should observe that the writing of tests has actually been a fairly minimal job—simply writing a piece of code each time that corresponds to the check that we'd make in the browser if we were testing by hand. We've mixed unit and integration tests without too much regard for coverage or test-driven design or any other software development religion, but we've still come out the other side of the process with enough tests to be reasonably sure that what we've done works, and a good basis for adding extra tests as we find bugs so that we can be sure that once they're fixed they stay fixed. Tests exist to make development easier and quicker, not to feed any ideological requirement. If you treat them that way, then you'll find that over time it actually becomes simpler to develop with them than without them.

We hope that we've given you a good feel for not only the mechanics of but also the motivation and philosophy behind extending a Catalyst application well, and that this will provide you with a frame of reference from which to understand how we see things and why we do things the way we do in the code going forward through the rest of the book.

Summary

In this chapter, we covered the development process that we recommend you take with Catalyst applications. One of Catalyst's real strengths is that it allows you to forget about your web application for a lot of the time and concentrate on the business logic underlying the data you will eventually display on the web page.

After refactoring the original LolCatalyst::Lite from Chapter 3 in the first half of the chapter, we went on to refactor it again to provide a pluggable infrastructure. This allowed us to create a further translator (Scramble, for aritenlg the psiotion of lteetrs isinde of wdors) and allowed us to add further translators without adding more code to either our web application or our model code. By this time we have a very good understanding of our business logic, and the URL action mapping is easy to provide through Catalyst's Chained dispatch type.

In the next chapter, we will cover sending your application out into the wild using a web server. This is done by using the built-in server, with FastCGI or mod_perl. We will also cover load-balancing solutions for distributing the computational load of your application, which in turn allows you to do zero-downtime, high-availability deployment. You can use any of the example applications in this book to test this for yourself.

CHAPTER 5

■ ■ ■

Deployment

In Chapter 2, we gave a brief overview of the common deployment scenarios for web application development and how they relate to deployment of Catalyst applications. In this chapter, in addition to providing a more detailed explanation of deployment scenarios for configuration of FastCGI and mod_perl under Apache, we will cover some other deployment scenarios using different engines and other web servers.

Using the Built-in Server

The built-in server is important! In the initial stages of developing your application, you should always use the built-in web server—that is, `script/myapp_server.pl`. In this respect, Catalyst differs from traditional CGI or mod_perl development, as most of the low-level details concerning your application have already been taken care of for you.

Occasionally on the Catalyst mailing list or on the #catalyst IRC channel, we encounter people who begin development on a real web server (usually Apache) because the development process for their previous (pre-Catalyst) projects had gone the same route. Don't do this—it's inefficient in terms of both use of developer time and use of resources on your computer. It's fine to rig up a test harness to test an external web server as part of your application's testing process. This has the advantage that you can do behavior testing as you go on the development server, rig up tests with Catalyst::Test or Test::WWW::Mechanize::Catalyst in your application's t/ directory, and then use an extra script to test your application on a live web server. If you want to do this, the tests in the Catalyst-Runtime distribution to look at are as follows:

- `optional_apache-cgi-rewrite.pl` *and* `optional_apache-cgi.pl`: These two test the CGI engine under Apache with and without the use of mod_rewrite.

- `optional_apache-fastcgi-non-root.pl` *and* `optional_apache-fastcgi.pl`: These two test the FastCGI engine under Apache with the application deployed at the server root and below root (i.e., at `http://my.host.name` and `http://my.host.name/myapp/`, respectively).

- `optional_http-server.t`: This tests the built-in server. You can also perform an equivalent test using Catalyst::Test or Test::WWW::Mechanize::Catalyst by running the test server for your application in one console and setting the environment variable `CATALYST_SERVER` in the other console. On a Unix system using the Bash shell, this would look like the following in the first command terminal:

```
$ script/myapp_server.pl
```

and like this in the second one:

```
$ CATALYST_SERVER=http://localhost:3000 prove -l t
```

On a Windows system, you'll need to do this on two lines (or wrap it up in a separate `.bat` file):

```
$ set CATALYST_SERVER=http://localhost:3000
$ prove -l t
```

▪Note Going forward, we'll set environment variables the Unix way: on a single line. If you're on Windows, you'll have to remember to do it the Windows way.

This technique will work for other web servers as well, but the advantage of using a script following the pattern of these `/t/optional_*` tests in the Catalyst-Runtime distribution is that all the server setup is taken care of automatically in the script.

- `optional_lighttpd-fastcgi-non-root.t` *and* `optional_lighttpd-fastcgi.t`: These two tests do the same thing for lighttpd as the Apache scripts do for Apache. Hopefully, one day someone will write a harness for testing the engines under the nginx web server as well.

Deploying with the Built-in Server

There is essentially one scenario in which it is desirable to deploy your application with the built-in server: when you have a single-user application, and you don't make significant use of asynchronous browser requests (e.g., Ajax calls), you can just run the test server and point your browser to `http://localhost:3000` (or `http://127.0.0.1:3000` if you're on a network that doesn't like you to use the localhost domain name). However, this reaches limits quickly. If you have a very small number of users on a local network, and you don't make use of asynchronous requests, then the standard built-in server is acceptable, although you'll almost certainly want to turn on the fork option with the `-fork` flag, which creates a new process for each request and therefore allows limited asynchronous requests to occur, so that two users can request a page concurrently:

```
$ script/myapp_server.pl -fork
```

If you don't do this, then things slow down pretty quickly with multiple concurrent requests. The built-in server is a *blocking* server—that is, it won't process a second request until it's finished processing the first request. Therefore, with multiple concurrent requests a queue forms, and each request will be processed only when the previous ones in the queue have finished. When you have logic in your application, that can take a little while to process (e.g., where you have computationally expensive logic to process), and this can cause things to slow down dramatically.

The built-in server also has a -k option for *keepalive*. The keepalive option means that if the browser sends the header Connection: Keep-Alive with its request, then the server will not disconnect immediately, but will maintain the connection with the client. While you could use this in conjunction with the -fork option to provide a more efficient environment for small-scale deployment with the built-in server, this is not recommended for two reasons: first, the built-in server uses HTTP 1.0, and second, its implementation of forking is relatively unsophisticated and uses more resources than necessary. However, we have deployed a couple of single-user web applications with no problems using the built-in server.

If you want really simple small-scale deployment, but you have significant use of asynchronous requests, or more than a small number of users, or complex logic, meaning requests can take a significant amount of time to process (*significant* might mean over half a second) and the built-in server is not quite good enough. Fortunately, Catalyst provides a second higher performance server based on the built-in server. It's called Catalyst::Engine::HTTP::Prefork, and can be installed from CPAN. All you need to do to use this engine instead of the default one is set the environment variable CATALYST_ENGINE to HTTP::Prefork and run the myapp_server.pl script as normal:

```
$ CATALYST_ENGINE=HTTP:Prefork script/myapp_server.pl
```

Our simple tests (using the ab tool provided by the Apache web server) indicate that for a simple page, the Prefork engine is about two to four times faster than the built-in server. Performance gains will be even greater for more complex controller logic or when requesting more than a single page concurrently.

Note that the Prefork engine doesn't need either the -fork option or the -k option. The -p option still works to run the server on a port other than the default. This engine has a number of additional options (discussed in the Catalyst::Engine::HTTP::Prefork documentation) that are not covered by the automatically generated script. However, the defaults are sensible, so in most cases you won't have to worry about this. The Prefork engine is fast enough and robust enough that a single instance should scale sufficiently that it can be used on its own or behind a front-end proxy. We'll show how to do this next.

HTTP::Prefork Engine Behind a Front-End Proxy

To take advantage of this setup, first you'll need to add the following line into the top-level package in your application (we commonly refer to this as MyApp.pm) before the __PACKAGE__ ->setup line:

```
__PACKAGE__->config( using_front_end_proxy => 1, );
```

Alternatively, you can set this in the application's configuration file, if it's likely to vary on a per-deployment basis.

Next you will want to set up the web server that will be handling the proxy requests. We'll cover how to do this for lighttpd, Apache, and nginx in the sections that follow, and then briefly discuss some other options.

Note The technical term for the front-end proxy is a *reverse proxy*.

Lighttpd

Lighttpd (pronounced "lighty") is an open source, high-performance web server that is well suited to be a low-memory-footprint, fast reverse proxy server. It also supports FastCGI, which we'll cover later in this chapter.

You can obtain lighttpd via your package manager on Linux systems, or you can obtain it via Fink or DarwinPorts, or compile it from source on OS X using the developer tools you installed to get Perl and CPAN working properly. If you're on Windows, we recommend you obtain a binary distribution of lighttpd from the project home page, unless you're comfortable with Windows build tools.

We'll cover compiling lighttpd from source here (on OS X, but the same procedure applies for Linux if you don't want to use the package manager). The source code for lighttpd is available from http://www.lighttpd.net/. If you compile from source, you'll also need the Perl Compatible Regular Expressions (PCRE) library, which is available from http://www.pcre.org/. For both of these, we use the generic procedure to compile from source on a Unix system. First, we extract the downloaded archive and change into the directory, and then we issue the commands in order:

```
$ ./configure
$ make
$ make test
$ sudo make install
```

Lighttpd doesn't appear to have a test suite that runs with the command make test, so skip that stage for lighttpd. By default, lighttpd installs to /usr/local/sbin with no default configuration file. For our current purposes, we'll put the lighttpd configuration file in our home directory in the etc subdirectory (i.e., ~/etc/lighttpd.conf on a Unix system). We also want lighttpd to serve static files without going through Catalyst. We'll need to let lighttpd know where to look for these files in our configuration later on, so we'll put the LolCatalyst::Lite application in the root of our home directory as well.

Here are the contents of the lighttpd.conf file, with comments:

```
server.modules = (
    "mod_access",
    "mod_proxy",
    "mod_fastcgi", # this is here for when we use fastcgi later
    "mod_accesslog"
)
```

```
server.document-root = env.HOME # this value doesn't really matter here as
                                # we're deploying our application from the
                                # server root.  Normally you'd put this in the
                                # virtual host configuration


server.errorlog     = "/tmp/lighttpd_error.log"
accesslog.filename = "/tmp/lighttpd_access.log"


server.bind = "127.0.0.1"
server.port = 8989 # this would normally be port 80 for a production web
                   # server, but would require starting the lighttpd process
                   # as root


# the configuration directive below says to serve every request other
# than those in the C</static> directory (relative to the root URI) with the
# proxy server, and correspondingly serve the pages in the /static directory
# with lighttpd directly.  This is more efficient than relying on
# Catalyst::Plugin::Static::Simple.


$HTTP["url"] !~ "^/static/" {


  proxy.server = ( "/" =>
                        ( (
                            "host" => "127.0.0.1",
                            # the default port for the built-in server
                            "port" => 3000                           ) )
                    )
  }
```

Next we can run the server:

```
$ /usr/local/sbin/lighttpd -f ~/etc/lighttpd.conf -D
```

The -f flag indicates the location of the configuration file, and the -D flag indicates not to go in the background (so we can press Ctrl+C to end the server).

If we visit http://localhost:8989 (or http://127.0.0.1:8989) after running the server, we get the text "503 Service Unavailable" in the browser window. This is because the back end is not running yet. We can remedy that, but before we do, we need to add the following line to lolcatalyst_lite.conf:

```
using_front_end_proxy = 1
```

This takes care of rewriting URLs from the back end to the front end.

Now in another terminal, change directory to LolCatalyst-Lite and run the following command:

```
$ CATALYST_ENGINE=HTTP::Prefork script/lolcatalyst_lite_server.pl
```

Then if you visit http://localhost:8989, you'll get the LolCatalyst::Lite application exactly as it was finished in the previous chapter.

On a proper server deployment, we'd want to write a stop-start script to spawn the back-end server as well as the front-end server. This is a good reason to use the Linux distribution–provided package for lighttpd for the front end, as it comes packaged with its own stop-start daemon.

Also on a larger scale deployment, we might want to consider load balancing, so that we have multiple back ends talking to the HTTP proxy. Load balancing with lighttpd is simple: you replace the configuration inside the proxy.server directive by adding one or more servers there. The following snippet shows how to start using lighttpd's load-balancing features with two servers. Note that you can have as many back-end servers as you want. If your application has lots of I/O bottlenecks, then having multiple back ends running on the same machine but on different ports is probably a good idea. If your application is memory and/or CPU intensive, then they should probably be on different machines.

```
proxy.server = ( "/" =>
                (
                    server1 =>(
                        "host" => "127.0.0.1",
                        "port" => 3000
                    ),
                    server2 =>(
                        "host" => "192.168.1.100",
                        "port" => 3000
                    )


                )
            )
```

For these server-type tasks, we'll want a script to start the server on boot, and stop or restart upon user intervention. On Unix, these are called *stop-start daemons,* and they are spawned by an init script. On Windows, being a more prosaic operating system, they are called *services,* and they are started using the service manager.

There's an init script suitable for use on most types of Unix systems on the Catalyst wiki. While it's for a FastCGI server, it can be easily adapted for use with HTTP::Prefork. An article with an entry on setting up an init script for the back-end server is available at http://dev.catalystframework.org/wiki/gettingstarted/howtos/deploy/lighttpd_fastcgi.

Mac OS X doesn't use the init.d system, opting for launchd and XML-based configuration files. Lingon (http://tuppis.com/lingon) is a convenient and user-friendly GUI for making system daemons on OS X. On Windows, you'll need a utility to make your server script into a service. A few are available, and ExeService (https://slion.net/view/Dev/ExeService) is popular and free.

Apache

The following instructions are for Apache 2 (tested on the stock Apache that comes with OS X Leopard). Some of them may also work for older versions of Apache, but there are no guarantees. We won't bother discussing compiling Apache from source, as that's well documented elsewhere than this book. As with Perl, unless you have a reasonably good reason to compile Apache from source yourself, use a binary version that comes with your distribution. The same advice goes for Windows (you'll have to obtain Apache from http://www.apache.org/dyn/ closer.cgi/httpd/binaries/win32/; Apache comes preinstalled on OS X).

Apache is the most popular web server in use on the World Wide Web. It's very flexible and has many features, and so is heavier weight than the alternatives outlined in this section. As such, configuration can become complicated, and Apache's memory footprint can be significantly bigger. Nonetheless, Apache's flexibility and excellent documentation make it a good choice under many circumstances (and frequently you don't get a choice). Despite its complexity, for this case it's pretty simple.

To get Apache serving static content for your application and acting as a reverse proxy for the dynamic content using the back-end server, add the following to the httpd.conf file (adjusting the path to static content):

```
Alias /static/ "/my/static/files/"
<Location "/static">
    SetHandler none
</Location>


ProxyRequests Off


<Proxy *>
Order deny,allow
Allow from all
</Proxy>


ProxyPass / http://127.0.0.1:3000
ProxyPassReverse / http://127.0.0.1:3000
```

For load balancing, you need the Apache module mod_proxy_balancer enabled. A complete proxy configuration using load balancing would look like this:

```
ProxyRequests Off


<Proxy *>
Order deny,allow
Allow from all
</Proxy>
```

```
<Proxy balancer://my_cluster>
    BalancerMember http://127.0.0.1:3000
    BalancerMember http://192.168.1.100:3000
</Proxy>
ProxyPass / balancer://my_cluster/
ProxyPassReverse / balancer://my_cluster/
```

Nginx

Nginx (pronounced "engine X") is an interesting web server. Written to be fast and lightweight like lighttpd, it's slightly newer and therefore may have had the opportunity to learn from the experience of the lighttpd developers (although this is speculation on our part). Nginx seems to be increasing in popularity relative to lighttpd, and there appears to be some collaboration and cooperation developing between the nginx developer community and the Catalyst developer community. But enough discussion—let's demonstrate how to reverse proxy with nginx.

You can install nginx via a package manager or by compiling from source. Note that while there are unofficial builds of nginx for Windows, these are experimental and require Cygwin (which is sort of a Linux compatibility layer for Windows). Therefore, we don't recommend using nginx on a Windows system.

Configuring and compiling nginx from source is simple, just like lighttpd:

```
$ ./configure
$ make
$ sudo make install
```

Now you have nginx installed at /usr/local/nginx, with the nginx executable in /usr/local/nginx/sbin and configuration in /usr/local/nginx/conf/nginx.conf. The configuration file comes with quite a bit preinstalled. Find the block of configuration as follows:

```
location / {
    root   html;
    index  index.html index.htm;
}
```

Add the following below this:

```
location /static {
        root /Users/kd/LolCatalyst-Lite/root;
}


location / {
    proxy_set_header Host $http_host;
    proxy_set_header X-Forwarded-Host $http_host;
    proxy_set_header X-Real-IP $remote_addr;
    proxy_set_header X-Forwarded-For $proxy_add_x_forwarded_for;
    proxy_pass  http://localhost:3000/;
}
```

Now you have static content served by nginx and the web application served by a back-end server running on localhost. Note the slightly odd syntax for specifying serving static files, in that the `static` directory in the root directive is missing in the `/static` location block for serving the static files.

Load balancing with nginx is slightly different from lighttpd, having more in common with the Apache way of doing things. First, you define a cluster of servers:

```
upstream my_cluster {
        server 127.0.0.1:3000;
        server 192.168.1.100:3000;
}
```

Then you point the `proxy_pass` definition at the cluster:

```
location / {
    proxy_set_header Host $http_host;
    proxy_set_header X-Forwarded-Host $http_host;
    proxy_set_header X-Real-IP $remote_addr;
    proxy_set_header X-Forwarded-For $proxy_add_x_forwarded_for;
    proxy_pass  http://my_cluster;
}
```

Note that you can specify an optional weight to each node in the cluster so as to specify the number of requests that each back-end server gets.

Other Options

We've covered only three of the most common web servers for use as a reverse proxy, but there are many others.

One of particular note is Varnish. There are a couple of detailed articles about Varnish as part of the 2008 Catalyst advent calendar: http://www.catalystframework.org/calendar/2008/14 and http://www.catalystframework.org/calendar/2008/17.

Squid is a proxy server that may be installed in a reverse proxy configuration. It's a fairly old proxy, but it's very powerful and widely used. For this reason, it's quite likely that you'll come across system administrators with expertise in configuration of Squid.

Perlbal is a Perl-based reverse-proxy load balancer and web server. It's also powerful, and there's a reasonable amount of expertise around.

Pound seems to be in roughly the same space as nginx as a lightweight open source reverse proxy, although our impression is that nginx is easier to use.

FastCGI Deployment

At the beginning of this chapter, we showed running the built-in server, either as a stand-alone or in front of a front-end proxy. FastCGI is an alternative to this and in fact is probably the most common way to deploy a Catalyst application. It's still one of the best ways, and it even has some advantages over HTTP::Prefork—particularly the ability to respawn processes by itself (HTTP::Prefork needs to be manually restarted if it stops). As we outlined in Chapter 1, FastCGI is just like a "normal" CGI script but wrapped in an event loop so that it's contained within a persistent process.

In this section, we'll look at FastCGI deployment on shared hosting. Here you have a single option called *dynamic* FastCGI. This is where the configuration is global for all FastCGI processes running on the web server. Following this, we'll cover deployment on your own server using the *static* FastCGI configuration. This is where FastCGI is set up inside the web server configuration. Finally, we'll examine *external* FastCGI deployment, where you configure the web server to listen to one or more external sockets or TCP/IP ports, and all the FastCGI setup is configured outside of the web server. We cover this setup on the three most common open source web servers: Apache, lighttpd, and nginx.

Deployment on Shared Hosting

FastCGI is usually your only option for deployment on shared hosting. You could use CGI, but it will be unacceptably slow. If your application gets even moderate use, the administrator will likely disable your account for excessive use of resources, because while fast and efficient, Catalyst has substantial startup overhead.

For a basic configuration of FastCGI on shared hosting, you'll want to install Catalyst using local::lib as described earlier (this can eat into disk quota, so clean up your .cpan directory when you're done), and then put the following .htaccess file in the virtualhost root directory:

```
RewriteEngine On
RewriteCond %{REQUEST_URI} !^/?script/myapp_fastcgi.pl
RewriteRule ^(.*)$ script/myapp_fastcgi.pl/$1 [PT,L]
RewriteRule ^static/(.*)$ static/$1 [PT,L]
```

This assumes that the distribution files are contained in the virtual server's root. Note that you may need to change the name of the fastcgi.pl script to have an .fcgi extension for some hosting providers. Here's an equivalent deployment at a non-root location (with the application's distribution directory contained within the same location in the virtual host's root directory):

```
RewriteEngine On
RewriteCond %{REQUEST_URI} !^/?myapp/script/myapp_fastcgi.pl
RewriteRule ^myapp/(.*)$ myapp/script/myapp_fastcgi.pl/$1 [PT,L]
RewriteRule ^myapp/static/(.*)$ myapp/static/$1 [PT,L]
```

Here we're basically deploying via a *rewrite rule*, meaning that when a user requests a page like http://example.com/myapp/path/to/action, this arrives at the web server, which rewrites the URL and internally requests http://example.com/myapp/myapp_fastcgi.pl/path/to/action. Finally, the web server sends the response back to the client with the Location header modified so that the client knows nothing about the internal rewriting.

FastCGI Deployment on Your Own Web Server

Having covered shared hosting, next we'll outline the various FastCGI options that we can use when we run our own web server. First, we'll provide an overview of the options, and then we'll provide concrete examples for each of the three most common web servers used with Catalyst: lighttpd, Apache, and nginx.

Deployment Methods

The .htaccess configuration for shared hosting presented earlier is an example of dynamic deployment of FastCGI. That is, the FastCGI process spawns on first request, and then all of the process management (e.g., the number of processes to start, the amount of time to keep the process running when there are no requests for the application, etc.) is configured elsewhere in the Apache configuration.

The static deployment method is somewhat similar to this. Essentially, all process management and spawning of the application script is the responsibility of the web server, and this is where it's all configured. There's not much difference between this and the dynamic option, except that in the case of the static method you don't need to use mod_rewrite (except for lighttpd, which we'll come to shortly), and if you have multiple applications on the same server, you have more fine-grained control over process management for each individual application. Compare this to the dynamic instance, where the process management configuration is global across the whole server. Finally, the fact that you don't need to use mod_rewrite reduces the amount of work that the web server does, so it has a small impact on the processing overhead for your application.

The external method is where you run the FastCGI process externally to the web server, and point your web server to a socket (a special file which is an endpoint for interprocess communication) or a TCP/IP port (which in this case can be seen as a networking construct for interprocess communication). With this method, you can run the FastCGI process on the same machine as the web server (with the socket of the port method) or on a different machine (only if using a TCI/IP port). Clearly, this method has the greatest flexibility and is the only one that can be used if you need to provide a load-balancing solution with FastCGI.

Apache

Two Apache modules deal with FastCGI: mod_fastcgi and mod_fcgid. The latter is a binary-compatible rewrite of the former, which is often used on shared hosting. As is common with software, and especially open source software (which makes it easier to learn from others' experience), mod_fcgid has some improvements, especially in the area of process management. However, mod_fcgid doesn't provide the FastCgiExternalServer directive, so it doesn't support the external method. Also, at the time of this writing it does not react well to applications that spawn external processes. This points to mod_fgcid being most suitable for shared hosting environments. Configuration of mod_fastcgi and mod_fcgid is essentially identical.

Having covered the dynamic option at the beginning of this section, let's now look at configuring the static and external ways.

Static Configuration

The directive to serve static content needs to come first in the virtual host configuration file:

```
DocumentRoot  /usr/local/lib/MyApp/root
Alias /static /usr/local/lib/root/static
```

Next, we set up the static server:

```
FastCgiServer /var/www/MyApp/script/myapp_fastcgi.pl -processes 3
Alias / /var/www/MyApp/script/myapp_fastcgi.pl/
```

The myapp_fastcgi.pl script takes a number of options, but the only one commonly used that makes any sense to use with a static server is the number of processes to spawn. Note that if you're running in a virtual host, the FastCgiServer directive needs to go outside the virtual host configuration in the global Apache configuration.

External Configuration

As mentioned before, mod_fcgid doesn't support this method. The deployment technique here is somewhat similar to using the HTTP::Prefork engine, although you don't need to set up your front-end web server as a reverse proxy.

First you need to run the FastCGI process. The first example uses sockets for interprocess communication:

```
script/myapp_fastcgi.pl -l /tmp/myapp.socket -n 5 -p /tmp/myapp.pid -d
```

Note that now you need to provide other options to start the FastCGI script as well. In addition to the -n option to indicate the number of processes to run, you need to provide a socket file (i.e., /tmp/myapp.socket) or a TCP/IP port to listen on (with the leading colon to tell the script that it's a port rather than a socket). The -d option tells the script to daemonize— that is, run as a background process that is not stopped when the user logs off the terminal. Note that the stop-start daemon script doesn't require you to issue the -d option.

Alternatively, and most important if you want your server running on a different machine from the web server, you'll need to use TCP/IP ports instead:

```
script/myapp_fastcgi.pl -l  host.name.or.ip.address:8080 -n 5 -p /tmp/myapp.pid -d
```

In general, for a production server you'll want to adapt the stop-start daemon script on the Catalyst wiki (mentioned previously) to avoid manual intervention to get your application running.

Next, you need to configure Apache to tell it where to send requests. First, you'll want to configure a user-friendly error page that informs the user when the back end is not running or is otherwise unreachable:

```
Alias /_errors /var/www/MyApp/root/error-pages
ErrorDocument 502 /_errors/502.html
```

Next, you'll want to serve static content directly through the web server, as previously:

```
Alias /static /usr/local/lib/root/static
```

Finally, you tell Apache where to listen to the socket or port. With a socket listener this is as follows:

```
FastCgiExternalServer /tmp/myapp.fcgi -socket /tmp/myapp.socket
Alias /myapp/ /tmp/myapp.fcgi/
```

And with a TCP/IP listener it's this:

```
FastCgiExternalServer /tmp/myapp.fcgi -host my.host.name.or.ip.address:8080
Alias /myapp/ /tmp/myapp.fcgi/
```

Note that it doesn't really make much sense to run the external server as a TCP/IP service if it's running on the same machine, but this might happen for historical reasons (e.g., server moves) from time to time.

Lighttpd

For lighttpd, the FastCGI module is handled by mod_fastcgi, which is included in the light-tpd distribution and compiled in by default. While with rewrite rules, it should be possible to configure lighttpd to do dynamic FastCGI deployment, this technique is only really useful for shared hosting environments. Seeing as how shared hosting is generally not available with lighttpd servers, we won't cover this.

The configuration for static and dynamic servers for lighttpd is rather similar. Recall that we provided a complete but basic lighttpd configuration option when discussing the HTTP::Prefork deployment method. We can recycle all of this right up to the $HTTP["url"] ! "/static/" line.

Static Configuration

Inside the appropriate virtual host container, we can serve static content directly with lighttpd and provide the FastCGI configuration in the same configuration block:

```
$HTTP["url"] ! "/static" { fastcgi.server = (
    "" => (
               "MyApp" => (
                          "check-local" => "disable",
                          "bin-path" =>
                              "/Users/kd/LolCatalyst-Lite/script/➥
lolcatalyst_lite_fastcgi.pl",
                          "socket" => "/tmp/myapp.socket",
                          "min-procs" => 2,
"max-procs" => 5,
                          "idle-timeout" => 20 )
               )
        )
}
```

Note that there's no point in using TCP/IP ports for an internally controlled FastCGI like this, as the web server and the FastCGI back end have to be on the same machine.

External Configuration

Here we use the same technique to get lighttpd to serve static content that we used with HTTP::Prefork. First, we run the Catalyst fastcgi.pl script externally as detailed previously (again, preferably via a stop-start script) and then configure as follows:

```
$HTTP["url"] !~ "^/static" {
    fastcgi.server = (
        "" => (
            "myserver1" => (
                "socket" => "/tmp/myapp.socket",
                "check-local" => "disable"
            )
        )
    )
}
```

Using a port is just as easy—replace the socket line in the preceding configuration with `port => [ port number ]`.

The technique for load balancing is essentially identical to when we demonstrated it using the HTTP::Prefork engine.

Note Load-balancing solutions are the simplest way to provide zero-downtime upgrades of your site. Simply kill the FastCGI or server process and set up the upgraded application for each socket or TCP/IP port in turn until all are replaced.

A WARNING ABOUT FASTCGI DEPLOYEMNT

One drawback of FastCGI is that it's a fairly vague standard, so the specification of how to implement FastCGI support on the web server is not set in stone. The main practical upshot of this occurs when you deploy your application in a non-root location (you have to switch on the rewrite module in lighttpd by adding `mod_rewrite` to the `server.modules` directive). If you're deploying your application at the `/myapp` directory, you'll need to add the following line to just before the FastCGI configuration (i.e., just before the `$HTTP["url"]` line):

```
url.rewrite = ( "myapp\$" => "myapp/" )
```

This enables URLs with and without trailing slashes to be treated by the application in the same way (and so allows the application to function properly!).

Nginx

As we mentioned before, nginx and lighttpd are similar web servers. However, nginx is slightly less flexible than lighttpd and Apache in that it supports only external FastCGI. Also, if you're using Catalyst prior to version 5.8, non-root deployment on nginx using FastCGI is not possible—it doesn't have the internal process manager that the other web servers have. For 5.8 and later, the principle is the same as for using the HTTP::Prefork engine.

Now on to the configuration. First, you run the FastCGI script the same as with every other external deployment. Then you replace the `location` block with all the proxy_set_header information with the following:

```
location / {
    include fastcgi_params;
    fastcgi_pass  unix:/tmp/myapp.socket;
}
```

Everything else (including serving static content) remains the same.

One more thing: because of the inconsistent way in which FastCGI is implemented across web servers, and the assumptions that Catalyst::Engine::FastCGI makes about how this is done, you'll need to replace one line in the file `fastcgi_params` in the nginx configuration directory (`/usr/local/nginx/conf/` on a default installation compiled from source). Replace this line:

```
fastcgi_param  SCRIPT_NAME        $fastcgi_script_name;
```

with this:

```
fastcgi_param  PATH_INFO          $fastcgi_script_name;
```

If you want to run on a TCP/IP port rather than a socket, you change the `fastcgi_pass` line to the following:

```
fastcgi_pass 127.0.0.1:8987;
```

The load-balancing solutions take the same form as for the proxy server configuration given in the "HTTP::Prefork Engine Behind a Front-End Proxy" section of this chapter.

A NOTE ON THE NUMBER OF PROCESSES TO RUN AND BENCHMARKING

Usually for a low-traffic application deployed on FastCGI you'll want to spawn two or three processes. Working out what to do when traffic increases is a little more complex. Apache comes with a useful tool called ab that can simulate a load for requesting particular pages. Here's a command to make 100 requests with a maximum of 5 concurrent for a standard Catalyst application:

```
$ ab -n 100 -c 5 http://127.0.0.1:3000/
```

You can use standard tools to then profile the memory usage during the time that your application runs. If you are getting too much CPU usage or memory use, you can adjust the parameters of your FastCGI back end as required.

The disadvantage of ab is that you can request only a page at a time, and complex workflows can't be simulated. One solution to this is to write a script using WWW::Mechanize to simulate a workflow and then run a number of instances of the script concurrently to simulate.

Other Web Servers That Support FastCGI

Catalyst should run on any other web server that supports FastCGI, with the proviso that you'll have to check that the environment variables passed to the FastCGI process are what Catalyst expects. One final note on this: when you're choosing a web server not in this list, investigate its reverse proxy support and FastCGI process management support.

Deployment on mod_perl

Although it is very powerful, mod_perl is an old technology, and back in the day (between around 1997 and the birth of modern web framework technology in the early twenty-first century) it was really the only way to get a persistent Perl interpreter running on your system. If you're new to this and don't have any legacy reason to do so, we suggest that you don't use mod_perl, and instead use one of the other techniques for deployment outlined in this chapter. mod_perl is pretty easy to configure for the simple instance, but it can get complex and is relatively memory-thirsty. If you make changes to your application, it also requires a full server restart, which can be inconvenient and almost always requires superuser privileges.

If you know mod_perl already, you more or less know how to install a Catalyst application. On an Apache server with mod_perl compiled in (mod_perl needs to be compiled in; it isn't a loadable module like mod_proxy mentioned earlier), configuration is simple. For an application called MyApp located at /usr/local/lib/MyApp, a simple configuration is as follows:

```
PerlSwitches -I/usr/local/lib/MyApp/lib
PerlModule MyApp


<Location />
    SetHandler          modperl
    PerlResponseHandler MyApp
</Location>
```

You'll also want to serve static content directly:

```
DocumentRoot /usr/local/lib/MyApp/root
<Location /static>
    SetHandler default-handler
</Location>
```

Note the configuration semantics here are very similar to those of nginx. Deploying to a non-root location on the server is just as simple:

```
PerlSwitches -I/usr/local/lib/MyApp/lib
PerlModule MyApp


<Location /myapp>
    SetHandler          modperl
    PerlResponseHandler MyApp
</Location>
```

And again, for static content:

```
DocumentRoot /usr/local/lib/MyApp/root
<Location /myapp/static>
    SetHandler default-handler
</Location>
```

Add this to the appropriate part of the Apache configuration, restart the Apache server, and you're good to go.

As we mentioned earlier, Apache is a large, complex, and flexible beast. mod_perl is doubly so, and it's usually overkill to deploy a Catalyst application with it, unless you actually want to do things to Apache's internal request handling for some reason. However, mod_perl is common in some production environments, and for this reason you may want to use it.

Using Apache As a Back End to a Front-End Proxy

Because mod_perl requires that your application is loaded into memory for every instance of Apache running, it's often advisable to have a single Apache instance serving to a front-end reverse proxy. This is because for a busy application, Apache can spawn quite a number of separate processes. The technique for doing so is basically identical to using the front-end proxy to the HTTP::Prefork engine described earlier in the chapter, except that you'll want to run the Apache instance behind rather than the Catalyst server. You can use internal Apache directives or firewall rules to restrict the Apache service to only responding to particular hosts. In this instance, as with the other two-tier deployment scenarios, you'll want the front-end proxy to serve static content, and the back end to serve the dynamic content.

Getting Your Code to the Server

Once you've written your code on your development machine and you're ready to push it to a web server to go live, you need to transfer it over to the server. There are a number of ways of doing this. Using rsync or version control checkout is probably best for an application that's deployed in one particular place, while using make dist is probably best for "white box" applications that may have many instances deployed across an organization or across the whole Internet, although sometimes it can make your sysadmin's life easier as well. We'll describe these options in the sections that follow.

Rsync

To copy files from one location to another efficiently, you can use rsync, "an open source utility that provides fast incremental file transfer" (as noted on the http://www.samba.org/rsync/ site). *Incremental* here means that rsync is efficient in the way that it determines what needs to be copied from one destination to another. You can use rsync over on a local machine, over the network with an rsync server, or through an SSH tunnel. Here we'll give an example of how to use rsync across the filesystem and across the network using the rsync server over ssh. Note that rsync comes included on most Unix systems (although it may need to be installed by your package manager) and that there are production-ready rsync builds for Windows systems.

Using rsync across the filesystem is simple:

```
$ rsync -avc ~/MyApp /usr/local/lib/MyApp/
```

This copies from the development directory to the deployment directory. Note that the trailing slash after the second MyApp and its absence after the first are both important. Because of the -v flag (for *verbose*), you will see the output indicating what files were copied from the development machine to the server. If you make any changes to the application in your home directory and then run this command again, only the new files and parts of the old files that have changed are transferred over. This is extremely efficient—especially over the network.

While you can run an rsync server on a remote machine, ssh is almost universally installed to enable remote access of server machines. So long as you have rsync installed on the remote machine as well as a configured ssh daemon, you can use ssh to transfer your data across like this:

```
$ rsync -avz -e "ssh -l your_username" MyApp  your.remote.host.name:/usr/local/lib/
```

This copies the contents the MyApp directory from the local (developer) machine to the deployment directory on the remote host.

You'll also probably want to set up public/private key–based authentication for ssh to avoid having to type in your password all the time. Rsync is pretty flexible, and thus it can get pretty complicated. Once you've started as per the preceding instructions, though, reading the manual to understand other options (e.g., excluding version control directories) is pretty easy.

Version Control Checkout

While usually slower than rsync (often a lot slower, depending on which version control software you're using), one valid way of getting your application to the server is to make a version control checkout. For stability purposes, you should use your version control software's implementation of tags.

A *tag* is a label for a particular release. In Subversion, this is just a directory where particular release versions of your application are copied over to a tags directory within the repository. In git, it's a representation of the state of commits at a particular point. However, with Subversion (or CVS), if your application requires traversing the filesystem (e.g., if you use the filesystem as a data store), you'll need to ensure that you exclude the .svn subdirectories in any code that you write that traverses subdirectories programmatically.

Once you have the version control checkout on the server, it should be a simple matter of getting new code to the server by issuing the following command (for a Subversion/Apache arrangement on a Unix system):

```
$ svn update && prove -l t && sudo /etc/init.d/apache restart
```

or this one:

```
$ svn update && prove -l t && sudo/etc/init.d/myapp restart
```

if you're using a stop-start daemon with FastCGI or a reverse proxy arrangement. In either case, the command updates the code. If the update is successful, it runs the tests, and if the tests pass, it restarts the server.

This can be convenient, but it does require discipline to ensure that you don't accidentally check out the wrong part of the code repository (e.g., a revision broken in some way).

make dist

We can bundle our application into a convenient archive for copying around the different machines with the command make dist. This kind of deployment works best for small applications—maybe you're the developer and sysadmin, and you don't feel the need to automate your deployment process. A Catalyst application follows the pattern of any other CPAN module. This means that making a tarball that contains everything you need for your application is quite easy. From the command line in the application root, you can do the following:

```
$ perl Makefile.PL
$ make
$ make manifest
$ make dist
```

This leaves a tarball in the application root that contains everything that you need to install the application on the server. Assuming you've been tracking dependencies for your application in `Makefile.PL`, you can use the `make installdeps` or `cpan .` method to get these dependencies installed on the server system.

When you get a tarball of your application, you can send it over to the server and then deploy it with the method that you've chosen. Assuming that you don't want to install to the system, this is a matter of issuing the following commands (for a Linux system):

```
$ tar zxvf MyApp-0.01.tar.gz
$ cd Myapp-0.01
$ perl Makefile.PL
$ make
$ make installdeps
$ make test
```

You'll want to make a decision about whether or not you install your application at the system level. We'll discuss this next.

To make install or Not to make install, That Is the Question

Whether 'tis nobler in the mind to have your code all in one place or by opposing, having all of your code dotted in predictable places on the filesystem (sorry!).

Hopefully this ~~obligatory~~ butchering of Shakespeare will indicate to you that this is an interesting question, and it warrants further examination. Essentially you `make install` your Catalyst application if you want it to be installed at the system level rather than the user level. You might want to do this if your employer has a policy that applications must be deployed at the system level, or if you find that you can't trust your system administrators to do the right thing. Being able to `make install` also means that your application can be distributed in a Linux distribution package such as a `.deb` file.

The process of installing your Catalyst application is the same as installing any other Perl module.

```
$ perl Makefile.PL
$ make
$ make test
$ make install
```

(Or `sudo make install` if you're installing to the system `perl`.)

Catalyst will then detect that your application has been installed at the system level, rather than running from within a distribution. It does this by looking for the presence of `Makefile.PL` at the directory above the script that runs the application (i.e., `myapp_server.pl` or `myapp_fastcgi.pl`). This is one of the reasons that you should never delete `Makefile.PL` in the application root directory.

Installing your application like this provides some insurance, as cpan changes the permissions of the files installed so that you can't accidentally overwrite them, and everything is installed in the appropriate location in $PERL5LIB (or %PERL5LIB% under Windows). You can then start your application server (e.g., myapp_server.pl or myapp_fastcgi.pl) from anywhere in the filesystem, rather than worrying about the actual location of the distribution directory.

You might want to provide per-user configuration of your application on the same machine after a make install of your application (e.g., for a white box/generic application). One way of doing that is as follows. Before the line __PACKAGE__->setup you place the following lines:

```
__PACKAGE__->config('Plugin::ConfigLoader'  => { file => 'myapp.conf' } );
__PACKAGE__->config( 'Plugin::ConfigLoader' => { file =>
                                        "$ENV{HOME}/etc/myapp.conf" } );
```

This allows the end user to maintain a configuration file in his home directory, with sensible defaults that can be overridden by the user. This in turn allows the end user to add new configuration items and provide new templates (by using a new value for the root configuration key if using the Template Toolkit view).

An installed application with a configuration that can be overridden by the user would lend itself well to automated deployment (probably with Apache, where its modularity and flexibility become a significant strength). The easiest way to achieve this would probably be with a dynamic FastCGI back end. Having said that, in general, these kinds of decisions are best left to system administrators rather than mere application programmers.

Dependency Installation

Dependencies in Catalyst are really important. In some programming circles, dependencies are seen as a bad thing. This is usually a wrong-headed attitude. Dependencies are exceptionally useful, as they represent another wheel that you don't have to reinvent. Why do the work when someone else has done it already? Most of the useful modules on CPAN (and some of the useless ones) are well tested and represent a robust and compelling solution to a particular software problem.

The Module::Install build system used by Perl modules, and in turn by Catalyst, provides a mechanism to track dependencies. (Recall that we introduced this system in Chapter 3.) Essentially, every time you use a new module in your code, you should add it (optionally with a minimum version number) to the Makefile.PL, for example:

```
requires 'Moose::Autobox';
```

or with a minimum version specified:

```
requires 'Moose::Autobox' => '0.09';
```

Remembering to put these in `Makefile.PL` is a little error-prone (if you're really in the coding zone, it's easy to forget). If you're on a Unix system and using the Bash shell, here's a rough-and-ready but useful technique to help you identify when you've forgotten. First, put the following in the `.bashrc` file in your home directory:

```
function find-perl-module-use() {
  dir=${1:-lib};
  ack '^\s*use\s+.*;\s*$' $dir | \
  awk '{ print $2 }' | \
  sed 's/();\?$\|;$//' | \
  sort | uniq;
  ack '^\s*use\s+base\s+.*;\s*$' $dir | \
  awk '{ print $3 }' | \
  sed 's/();\?$\|;$//' | sort | uniq;
}
```

Next, you'll want to install App::Ack from CPAN. This is a grep replacement written in Perl. You can install the function with this command:

```
$ source ~/.bashrc
```

Now from your application root, you can run the command `find-perl-module-use`. For the `LolCatalyst-Lite` root directory in Chapter 3, we get the following output:

```
Acme::LOLCAT
Catalyst::Runtimebase
parent
strict
warnings
'Catalyst::Model::DBIC::Schema'
'Catalyst::View::JSON'
'Catalyst::View::TT'
'DBIx::Class'
'DBIx::Class::Schema'
```

The `warnings`, `strict`, and `base` items are spurious and can be ignored. `parent` is also somewhat spurious (`parent` is a dependency of Catalyst::Runtime). You should check that the remaining items are included in the `Makefile.PL`. You'll need to read the documentation to determine if you need to specify a minimum version (e.g., if you're using Catalyst::Runtime version 5.8 and taking advantage of its features, you'd specify `requires 'Catalyst::Runtime => '5.8'`).

As a side note, you could have a look at Acme::Magic::Pony as an alternative solution to tracking and installing dependencies. But then discard it immediately. Seriously folks, the Acme namespace on CPAN is interesting, and it contains a lot of code that should absolutely never be used in production. On the other hand, it also contains a lot of interesting proof-of-concept code that sometimes stretches Perl to its limits and points to creative solutions to common and not-so-common programming problems.

The cpan . Command

Running the command cpan . from the command prompt in the application root will install all your dependencies, but it will also install the application at the system level. Usually this isn't what you want, although cpan . is a nice, simple, one-step process if this is what you want to do. The alternative is make installdeps.

The edited output from cpan . for our Acme::Makefile application (with simply four different Acme:: modules specified as requires in Makefile.PL) looks like this:

```
$ cpan .
You are visiting the local directory
  '.'
   without lock, take care that concurrent processes do not do likewise.
[output snipped ]
   CPAN.pm: Going to build /tmp/Acme-Makefile/.


include /private/tmp/Acme-Makefile/inc/Module/Install.pm
include inc/Module/Install/Metadata.pm
include inc/Module/Install/Base.pm
Cannot determine perl version info from lib/Acme/Makefile.pm
include inc/Module/Install/Catalyst.pm
*** Module::Install::Catalyst
[ output snipped ]
*** Checking for Perl dependencies...
[Core Features]
- Catalyst::Runtime              ...loaded. (5.710 >= 5.71000)
- Catalyst::Plugin::ConfigLoader  ...loaded. (0.210)
- Catalyst::Plugin::Static::Simple ...loaded. (0.200)
- Catalyst::Action::RenderView    ...loaded. (0.080)
- parent                          ...loaded. (0.221)
- Config::General                 ...loaded. (2.400)
- Acme::Drunk                     ...missing.
- Acme::CorpusScrambler           ...missing.
- Acme::EyeDrops                  ...missing.
- Acme::Curse                     ...missing.
==> Auto-install the 4 mandatory module(s) from CPAN? [y] y
```

The list of modules tells us what's already installed on our system and what's not—we can see that the four Acme:: modules are not. From here on, things are the same as pretty much any other CPAN installation, except for perhaps this output during the installation of Acme::EyeDrops:

```
                      ######
        #####        #########
     ##########      ###########
     #########      #############
      #######    ################
     ########  ###################
     ####### #####################
     #############################
       ############################
      ##############################
       #############################
       ######################### ##
        ## ############### #### ##
          ####   ########   ### #
          ###   #### ###    ###
          ###   ##### ##     ##
          ###   ####  ##     ##
          ##    #     ##     ##
          ##    #    #       #
          ##    #  #         #
          #       ###        #
          #      ## ##        #
          ##    ####  #      ##
         ####               ####
```

Note that you have relatively little control over your installation when you use `cpan .`; it uses your existing configuration of the CPAN shell, and if there is a problem with any of the tests in your dependencies, you'll have to either install them by hand or drop into the CPAN shell to resolve them. Finally, usually you won't want to install your module to the system libraries. Therefore, for normal cases, you'll want to use the slightly more complicated `make installdeps`.

make installdeps

`make installdeps` (*installdeps* being an abbreviation of "install dependencies") is a slightly more complex but more useful tool to install your application's dependencies. It works as follows:

```
$ perl Makefile.PL
$ make installdeps
```

This sidesteps the need to run a bare `make` that would otherwise clutter the distriubution's directory with the `blib` directory, which is not harmful to have, but you don't want it to get in the way. For example, you wouldn't want to check it into your version control repository, especially for a big project. The `make installdeps` command sidesteps the building of this staging area, so there's no pollution to your distribution directory except for the addition of the `Makefile.PL` after you run `perl Makefile.PL`.

> **Note** `blib` is an abbreviation for "build library," a staging area for the installation of your code where architecture-specific material goes. `blib` is only really important for libraries with code for other programming languages, and it is most commonly used with C.

Remember, if you experience any problems installing CPAN modules, then it's likely that you'll have to move over to the CPAN shell to investigate any failing modules. Once you've run `make installdeps`, run `make realclean` to remove the generated `Makefile.PL`.

make catalyst_par

PAR (which stands for Perl Archive (PAR) is a useful way of bundling your application and all its dependencies and distributing it as either a `.par` archive or a binary executable. Starting with a fresh application, here's how to make the `.par` file:

```
catalyst.pl MyApp
cd MyApp
perl Makefile.PL
make catalyst_par
```

This will create the file `MyApp.par`, which we can run on another system using the same version of `perl`. Note that if any modules containing C code are in the archive, the other system needs to be binary compatible. You could run the development server off this PAR with the following command:

```
perl –MPAR=/path/to/MyApp.par script_myapp_server.pl
```

> **Note** PAR unarchives your modules and its dependencies into your temporary directory, and so does not by default store persistent state on the filesystem. If you need persistent state stored, you will need to store these files outside the PAR archive or its generated binary.

The binary is the archive with an embedded Perl interpreter for compatible systems without Perl or the wrong version installed. Generate a `myapp.bin` executable like this:

```
pp myapp.par -o myapp.bin
```

This is then run very similarly to the `.par` file:

```
./myapp.bin script/myapp_server.pl
```

PAR can be useful, but it is a bit fragile. It may not be easy to get it working on your system, but when it works, it's great.

Summary

In this chapter, we described most of the wide variety of ways you can deploy an application and get your code to the server. There was a lot of information in this chapter, and you might have many choices to make, so it may bear rereading.

In the first half of the chapter, we discussed a number of deployment options for your application, starting with the built-in server. We went on to discuss using Catalyst::Engine:: HTTP::Prefork with either an Apache, a lighttpd, or an nginx web server as a front-end proxy. We then covered using FastCGI on shared hosting (dynamic FastCGI deployment with global web server configuration), static FastCGI (with the FastCGI process configured in the web server configuration file), and external FastCGI deployment (with one or more FastCGI listeners on either a socket or a TCP/IP port, with the FastCGI processes configured externally to the web server). We finished off by looking at mod_perl deployment and briefly mentioned a couple of less common deployment options.

In the second half of the chapter, we covered getting your code to the server through a number of methods. Bundling your application as a binary executable looks attractive, but it can be unreliable and require troubleshooting.

In the next chapter, we'll look at using Catalyst with relational databases. In particular, we'll focus on the DBIx::Class object relational mapper and how to use it with Catalyst and the Template Toolkit.

■ ■ ■

## CHAPTER 6

Database Models

In a previous chapter, we looked at a simple Catalyst model for translating inputted text into LOLspeak. In Chapter 3, we also described the Catalyst AuthDBIC helper, which creates a complete model and database for you, to store your users in.

In this chapter, we will explore the database created by the AuthDBIC helper and how to expand it to store other useful data about users. Along the way, we will look at how to create your own database from scratch and how to set up a Catalyst controller to do some simple create, read, update, and delete (CRUD) operations on your database tables. First, we cover the various types of databases available and help you decide which one to use. We move on to discuss some existing models for Catalyst that provide interfaces to databases. We wrap up the chapter by explaining the database schema for the AuthDBIC helper and discussing some variations.

Choosing and Connecting to a Database

A wide range of database systems (properly called relational database management systems [RDBMSs]) are available for you to use. The one you choose will depend a great deal on the sort of application you are writing, what operating systems you have available, and how much you want to pay.

In this section, we'll first review some popular database options and why you might select each one, and then we'll move on to demonstrate how to connect to the database from Perl.

Popular Database Systems

The following list presents some well-known databases and why you might elect to use them.

- *Oracle (http://www.oracle.com/database/index.html)*: This is commercial software. Use it if you are writing an application inside a company and it is already available and accessible. Also use it if you want good commercial support. There is a free version for personal use, but check the terms and conditions carefully. Oracle runs on a wide variety of operating systems, including various versions of Windows, Linux, BSD, Solaris, AIX, and HP-UX. Older versions are somewhat non-SQL-standard.

- *DB2 (http://www-01.ibm.com/software/data/db2/)*: Again, this is commercial software. License and issues are similar to Oracle, although its SQL is mostly standards compliant. It's made by IBM.

- *Microsoft SQL Server (http://www.microsoft.com/sqlserver/)*: SQL Server runs on various Windows versions only. The caveats are the same as for the other commercial offerings. Additionally, in this case it can be tricky (but not impossible) to access using clients on Unix systems.

- *PostgreSQL (http://www.postgresql.org/)*: Often abbreviated as PG, this is free, open source software. Use PostgreSQL if it's already available on whatever hosting you have chosen for your application. Also use it if you are starting from scratch and have a small budget. Commercial support is available, and it runs on a wide variety of operating systems, including various versions of Windows, Linux, BSD, Solaris, AIX, and HP-UX. It is mostly the SQL standard, with some interesting additions.

- *MySQL (http://www.mysql.org)*: Again, this is free, open source software, and the advice from the preceding PostgreSQL entry applies here. MySQL is less powerful and full featured than PG, and it has more gotchas. Traditionally it's used for fast and simple storage. It's catching up with the rest of the world on SQL support.

- SQLite (*http://www.sqlite.org*): This is free software. Use it if you need a stand-alone database that is easy to use and install. It stores the data in a single transportable file, and it runs on all major operating systems. It implements a useful subset of SQL and is an excellent choice for use during development, but it will not cope well with multiple concurrent users making writes to the database without significant fiddling around.

In this chapter, we will use the SQLite database, because as we said, it is truly excellent for initial development. Note that code we will produce will work for all the other database systems mentioned, with minimal code modification. If you have any difficulties getting it running on an alternative system, check the generated SQL and refer to the relevant documentation.

Connecting to the Database from Catalyst

To connect to and use your database with Perl, you will first need to install the CPAN module DBI and the database driver (DBD) for the particular database you have chosen. You probably already did this in Chapter 3 when we set up authentication. In any case, you'll need to ensure that the following CPAN modules are installed on your system:

- Catalyst::Helper::Model::DBIC::Schema (this brings in DBIx::Class and the required SQLite libraries)

- DBIx::Class::TimeStamp

- SQL::Translator

- Email::Valid

Some of these modules may take a little while to install, depending on the initial state of your CPAN installations and the speed of your computer.

DBD:SQLite comes with its own embedded SQLite library. The fact that you install this module and then have to do nothing else to have a working database is one of the things that makes it so useful for development and for some production uses.

Note SQLite is used for the storage layer in many embedded devices.

DBI gives us the bare bones of database usage. Using plain DBI allows us to send hand-written SQL statements to the database server. We will get the results as arrays of scalar values, or hashrefs of column name/value pairs.

CPAN also contains several premade Catalyst model modules for connecting to databases:

- *Catalyst::Model::DBIC::Schema*: DBIx::Class is an object-relational mapper (ORM). It is widely used with Catalyst and highly respected. We will be using it for the rest of this chapter.

- *Catalyst::Model::DBIDM*: This model uses the DBIx::DataModel layer on top of Perl DBI that provides Unified Modeling Language (UML)–style database schema declaration in Perl.

- *CatalystX::CRUD::Model::RDBO*: This model provides a database model for CRUD functionality using CatalystX::Crud and the Rose::DB::Object ORM system.

- *Catalyst-Model-CDBI-Plain*: Class::DBI is the ancestor of DBIx::Class. This model is for using existing Class::DBI code inside Catalyst. Note that DBIx::Class has a Class::DBI compatibility layer included, so if you have legacy Class::DBI code, you should consider which of these two libraries to use: Class::DBI or DBIx::Class. A good rule of thumb is that if you want to continue adding functionality to Class::DBI code, then you should use the DBIx::Class compatibility layer. If you are certain that development has ceased for the Class::DBI classes, then you should use whichever back end you are most comfortable with.

- *Catalyst::Model::DBI*: This model creates a simple interface to DBI for Catalyst. It lets you write plain SQL in your Perl code. This is generally considered a bad idea. It is preferable to generate SQL so it is consistent and easy to maintain.

A good many more modules are available, which we won't go into here. Look on CPAN in the Catalyst::Model namespace to see them all.

Designing and Creating the Sample Application Database

We will be re-creating the authentication database of the sample application from Chapter 3 from scratch, so let's start a new application:

```
catalyst.pl DBAuthTest
```

Initially, we'll be exclusively concerned with the database, and not with Catalyst at all, so we'll create a directory for our SQLite database before we proceed.

```
cd DBAuthTest
mkidr db
cd db
```

Now we're ready to start using Catalyst with DBIx::Class. We'll begin by looking at a simple database design. The AuthDBIC helper from Chapter 3 creates three database tables to store the users of your application in. The SQL statements to produce those tables look like this:

```
CREATE TABLE roles (
    id   INTEGER PRIMARY KEY AUTOINCREMENT,
    role TEXT UNIQUE
);
CREATE TABLE users (
    id       INTEGER PRIMARY KEY AUTOINCREMENT,
    username TEXT UNIQUE,
    email    TEXT,
    password TEXT
);
CREATE TABLE user_roles (
    user_id INTEGER REFERENCES users(id),
    role_id INTEGER REFERENCES roles(id),
    PRIMARY KEY(user_id, role_id)
);
```

This database schema uses the SQLite SQL syntax. See http://www.sqlite.org/lang.html for a detailed explanation.

Each table has a set of columns, one for each piece of data it will contain. Each column should contain one piece of data only. One or more columns in the table should contain data that is unique for each row in the table, and preferably one that will not change over the life of the application—this is called the PRIMARY KEY. If the table has no such columns, we can add an artificial one containing an INTEGER, which the database will increment by one for us every time we enter a new row. This is called an AUTO INCREMENT field.

The primary key is not restricted to being just one column. The user_roles table contains only rows with unique user_id and role_id pairs, so the primary key can consist of those two columns.

The column or columns in the primary key will form a UNIQUE INDEX, and the database will automatically create this index. It will prevent entry of rows with duplicate primary keys. A table may also have more columns designated as unique indexes. For example, in the preceding user table, the username column description contains the word UNIQUE, which causes the database to create another unique index just for that column.

The strength of relational databases lies in their ability to connect tables together via FOREIGN KEYs. The third table in the Auth schema is a helper table used to link the users and roles tables together, in a many-to-many relationship. It allows us to indicate that each user can have more than one role, and each role can have more than one user. The keyword REFERENCES creates a database constraint on a column that restricts it to containing only values of the given column on the given table. DBIx::Class::Schema::Loader can pick up on these references automatically, if specified in the SQL, and if the database you're using has proper foreign key support. Alternatively, you can add the relationships in the perl code manually instead.

We can create this database as an SQLite database by saving the CREATE TABLE statements into a plain text file named authdb.sql and running it against SQLite's command-line tool:

```
sqlite3 auth.db < authdb.sql
```

auth.db is the name of the SQLite database file that will be created.

■**Note** For an introduction to SQLite's command-line tool, visit `http://www.sqlite.org/sqlite.html`.

Creating the Catalyst Model

Now that we have our database layout created and an actual database available in the `auth.db` file, we can create a Model class and a set of DBIx::Class schema classes all at once using the available helper, Catalyst::Helper::DBIC::Schema.

■**Tip** The database code in this chapter relies on functionality in DBIx::Class::Schema::Loader version 0.4006 or later. To make sure that you have the correct version installed, issue the following command from the prompt:

```
perl -MDBIx::Class::Schema::Loader\ 9999
```

This command looks for version 9999 of the module. As you can pretty much guarantee that no CPAN module will be at version 9999, then this will output an error with the version of the module that is installed in the text.

Using the helper means that we can use our application's create script to do all the work for us, creating our Catalyst Model and the underlying database schema:

```
script/dbauthtest_create.pl model AuthDB DBIC::Schema Auth::Schema\
    create=static dbi:SQLite:db/auth.db
```

To understand these arguments, we can take a look at the create script's documentation, `script/dbauthtest_create.pl`, which gives us some examples:

```
dbauthtest_create.pl model SomeDB DBIC::Schema MyApp::Schema \
    create=dynamic  dbi:SQLite:/tmp/my.db
dbauthtest_create.pl model AnotherDB DBIC::Schema MyApp::Schema \
create=static dbi:Pg:dbname=foo root 4321
```

The arguments are as follows, in order:

- `model`: This is the type of Catalyst component we are creating. This argument will create files in the `lib/DBAuthTest/Model/` subdirectory of our project.

- `AuthDB`: This is the name of the model that will be created, thus the file `lib/DBAuthTest/Model/AuthDB.pm` is produced.

- `DBIC::Schema`: This is the name of the Catalyst helper that will actually be used to create the new model files. It will be expanded to Catalyst::Helper::Model::DBIC::Schema, which we installed earlier.

- `Auth::Schema`: This is the name of the DBIx::Class Schema that actually represents the database tables. It will be created in `lib/Auth/Schema.pm`.

- `create=static`: The DBIC::Schema helper has two modes: either it can output a set of actual files on disc representing your schema or it can create them in memory every time your application runs.

  - `create=static` creates the files on disc.

  - `create=dynamic` creates the files in memory.

  The static mode is preferred as it puts less load on the application and guards you from being surprised when someone changes the database layout. If the database layout changes, and the dynamic mode picks up the changes, you will get an error somewhere in the depths of your Catalyst application code. In static mode, the error will occur in the database layer, where it is more easily diagnosed. In other words, *don't rely on implicitly generated code unless you really have to.*

  This argument can be omitted completely, in which case the helper will not create files on disc or in memory; it will assume that the schema files already exist.

- `dbi:SQLite:db/auth.db`: This is the connection string for the database. It is in the format used by the DBI module and its various DBDs. For a longer explanation of what it may contain, see the documentation for your DBD.

  The string always begins with the letters `dbi` (or `DBI` in capitals depending on the `DBD` module that you're using), followed by a colon, followed by the name of the database driver you wish to use, then another colon, and finally any other arguments the driver supports.

  For SQLite, the driver is DBD::SQLite. It only needs to name the file that the SQLite database is stored in. For MySQL, you will need the DBD::mysql driver, which takes a few more arguments than SQLite:

  ```
  dbi:mysql:mydatabase myuser mypassword
  ```

  or

  ```
  dbi:mysql:host=dbhost.com;dbname=mydatabase myuser mypassword
  ```

Tip If you need to dump a complex database or make your own files and make use of some of the more advanced features of DBIx::Class or DBIx::Class::Schema::Loader, leave out the `create=static` argument and see Chapter 11 for basic and more advanced direct usage of DBIx::Class::Schema::Loader. You'll also want to omit the `create` option if you've written your own DBIx::Class schema by hand.

In the lib/ directory of our application, we can now see the files of the DBIx::Class schema:

```
lib/Auth
lib/Auth/Schema
lib/Auth/Schema/Result/Roles.pm
lib/Auth/Schema/Result/Users.pm
lib/Auth/Schema/Result/UserRoles.pm
lib/Auth/Schema.pm
```

Exploring the DBIx::Class Schema Files

The DBIC::Schema helper uses a module called DBIx::Class::Schema::Loader to examine an existing database and create a set of DBIx::Class schema classes from it.

As you can see from the list of files shown in the previous section, there is one file for each SQL table we created, Users, Roles, and UserRoles. DBIx::Class::Schema::Loader has intelligently capitalized the names using Perl's CamelCase convention for package names.

There is also one extra file, the Schema file. This is the one that ties the rest together, so we'll look at it first. We'll then move on to cover the Result files.

The Schema File

The Schema file is fairly short:

```
package Auth::Schema;

use strict;
use warnings;
use base 'DBIx::Class::Schema';

__PACKAGE__->load_namespaces;

# Created by DBIx::Class::Schema::Loader v0.04005 @ 2009-04-24 08:13:43
# DO NOT MODIFY THIS OR ANYTHING ABOVE! md5sum:ke33JRTDsUl78dyUT25zwg

# You can replace this text with custom content,
# and it will be preserved on regeneration


1;
```

Note the indication that this is an autogenerated file and that you should edit only below that line. This is very important if you need to update your database structure and regenerate your schema during development. However, you may want to forgo this facility as well. If that is the case, it's best to delete the comments at the end of the package and never use the auto-generation facility again for your database classes.

The package itself inherits from DBIx::Class::Schema, and makes one call: load_
namespaces. The default behavior of load_namespaces is to load all the files it finds in the
Result and ResultSet namespaces under the namespace of the Schema itself. The ResultSet
namespace is for custom methods, and we haven't made any of these yet, so next we'll look
at the Result files.

The Result Files

The Result files, as indicated previously, contain the information about our database. Each
Result file, called a Result class, represents a single result row of a query based on the table it
describes. The Users Result class starts like this:

```
package Auth::Schema::Result::Users;

use strict;
use warnings;

use base 'DBIx::Class';

__PACKAGE__->load_components("InflateColumn::DateTime", "Core");
__PACKAGE__->table("users");
```

Inheriting from DBIx::Class gives it the ability to load components. The main component,
which is always needed for a table result class, is Core. The helper also adds the InflateColumn::
DateTime component. We will look at this and some other useful components later.

The table call sets the name of the table DBIx::Class should use to make queries on based
on this class.

After the table, the available columns are described:

```
__PACKAGE__->add_columns(
  "id",
    { data_type => "INTEGER",
      is_nullable => 0,
      size => undef,
      is_auto_increment => 1
    },
  "username",
    { data_type => "TEXT", is_nullable => 0, size => undef },
  "email",
    { data_type => "TEXT", is_nullable => 0, size => undef },
  "password",
    { data_type => "TEXT", is_nullable => 0, size => undef },
);
```

Each column is listed, together with a hashref of column_info about the column. This is
mainly used by the deployment code of the DBIx::Class, when creating new database tables
based on the Schema. It is also useful to remind developers what sorts of data the database columns may contain, especially if someone else is maintaining the database. See the
"Deploying to a Different Database System" section later on in this chapter for how to create
tables in another database using this information.

The data_type column_info key is not restricted, so you may enter any type support by the type of database you have chosen.

```
data_type => "INTEGER"
```

The schema may also be deployed to other types of database, and the code does its best to convert the data_type into one for the target database (more on this in the "Deploying to a Different Database System" section).

This key is used by the deployment mechanism in DBIx::Class to create an autoincrementing field. These are often used to create a unique primary key.

```
is_auto_increment => 1
```

■**Note** The names of the columns are created as accessors to get and set values for that column on each result object. This means they must be valid Perl identifiers. If the column names in your database are not valid, add an accessor key that will be used to create the accessor method instead.

Next, the primary key and indexes are described:

```
__PACKAGE__->set_primary_key("id");
__PACKAGE__->add_unique_constraint("username_unique", ["username"]);
```

set_primary_key takes a list of one or more column names that together are the unique primary key of a row.

The primary key is used by DBIx::Class to uniquely identify a row. For example, when you UPDATE some changed values of a row, it is used in the WHERE clause of the SQL statement.

DBIx::Class also fetches the primary key values from the database for you, if not supplied when you create a new row object.

Unique indexes are added by providing an index name and an arrayref of column names to add_unique_constraint. These can be used to find unique rows.

Relationships

In order to use DBIx::Class effectively, it should be taught about the relationships among our tables. We can even tell it about relationships that don't actually exist in the database definition of the tables, and use those.

Our example Auth database contains FOREIGN KEY statements, which the model creation script has turned into relationships for us. We will describe the created ones here. Add these to your own classes, under the "do not modify" line if you are missing them.

Relationships are described using the various relationship methods. These are documented in DBIx::Class::Relationship.

To define a one-to-many relationship—for example, to indicate that the user has one or more roles defined in the user_roles table—we use the has_many method. This relationship should already be in the Auth::Schema::Result::Users module:

```
__PACKAGE__->has_many(
  "user_roles",
  "Auth::Schema::Result::UserRoles",
  { "foreign.user_id" => "self.id" },
);
```

- user_roles: The first argument is a name for the relationship. This should be a valid Perl identifier, as it will be used as the relationship data accessor from a result object of this class. It is also used when asking DBIx::Class to create a query with a join from this table to the user_roles table. When used, the accessor will return a set of one or more results, so its name should be plural.

- Auth::Schema::Result::UserRoles: This is the name of the DBIx::Class Result class representing the table we are creating a relationship to.

- { "foreign.user_id" => "self.id" }: This is the condition to use to join the two related tables. In this case, the foreign class, UserRoles, contains the id of this class in its user_id column.

has_many describes only one side of the relationship: how to get a list of user_roles entries for a given user. To retrieve data in the other direction, user_roles to a particular user, we need to use a different type of relationship, belongs_to.

The belongs_to relationship is defined in the Auth::Schema::Result::UserRoles class to add an accessor to fetch the user object:

```
__PACKAGE__->belongs_to(
  "user_id",
  "Auth::Schema::Result::Users",
  { "id" => "user_id" }
);
```

The created relationship may look slightly different depending on the version of DBIx::Class::Schema::Loader that you are using.

The arguments to belongs_to are very similar to those of has_many:

- user: This is again the relationship name, and it is used to create an accessor and for making joins between this table and the referenced table. In older versions of DBIx::Class::Schema::Loader, this was output as user_id, the same as the name of the column it is using. If the relationship name and the accessor name match, then fetching the plain column value (the numeric ID) becomes more difficult.

- Auth::Schema::Result::Users: This is the package name of the table we are creating a relationship to.

- { "foreign.id" => "self.user_id" }: This is the same condition as for the has_many relationship, but in reverse.

By defining these two relationships in the two related classes, we have created a one-to-many relationship from both sides. There should also be another belongs_to in Auth::Schema::Result::UserRoles for the link to the roles table:

```
__PACKAGE__->belongs_to(
  "role",
  "Auth::Schema::Result::Roles",
  { "foreign.id" => "self.role_id" }
);
```

Relationship Bridges

As mentioned back at the beginning of the chapter, the user_roles table is a supporting table to allow us to connect many users to many roles effectively. The actual contents of this table are rarely needed, as usually we will want to get a list of roles that a user has directly from the roles table.

To achieve this, we can use the many_to_many relationship bridge method. We'll explain this after writing some more code. Add the following in AuthSchema::Users::Result below the "do not modify" line:

```
__PACKAGE__->many_to_many('roles', 'user_roles', 'role');
```

many_to_many takes three arguments:

- roles: This is the name of the relationship, and it will be created as an accessor method. It should be a valid Perl identifier.

- user_roles: This is the name of a relationship that already exists. In this case, it is the name of the has_many relationship we created earlier.

- role: To complete the bridge, we need to name a relationship that exists in the module pointed at by the user_roles relationship we already named. We want the name of the belongs_to relationship, role. In Users.pm, user_roles connects to the Auth::Schema::Result::UserRoles class. In UserRoles.pm role connects to the Auth::Schema::Result::Roles class. So to get a list of roles for user 1, we would run the following code:

```
my $user = $schema->resultset('Users')->search( { id => 1});
my $roles = [$user->roles];
print "Fred has the " . $_->role . " role\n"  for $roles;
```

Hopefully we have now explored enough of the exported DBIx::Class schema structure to give you a good idea of what is going on. More documentation can be found in the DBIx::Class documentation on CPAN.

Components

A *component* is a code module that adds some extra functionality to a row object. For example, DBIx::Class::InflateColumn::DateTime implements the inflate functionality to return Date-Time objects from accessors for columns that are marked as containing datetime type data. It also implements deflate, which allows you to pass a DateTime object to a column accessor, and it will be output into the database as the appropriately formatted string to represent that datetime.

We will demonstrate the use of DBIx::Class components by adding the DBIx::Class::TimeStamp component. This component builds on DBIx::Class::InflateColumn::DateTime to automatically maintain a table column containing a datetime field. That is, every time an update is done to any column in the table, the TimeStamp component can update a datetime column with the current date and time. It can also set the current date and time when a new row is created.

To explain, we will introduce a new column, last_modified. This is going to contain the date and time that a user last updated her profile. First, we update the SQL in authdb.sql to add the column to the users table:

```
CREATE TABLE users (
    id           INTEGER PRIMARY KEY AUTOINCREMENT,
    username     TEXT UNIQUE,
    email        TEXT,
    password     TEXT,
    last_modified DATETIME
);
```

We update the copy of the table in the SQLite database by manually running an ALTER TABLE statement with the following command (from our application's root directory):

```
sqlite3 db/auth.db "ALTER TABLE users ADD COLUMN last_modified DATETIME"
```

We have to get the DBIC Schema files in sync with the new database, so we rerun the DBIC helper to update the Result class files and add the new column:

```
script/dbauthtest_create.pl model AuthDB \
DBIC::Schema Auth::Schema create=static dbi:SQLite:db/auth.db
```

We should now see that a new column has appeared in the Auth::Schema::Result::Users class:

```
"last_modified",
{ data_type => "DATETIME", is_nullable => 0, size => undef },
```

Actually, we forgot to include the new DBIx::Class::TimeStamp component in the schema files. Luckily we can try again:

```
script/dbauthtest_create.pl model AuthDB DBIC::Schema Auth::Schema \
    create=static components=TimeStamp dbi:SQLite:auth.db
```

Now if we look in any of our Result files (e.g., in Auth::Schema::Result::Users), we see the following:

```
__PACKAGE__->load_components("InflateColumn::DateTime", "TimeStamp",➥
"Core");
```

DBIx::Class::TimeStamp overrides the insert and update methods to write the current date and time into a column value. TimeStamp will update or set only on columns we ask it to change. It relies on the column information in the Result files indicating which columns need to be updated, so we alter the Users.pm file.

The two configuration keys used by the TimeStamp component are `set_on_create` and `set_on_update`. It uses these to determine when to update a column's value. However, we shouldn't edit column definitions in the Result classes if we want to be able to rerun DBIx::Class::Schema::Loader again, so instead we can add the following, after the "do not modify" comment line:

```
__PACKAGE__->add_columns('last_modified',
  { %{__PACKAGE__->column_info('last_modified') },
  set_on_create => 1,
  set_on_update => 1
});
```

This code comes after the existing `last_modified` column definition, and so it adds to the previous definition in the file. It includes the existing definition by fetching it using `column_info` on the package. This existing definition and the new keys, `set_on_create` and `set_on_update`, make up the new definition for this column.

`last_modified` will now default to the date the user is created, and it will be re-updated to the current date every time we `update` that row. The actual effect of components will be shown later.

Now you've seen most of the elements that make up a DBIx::Class schema representing a simple set of tables. You can use these ideas to add your own tables to the schema as described. You've seen how to add components, but not what they are for yet, which is a mystery that will be solved later on in this chapter.

Deploying to a Different Database System

The previous section described how to maintain your Result classes by updating them after changes are made to the database itself. This is a useful technique if the database is being maintained by someone else or is shared across applications in some way.

You can also do the reverse—that is, make a DBIx::Class::Schema and use that to deploy to a different database—either a different SQLite instance or to an entirely new database system. You can do this because DBIx::Class comes with its own Parser module that can introspect the Result classes and create an SQL::Translator schema. SQL::Translator can output SQL for various types of databases, based on that schema. Luckily, DBIx::Class has all this functionality built in and ready to use, so you don't need to worry about the mechanics of it too much.

To use this functionality, you will need to make sure that you have installed SQL::Translator as instructed at the beginning of this chapter. To set up a new SQLite database with tables that match the ones described in your schema, use the `deploy` method on a DBIx::Class::Schema object. You can do this from the command line as follows:

```
perl -Ilib -MAuth::Schema -e \
 'my $schema = Auth::Schema->connect("dbi:SQLite:another_auth.db");
  $schema->deploy;'
```

Alternatively, you can use a Perl script to achieve the same. Save this script in the `scripts` directory of your application and call it `deploy.pl`:

```
#!/usr/bin/env perl
use strict;
use warnings;
```

```
## Tell perl which directory Auth::Schema is in:
use FindBin qw($Bin);
use lib "$Bin/../lib";
use Auth::Schema;

## Collect the database type, name, user, and password
## from the command line:
my $newdb_type = shift;
my $newdb_name = shift;
my $newdb_user = shift;
my $newdb_pass = shift;

## Create the schema object using the database connection info from above:
my $schema = Auth::Schema->connect(
                    "dbi:${newdb_type}:${newdb_name}",
                    $newdb_user, $newdb_pass);

## Call the deploy method on the schema object:
$schema->deploy();
```

To use this script, save it as scripts/deploy.pl and call it as follows:

```
perl scripts/deploy.pl SQLite another_auth.db
```

or use the following for MySQL:

```
perl scripts/deploy.pl mysql myauthdatabase myuser mypassword
```

Looking in the SQLite database with .dump shows us a similar table structure as in auth.db:

```
sqlite3 another_auth.db ".dump"
```

It may not be exactly the same, as SQL::Translator defaults to outputting SQL suitable for older versions of SQLite. See its documentation for how to make it more modern.

You can also create SQL files for a whole set of different databases, to use in install routines later:

```
perl -Ilib -MAuth::Schema -e \
 'my $schema = Auth::Schema->connect("dbi:SQLite:another_auth.db");
  $schema->create_ddl_dir;'
```

By default this will create three files:

```
./Auth-Schema-1.x-MySQL.sql
./Auth-Schema-1.x-PostgreSQL.sql
./Auth-Schema-1.x-SQLite.sql
```

Now the application can be deployed to any of these systems without needing SQL::Translator installed.

To create SQL files for a database not in this list, make another little script:

```perl
#!/usr/bin/env perl
use strict;
use warnings;

## Tell perl which directory Auth::Schema is in:
use FindBin qw($Bin);
use lib "$Bin/../lib";
use Auth::Schema;

## Collect the database type from the command line:
my $db_type = shift;

## Create the schema object using any db connection info:
my $schema = Auth::Schema->connect("dbi:SQLite:db/auth.db");

## Call the create_ddl_dir method on the schema object:
## The first argument is an arrayref of database types to export.
$schema->create_ddl_dir([ $db_type ]);
```

Save it as script/create_sql.pl and call it like this, to produce ./Auth-Schema-1.x-DB2.sql:

```perl
perl script/create_sql.pl DB2
```

Note that the database type name in this case needs to match the names of the SQL::
Translator Producer classes, not the DBI DBD:: classes. For example, if you were going to use
MySQL, your script would use MySQL as a shortcut for SQL::Translator::Producer::MySQL and
not mysql as a shortcut for DBD::mysql.

Dealing with Data

The database is set up, so we can now start looking at how to get data from our database into
our application.

To use DBIx::Class, you need to understand *resultsets*. A basic resultset is returned from
Catalyst's $c->model call. To obtain this, we pass it the namespace of the Catalyst model and
then the name of the Result class we want to use prepended with a double colon.

```perl
my $users_rs = $c->model('AuthDB::Users');
```

This is an alternative to more unwieldy syntax:

```perl
$c->model('AuthDB')->resultset('Users');
```

The resultset, which inherits from DBIx::Class::ResultSet, is used for creating, finding,
updating, and deleting rows in the database. Single row objects can be retrieved by finding or
searching for them. Row objects will inherit from DBIx::Class::Row as well as the Result class
for the particular table the row was retrieved from.

Creating a resultset runs no queries on the database; it just stores a query ready for use.

> **Tip** The ability to see the SQL generated by DBIx::Class is very valuable for debugging and learning. If you want to see the SQL code generated by DBIx::Class, you can run the code with the environment variable DBIC_TRACE set to 1, for example:

```
$ CATALYST_DEBUG=0 DBIC_TRACE=1 \
   script/dbauthtest_test.pl /authusers/1/profile
SELECT me.id, me.username, me.email, me.password, me.last_modified FROM users ➥
me WHERE ( me.id = ? ): '1'
SELECT me.id, me.role FROM roles me:
SELECT role.id, role.role FROM user_roles me  JOIN roles role ON role.id = ➥
me.role_id WHERE ( ( role.id = ? AND me.user_id = ? ) ): '1', '1'
SELECT role.id, role.role FROM user_roles me  JOIN roles role ON role.id = ➥
me.role_id WHERE ( ( role.id = ? AND me.user_id = ? ) ): '2', '1'
SELECT role.id, role.role FROM user_roles me  JOIN roles role ON role.id = ➥
me.role_id WHERE ( ( role.id = ? AND me.user_id = ? ) ): '3', '1'
  <html>
[rest of output cut]
```

Note how we set the CATALYST_DEBUG variable to 0 so that we suppress Catalyst's normal debug output as well.

In this section, we'll cover creating a simple user interface for updating the records in a database by hand. There are other Catalyst extensions designed for this functionality, most notably Catalyst::Controller::HTML::FormFu (http://search.cpan.org/perldoc/Catalyst::Controller::HTML::FormFU) which has excellent online documentation) or Reaction (more complex and introduced in Chapter 12). However, these CRUD frameworks require learning how the software libraries work and, often, nontrivial functionality for editing and creating database records usually requires large amounts of customization and fighting against the library author's assumptions if they differ from yours (this assumption doesn't apply to Reaction, but instead the learning curve is steep). Therefore, it's generally recommended that you know how to create, retrieve, update and delete records manually, which is what we cover here.

Simple CRUD

As noted earlier in the chapter, CRUD stands for create, read, update, and delete, which describes all the essential operations that can be done on rows of a database. We will create a simple set of Catalyst actions to do these operations on our Auth database.

We can use Chained actions to good effect here. We covered these in Chapter 4 and describe them in some detail in Chapter 7. We'll make a controller for CRUD operations on our users table.

```
script/dbauthtest_create.pl controller AuthUsers
```

Since we will also need a view to show our output, we create a new TT view:

```
script/dbauthtest_create.pl view Web TT
```

All actions in the controller will need access to the ResultSet of users, so we can create a base action that always loads the resultset, ready for use. We edit DBAuthTest::Controller::AuthUsers, remove the `index` action, and add the following action:

```
sub base : Chained('/'): PathPart('authusers'): CaptureArgs(0) {
  my ($self, $c) = @_;
  $c->stash(users_rs => $c->model('AuthDB::Users'));
}
```

▓**Note** There's a mistake that's easy to make here. If we accidentally put a space between the attribute and the opening parenthesis (i.e., `Chained ('/')`) we'll get an error that states that "(is not a valid attribute separator."

Creating a User

To allow a new user to sign up to our application, we need to first show the user a form to enter the data. We create a new action to display the form and a Template Toolkit file to create the form. First, we can create the action in DBAuthTest::Controller::AuthUsers:

```
sub add : Chained('base'): PathPart('add'): Args(0) {
  my ($self, $c) = @_;

}
```

The template uses the `result_source` method available on the resultset object, which returns the ResultSource representing the table. To get the names of the columns we defined in the Result class, we call the `columns` method on it. This way, we can add columns to our database definition and the form will automatically update to contain the new ones.

This is the template, in `root/authusers/add.tt` (create the `authusers` subdirectory under root first):

```
<html>
  <head>
    <title>Add user</title>
  </head>
  <body>
    <form action="[% c.uri_for(c.controller('AuthUsers').action_for➡
('add')) %]" method="post">
      [%# Simple column set %]
      [% FOREACH col = users_rs.result_source.columns %]
      <div>
       <label>[% col %]
         <input type="text" name="[% col %]"/>
       </label>
      </div>
```

```
      [% END %]
      <input type="submit" value="Create"/>
    </form>
  </body>
</html>
```

Note The preceding is a very simple user creation form, following best practices: for a real application we would display two password fields and two e-mail fields for variation.

The action that the form submits to is created using the uri_for method in the context object, passed to the template as c. It will produce a URL like http://localhost:3000/authusers/add.

Now we write the code to create the user from the submitted values. The request parameters will be named after the accessors for our database columns, and we can also use these to create a new user using the create method.

We add this code to the existing add action and check for an attempt to create a new user vs. just loading the form using the HTTP method from the request:

```
sub add : Chained('base'): PathPart('add'): Args(0) {
  my ($self, $c) = @_;

  if(lc $c->req->method eq 'post') {
    my $params = $c->req->params;

    ## Retrieve the users_rs stashed by the base action:
    my $users_rs = $c->stash->{users_rs};

    ## Create the user:
    my $newuser = $users_rs->create({
      username => $params->{username},
      email    => $params->{email},
      password => $params->{password},
    });
  }

}
```

Here we'll use plain text passwords. Catalyst::Helper::AuthDBIC stores encrypted passwords, and we'll show how to set up password encryption in Chapter 8.

Note In a real application, as well as encrypting your password, you would also verify the two copies of passwords and e-mail addresses against each other to protect against user error.

We should, of course, attempt to check that the data entered into the form is in a sane format to store in our database. We can do this in various ways. To check the validity of an e-mail, we'll use the CPAN module Email::Valid, which you should install if you haven't already. The cheap and easy way to validate in Catalyst just adds more code to add to check the values. To do this, you would add the following before the "create the user" comment:

```
## VALIDATE THE DATA
use Email::Valid;
if(!Email::Valid->address($params->{email})) {
  $c->stash( errors => { email => 'invalid' });
  return $c->res->redirect($c->uri_for($c->controller()->action_for('add')));
  # empty argument to $c->controller() defaults to the current controller.
}
```

We're not going to do this, though. It's much better to have the validation closer to the database layer. This makes it possible to reuse the database model in another application and still have identical checks on the inputs.

The create method on a resultset calls new on a Result class and then insert to create the database row. We can prevent new from succeeding when the data is invalid by overloading it in our Auth::Schema::Result::Users class below the "do not modify" line:

```
use Email::Valid;
sub new {
  my ($class, $args) = @_;

  if( exists $args->{email}
      && !Email::Valid->address($args->{email}) ) {
      die 'Email invalid';
  }

  return $class->next::method($args);
}
```

and we remove the original VALIDATE THE DATA section in DBICTest::Controller::AuthUsers.

The create call will die if the e-mail is not a valid address, so we'll need to catch that in our code, unless we want the user to see the standard Catalyst error page. Change the create call in the AuthUsers controller to

```
## Create the user:

my $newuser = eval { $users_rs->create({
  username => $params->{username},
  email    => $params->{email},
  password => $params->{password},
}) };
if($@) {
  $c->log->debug(
       "User tried to sign up with an invalid email address, redoing.. ");
  $c->stash( errors => { email => 'invalid' }, err => $@ );
  return;
}
```

We return when there is an error, which will cause the add form to be redrawn. We can also update the form template in root/authusers/add.tt to add a warning, using the errors we added to the stash.

We also output the actual code error into a comment on the page, so the developer can check and make sure the error condition is actually from our die call and not some other coding error.

```
<!-- [% IF err %][% err %][% END %] -->

[% FOREACH col = users_rs.result_source.columns %]
  <div>
   <label>[% col %]
     <input type="text" name="[% col %]"/>
   </label>
   [% IF errors.$col %]
     <span style="color: red;">[% errors.$col %]</span>
   [% END %]
  </div>
[% END %]
```

After the user has been created, we need to send them to a useful page. We can redirect the browser to a page to view the newly created user. Add the following to the bottom of the add action in DBICTest::Controller::AuthUsers, just after the error-checking if statement:

```
## Send the user to view the newly created user
return $c->res->redirect( $c->uri_for(
  $c->controller('AuthUser')->action_for('profile'),
  [ $newuser->id ]
) );
```

After the create method returns, $newuser contains a row object representing the user we just created. The autoincrementing primary key has been fetched from the database for us and put into the id value, so we can use it to uniquely identify our user.

```
$newuser->id
```

The uri_for call in the redirect should be a URL similar to

```
http://localhost:3000/authusers/1/profile
```

where 1 is the ID of the newly created user. This leads us neatly to the "read" part of CRUD.

However, since we haven't written our action yet, uri_for will return the following:

```
http://localhost:3000/authusers/ARRAY([...])
```

DEBUGGING NOTES

Before you actually move on to writing the user display code, start the application using the `script/dbauthtest_server.pl` script. Visit the `http://localhost:3000/authusers/add` URL in your browser and try to add a user.

Fix any syntax errors or typos in your code, and keep trying until the browser tries to redirect you to the `http://localhost:3000/authusers/1/profile` URL.

To be quite sure that you have successfully entered a user in the database, you can investigate directly using the `sqlite3` command-line tool:

```
sqlite3 db/auth.db ".dump"
```

This will output a series of SQL statements representing all the data in the database. If one of them is an `INSERT into users ...` statement, you have succeeded.

You can also check your code by comparing it to the source code for the book available at `http://www.apress.com`.

Displaying Users

To display a single user (e.g., as the page after the `add` user process), we first create another `Chained` action in the DBICTest::Controller::AuthUsers class, which will fetch the user object represented by its `id` in the URL. Note we catch the extra URL argument in the first line of the subroutine.

```
sub user : Chained('base'): PathPart(''): CaptureArgs(1) {
  my ($self, $c, $userid) = @_;

  my $user = $c->stash->{users_rs}->find({ id => $userid },
                                         { key => 'primary' });

  die "No such user" if(!$user);

  $c->stash(user => $user);
}
```

The `userid` is taken from the URL by `CaptureArgs` and is passed into the action sub as an argument. We use the `find` method of the DBIx::Class::ResultSet (users_rs) to fetch the one matching unique row with that ID. As we already know that we want to match using the primary key column, we also pass the `{ key => 'primary' }` attributes hashref to `find`, to give it a hint.

When we run `find` it will try its best to find a row matching the given arguments. Unless given an exact key to search against (e.g., `primary` or the name of one of the unique constraints), it will attempt to match the set of columns passed to it against the primary key definition and the unique constraints definitions, and to find a best fit.

If a single matching row in the database is found, it is returned as a Row object, which inherits from both DBIx::Class::Row and your Result class. If no row is found, `find` returns `undef`. If multiple rows match, `find` will output a warning:

```
Query returned more than one row
```

If, for some reason, the $userid variable does not contain the primary key of one of the existing rows, find will return undef.

As with add, we should attempt to validate the $userid value passed to the user action. Simple validation could look like this:

```
my ($self, $c, $userid) = @_;
if($userid =~ /\D/) {
  die "Misuse of URL, userid does not contain only digits!";
}
```

Using die is correct error handling here. It should only die if the user did something silly or the system is broken. Either way, the application will produce the stacktrace (in debug mode) or the "something is wrong" page (in nondebugging mode). Alternatively, use the end action from Chapter 3 as a basis for providing a custom error page.

We just test if the userid has any nondigit characters in it using a regex. Calling die here will cause the action to end abruptly and drop through to the end action, where the error can be read from $c->errors.

This action on its own does not produce a page; it is the middle part of a chain. To actually display the user using the found user object, we create the profile action.

```
sub profile : Chained('user') :PathPart('profile'): Args(0) {
  my ($self, $c) = @_;


}
```

Since the user object is already loaded into the stash in the user action, which profile is chained to, this action needs to do nothing but set the template it uses (or use the default one). All we need to do now is add the template, in root/authusers/profile.tt.

```
<html>
  <head>
    <title>Profile of [% user.username %]</title>
  </head>
  <body>
    [%# Simple column set %]
    [% FOREACH col = users_rs.result_source.columns %]
      <div>
        <span>[% col %]</span>
        <span>[% user.$col %]</span>
      </div>
    [% END %]
  </body>
</html>
```

This displays a simple set of column/value pairs to the viewer. If the user looking at the profile page is also the user displayed in the profile, we can allow the user to edit the data about herself as well.

ADD A USER

Now you have a couple of working application pages. Restart the application and give it a try:

```
script/dbauthtest_server.pl
```

View http://localhost:3000/authusers/add in your browser. Ignore the extra id and last_modified fields for now; these are just visible because you created a very simple form using all available fields.

Enter values for username, e-mail, and password, deliberately using an invalid e-mail (i.e., just "test"). You will be redirected back to the add page with a red "invalid" showing next to that field.

Try again with a proper e-mail address. This time you will be redirected to the http://localhost:3000/authusers/3/profile page. The number is the database ID of the user, and it will be different depending on how many attempts to create a user you made. This page will show you all the values for the user in the database. The id field is filled in from the autoincremented value in the primary key field.

Here you also see the results of adding the DBIx::Class::TimeStamp component earlier. The last_modified field will be displayed with the date the user was added, even though you didn't put any value in that field on the add form.

Updating Users

The user should be able to update the data about herself and change her password if needed. We can either create a separate page for editing or add the form to the profile if the user ID of the profile matches that of the current user.

We will probably also want to allow users with the admin role set to be able to edit users. We haven't looked at how to add roles yet; we will do so later.

Templates do not have to always represent entire pages; we can also use them to contain just parts of pages. Page parts are useful to avoid repeatedly writing the same pieces of HTML and templating code. We're going to create one for the update form, so we can put it in several pages. To do this, we first create a new directory, root/components. Next, we add a template just for editing a user profile, in root/components/edit_user.tt:

```
<form action="[% c.uri_for(c.controller('authusers').action_for('edit'),
[user.id]) %]" method="post">
  [% FOREACH col = users_rs.result_source.columns %]
  <div>
    <label>[% col %]
      <input type="text" name="[% col %]" value="[% user.$col %]"/>
    </label>
    [% IF errors.$col %]
      <span style="color: red;">[% errors.$col %]</span>
    [% END %]
  </div>
  [% END %]
  <input type="submit" value="Update"/>
</form>
```

Now we can add the template to the existing profile page, just after the existing display:

```
<hr/>
[% PROCESS components/edit_user.tt %]
```

This will display for everyone. To restrict display to the current user, we need to know who the current user is. When using the Authentication plug-in, as we showed in Chapter 3, the current user object is returned from $c->user->object. We can access it from the c context object in the template:

```
[% IF c.user.object.id == user.id;
    PROCESS components/edit_user.tt;
    END;
%]
```

The editing part of the profile page submits the results back to the edit action, so we need to add that one. The edit action is also chained to the user action, as it needs a specific user to update.

```
sub edit : Chained('user') :PathPart('edit'): Args(0) {
  my ($self, $c) = @_;

  if(lc $c->req->method eq 'post') {
    my $params = $c->req->params;
    my $user   = $c->stash->{user};

    ## Update user's email and/or password
    $user->update({
        email => $params->{email},
        password => $params->{password},
    });

    ## Send the user back to the changed profile
    return $c->res->redirect( $c->uri_for(
      $c->controller('AuthUsers')->action_for('profile'),
      [ $user->id ]
      ) );
  }
}
```

update is a method on DBIx::Class::Row that takes a hashref of new column name/value pairs. It will assign the values given to the appropriate columns in the object and then run the actual UPDATE SQL statement.

We can set all the values passed in from the form, regardless of whether the user has changed them. DBIx::Class will run the UPDATE statement only if it determines that any of the values have actually changed. It will also update only the changed values.

This action currently has no security. Although we are showing the edit form only to the owner of the profile, that does not stop another user from guessing the names of the inputs. A user could easily look at the HTML for their own edit user form and post it to a URL containing the ID of another user, thus changing the other user's password or e-mail and stealing the account.

We add the same check we did in the template, before the update:

```
## Check user is allowed to update this profile
if($c->user->object->id != $user->id) {
    die "Malicious attempt to update another user by: ". $c->user->username;
}
```

Adding Roles

To be able to give users certain roles, we first need to create some roles. We can do this by either creating a new CRUD controller for the roles and adding actions similarly to our existing `AuthUsers` controller, or, since this is probably an infrequent operation, falling back on a command-line script.

The command-line script is available only to users/admins who have direct access to the server the application is running on, or at least access to the database it is using. If you would like to give role-maintenance access to application users, add the new controller.

The advantage to having a non-Catalyst-bound set of DBIx::Class result classes now becomes useful, as you can talk to the database via those classes without needing to load Catalyst itself.

The script is similar to the script shown in the "Deploying to a Different Database" section, and you start it like this:

```
#!/usr/bin/env perl

use strict;
use warnings;

use FindBin qw($Bin);
use lib '$Bin/../lib';
use Auth::Schema;

## Add a debugging module:
use Data::Dumper;

## Get the name of the new role from the command line:
my $rolename = shift;
```

```
## Now create a schema object, by passing the database connection information:
my $schema = Auth::Schema->connect('dbi:SQLite:db/auth.db');

## Fetch the ResultSet for the Roles class:
my $roles_rs = $schema->resultset('Roles');

## This is the equivalent to the catalyst model code:
# my $roles_rs = $c->model('AuthDB::Roles');

## Create the role row in the database:
my $newrole = $roles_rs->create({ role => $rolename });

## Print the results just to check:
print "Created role: ", Dumper({ $newrole->get_columns });
```

And that's it.

Note the last line, which introduces a new method from DBIx::Class::Row, get_columns. get_columns conveniently returns all the column names and values in the row object, in a hash.

We save the script in script/createrole.pl and run it, passing it a role name:

```
perl script/createrole.pl admins
```

You should get output like this:

```
Created role: $VAR1 = {
        'id' => 1,
        'role' => 'admins'
      };
```

Now we can make our users into admins.

Adding Roles to Users

We can create users, and we can create roles. We can also give users particular roles. To do so, we update the base action in DBICTest::Controller::AuthUsers to fetch a resultset of available roles that we can use in our templates:

```
sub base : Chained('/'): PathPart('authusers'): CaptureArgs(0) {
  my ($self, $c) = @_;

  $c->stash(users_rs => $c->model('AuthDB::Users'));
  $c->stash(roles_rs => $c->model('AuthDB::Roles'));
}
```

We may want to add users to roles in various pages, maybe in the Roles CRUD, or when adding or updating a user. So we'll make another template component by adding this template in root/components/roles.tt:

```
<div class="roles">
  <form
    action="[%-
      c.uri_for(c.controller('authusers').action_for('set_roles'), [user.id]) %]"
    method="post">
    <select name="role" size="5" multiple="multiple">
    [% WHILE (role = roles_rs.next) %]
      <option value="[%role.id%]" [%-
        IF user.has_role(role) %] selected="selected" [% END %]>
    [% role.role %]</option>
      [% END %]
    </select>
    <input type="submit" value="Set"/>
  </form>
</div>
```

This creates a form just for updating/setting roles for a specific user. The form will output a `select` control that displays all the existing roles and preselects any that the user already has. It will allow us to pick multiple roles to set.

Next, we need to implement the has_role method that we are using in the template to check if a user already has a certain role. In the Auth::Schema::Result::Users class, we add this method, under the "do not modify" line:

```
sub has_role {
  my ($self, $role) = @_;

  ## $role is a row object for a role.

  my $roles = $self->user_roles->find({ role_id => $role->id });
  return $roles;

}
```

We're just adding a shortcut. `$user->roles` calls the many_to_many relationship bridge created originally. This code returns a ResultSet containing a query to fetch only the roles that the given user has. `find` on that resultset will search only in that subset of roles. If no such role is found, it will return undef (false).

We also need to create the action this form submits to, in order to add/update the list of roles. We call it set_roles, and we add the action to DBICTest::Controller::AuthUsers:

```
sub set_roles :Chained('user'): PathPath('set_roles'): Args() {
  my ($self, $c) = @_;

  my $user   = $c->stash->{user};
  if(lc $c->req->method eq 'post') {

      ## Fetch all role ids submitted as a list
      my @roles = $c->req->param('role');
```

```
       ## Remove any existing roles, we're replacing them:
       $user->user_roles->delete;

       ## Add new roles:
       foreach my $role_id (@roles) {
         $user->user_roles->create({ role_id => $role_id });
       }
    }

    $c->res->redirect($c->uri_for($c->controller()->action_for('profile'),
       [ $user->id ] ));
  }
```

While it can be useful to add code in the controller like this just to test stuff out, we're again violating the *thin controller/fat model* design, as we have lots of database code in the controller. Throughout your Catalyst programming experiences, you'll probably find that you'll allow the controller to put on too much weight from time to time. The solution is to move the offending code over to the model. So we'll move the complex bits of role assignment into Auth::Schema::Result::Users below the "do not modify" line:

```
sub set_all_roles {
  my ($self, @roleids) = @_;

  ## Remove any existing roles, we're replacing them:
  $self->user_roles->delete;

  ## Add new roles:
  foreach my $role_id (@roleids) {
    $self->user_roles->create({ role_id => $role_id });
  }

  return $self;
}
```

and change the set_roles action in the controller to the following:

```
sub set_roles :Chained('user'): PathPath('set_roles'): Args() {
  my ($self, $c) = @_;

  my $user    = $c->stash->{user};
  if(lc $c->req->method eq 'post') {

      ## Fetch all role ids submitted as a list
      my @roles = $c->req->param('role');

      $user->set_all_roles(@roles);
  }

  $c->res->redirect($c->uri_for($c->controller()->action_for('profile'),
     [ $user->id ] ));
}
```

■**Note** The many_to_many relationship bridge creates a set_roles method on the user object for us. However, it takes only a list of role objects, not IDs, so we can't use it here. People frequently have trouble understanding many_to_many relationship bridges for reasons like this. As you use it more often, it will make more sense.

Now all we need to do is to add our roles.tt component to a page and see if it works. Add it to the bottom of the root/authusers/profile.tt template:

```
[% PROCESS components/roles.tt %]
```

ADD ROLES TO A USER

Make sure all the files you just edited and added are saved, and restart your application. Visit again the profile of an existing user (e.g., http://localhost:3000/authusers/2/profile). You should see a select box five rows tall that lists just the one existing role, admins. It should be unselected, as your users have no roles yet. Then follow these steps:

1. Choose the role and click the Set button. The page should reload with the admins role preselected.

2. Add some more roles using the createrole.pl script.

3. Look in the database to see the effect:

```
sqlite3 db/auth.db ".dump"
```

Removing a User

The last CRUD action left to implement is delete (although we'll add function to list all records to finish). Delete functions should always be written with care, especially if your application allows users to *own* objects in the database. Deleting a user will also delete comments the user has created, posts the user has made, and so forth. In a real-world application, we should probably restrict real delete to admins, and allow users only to mark themselves inactive. However, implementing the more secure procedure is left as an exercise for the reader.

One way to do a real delete of the row is to add a "Delete Me" button or link to the user's profile page for him to use:

```
<a href="[%-
  c.uri_for(c.controller('authusers').action_for('delete'), [ user.id ]) %]">
Delete Me</a>
```

This will produce the URL http://localhost:3000/user/1/delete.

Next, we add an action in Controller::AuthUsers to remove the user from the database:

```
sub delete :Chained('user'): PathPart('delete'): Args() {
  my ($self, $c) = @_;
```

```
    my $user = $c->stash->{user};
    $user->delete();

    return $c->res->redirect( $c->uri_for('/') );
}
```

Calling `delete` on a DBIx::Class row object will send a `DELETE` statement to the database. It will delete the row based on its primary key, so in the case of our `users` table, we get the following SQL:

```
DELETE FROM users WHERE id = ?
```

▌Note Remember, as mentioned earlier in this chapter, you can see what SQL your database class is generating with the `DBIC_TRACE` environment variable. If you start your server as follows, you'll see SQL interspersed with the rest of the debug output:

```
CATALYST_DEBUG=0 DBIC_TRACE=1 script/myapp_server.pl
```

Being able to view SQL like this is very useful for troubleshooting. Remember, you can also turn debugging on with `CATALYST_DEBUG=1` if that's more convenient at the time.

The code will then also try and delete any `has_many` related rows. This will remove any entries in `user_roles` for the user. It will not remove the roles themselves, as other users can still have those roles.

The database itself will have better support for deleting related rows than DBIx::Class, so always set up constraints there if possible. Deploying the database schema via `deploy` will create constraints for you, by inferring them from the relationships.

Again, we should note that our code is really just for illustrative purposes. In production applications, it is probably better not to have a Delete Me link or button. Instead, allow the user to mark a record for deletion, and leave the power of deletion to admin users behind the scenes.

Listing All Users and Their Roles

The final CRUD action to implement is to list all records in the database. Admins of your application will probably need an overview of all the existing users. It can also be used to do administration such as deleting multiple users at once. The list view helps us here.

As input, all the list view needs is our `users_rs`, so we chain it to the `base` action for the AuthUsers controller:

```
sub list : Chained('base'): PathPart('list'): Args(0) {
  my ($self, $c) = @_;

}
```

The template for this action, in root/authusers/list.tt, lists all the users in the database by iterating over the resultset:

```
<html>
  <head>
    <title>All users and their roles</title>
  </head>
  <body>
    <table>
     <tr><th>UserId</th><th>Username</th><th>Email</th></tr>
     [% WHILE (user = users_rs.next) %]
       <tr>
         <td>[% user.id %]</td>
         <td>[% user.username %]</td>
         <td>[% user.email %]</td>
       </tr>
     [% END %]
     </table>
  </body>
</html>
```

The next method on a resultset runs the SQL query, if it hasn't been run yet. Then it returns the next row as a row object. The resultset keeps track of the position in the set of rows. When the last row is reached, next will return undef.

To return all the roles a user already has, we can call the roles accessor to use the many_to_many relationship bridge. In list context, which Template Toolkit uses, it will return a list we can loop over. Note the two different ways that a resultset iterator and a list are called. In the first instance, we have [% WHILE (user = users_rs.next) %], while in the second we do it in a FOREACH loop shown in the next code snippet. The parentheses in the WHILE loop are required.

We add another header to the list in the table and then add another cell to list the roles:

```
<tr><th>UserId</th><th>Username</th><th>Email</th><th>Roles</th></tr>


    <td>
    <ul>
    [% FOREACH role = user.user_roles %]
     <li>[% role.role_id.role %]</li>
    [% END %]
    </ul>
    </td>
```

Finally, we restart our application and view the results at http://localhost:3000/authusers/list.

Summary

In this chapter, we covered the basic usage of DBIx::Class with Catalyst. We gave a tour of different database systems, and we set up an example SQLite database. From there, we created a new Catalyst application and developed a DBIx::Class::Schema model for our application. We showed the use of DBIx::Class components for automatic insertion of data into the database with DBIx::Class::TimeStamp and described the main relationship types in DBIx::Class: belongs_to, has_many, and many_to_many. We then showed a practical example of how this all fits together by implementing create, retrieve, update, delete, and list functionality in our application using the Template Toolkit.

In the next chapter, we will look at the Catalyst dispatcher. First we'll cover the request cycle, and then we'll examine the various ways of URL/path action mapping that can be used in Catalyst. We'll look at the various dispatch methods used by "legacy" Catalyst (:Path, :Local, and :Regexp), and then we'll explain in detail the Chained dispatch type that we've already touched on in this chapter and in Chapter 4.

CHAPTER 7

■ ■ ■

The Catalyst Dispatcher

We looked at Catalyst's approach to dispatch in Chapter 1 when comparing it to other frameworks. You've also seen most, if not all, of the dispatch types available by default at this stage of the book. Now we will look at the dispatcher in much more detail.

The dispatcher provides the rules to indicate which code runs when given a specific request. As we mentioned in Chapter 1, Catalyst has self-contained controllers that do not require an external file to the dispatch rules. This is a powerful technique that is in part responsible for the ease with which Catalyst applications can be extended.

Figure 7-1 shows a flowchart representing what happens in the dispatch cycle. In the first part of this chapter, we'll walk through this process more or less in the order that it's shown in the flowchart.

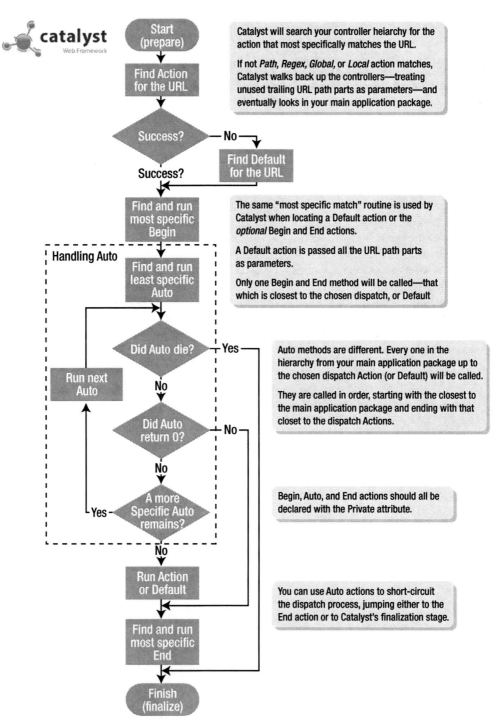

Figure 7-1. *Flowchart representing the Catalyst request cycle from the initial request to serving the document to the client (Source: Catalyst Wiki:* http://dev.catalyst.perl.org/wiki/)

How Catalyst Prepares Before Dispatch

Before Catalyst works out the dispatch logic, the request is prepared via the prepare method in Catalyst.pm. The first thing done to prepare the request is to corral all of the information from the engine into the context object (usually $c, or if you're overriding a method in MyApp.pm, you'll want to call it $self, which we do in the "The Chained Dispatch Type" section of this chapter).

First, prepare gathers all the information from the latest request from the current engine (be that the built-in server, FastCGI, mod_perl, or others) and assigns it into the context object. The methods called during this process are as follows. These methods all need to apply rules for the specific engine currently under use in order to work properly.

- prepare_request
- prepare_connection
- prepare_query_parameters
- prepare_headers
- prepare_cookies
- prepare_path
- prepare_read

You won't come across most of these methods in ordinary use of Catalyst, but because the request path is so fundamental to the dispatcher, we should note that prepare_path splits up the request base (i.e., $c->req->base), the portion of the request URI that doesn't have anything to do with the Catalyst application, from the request path (i.e., $c->req->path), which does.

After dealing with the parts of the context object that require engine-specific logic, Catalyst now deals with the request body via the prepare_body method and stores the current request method (i.e., GET, POST, etc.) via get_method.

The Basic Dispatch Process

At this point, Catalyst has calculated $c->req->path and now has to work out what to do with it. Catalyst searches the controller hierarchy (depth first, with the exception of auto) for the action that most specifically matches the URL. An action is a subroutine in a Catalyst controller with one or more attributes. Subroutine attributes are a part of the subroutine declaration and are a list of labels for the subroutine, as follows:

```
sub do_stuff :Attribute1 :Attribute2 :Attribute3('with_argument') { ...
```

Note The first : for the attributes is compulsory, whereas the following are optional.

As you can see from the preceding code example, subroutine attributes can also have an argument (make sure there's no space before the parenthesis containing the argument, or your application will not compile).

The built-in subroutine attributes for Catalyst controllers are implemented in the Catalyst::Controller module, where the parse_XXX_attr methods provide the attributes for the dispatcher. You can make your own with a base controller (we'll cover this in Chapter 10). The types of actions built into Catalyst are Private, Local, Global, Path, LocalRegex, Regex, and Chained.

Of these the first three do not take any arguments. A Private action is one that cannot be accessed by visiting a particular URL; it can be invoked only through a forward or a detach within a controller. In fact, this is not quite true. For backward-compatibility reasons, default : Private and index : Private are special, publicly accessible private actions. We don't use these any more—instead of sub default : Private, we use something like sub default : Path, and instead of sub index : Private, we use sub index : Path Args(0). However, these can have any name you like, for example, sub do_404 : Path and sub homepage : Path Args(0).

Using the Path attribute for the index and default actions, compared to the old method of special private actions, creates consistency across all of our controller actions. For example, if we had the following subroutine definition in our application's Controller::Root, it would run if we requested /something or something_else, so long as we didn't actually have any definition that explicitly caught these arguments:

```
sub level1_catchall : Path : Args(1) { ...
```

We can also provide an argument to the Path attribute as follows:

```
sub doit :Path('dog') :Args(1) { ...
```

So if the preceding line is in Controller::Root, and we request /dog/labradoodle, the value of $c->action will be doit, and $c->req->path will be an array reference whose only element is labradoodle.

In general, doing this kind of thing is preferable to providing an action with the :Local attribute, as it makes it much easier to refactor the URLs where the dispatcher will land. The same advice goes for Global, which has the same function as local but matches one level higher in the namespace. For example, say we want to have a more generic "pet" URL instead of "dog." All we have to do is change our action as follows:

```
sub doit : Path('pet') :Args(1) { ...
```

We can illustrate why this is an advantage by using $c->uri_for in a more introspective way. The complete code for our action as follows illustrates this:

```
sub doit : Path('pet') :Args(1) {
    my ($self, $c) = @_;
    $c->stash( this_uri =>
        $c->uri_for(
            $c->action => $c->controller->action_for('doit'), $c->req->path ),
    );
}
```

Path is also configurable in the package configuration (we'll look at this at the end of the Chained dispatch explanation in the "Overriding the Public Dispatch Paths with Configuration" section at the end of this chapter). Assuming that doit is in Controller::Root, the value for uri_for will be http://localhost/pet/labradoodle for the request /pet/labradoodle. If we wanted to generate the same URI from a different controller, we'd use the code $c->controller('Root')->action_for('doit').

Having explained this, we need to let you know about a little bit of complexity that you introduce by using action_for. First, if the action_for call returns undef, then uri_for will generate the URI for the current namespace, which is probably not what you want. Second, you can use action_for in Template Toolkit templates. Because Template Toolkit sometimes has issues working out what to do with array references, it's generally better to pass URIs generated in this manner from the stash rather than generating them in the template.

Two Special Dispatch Types: begin and auto

So now that we've clearly stated some best practices and introduced the simplest dispatch types, we can return to the rest. When Catalyst goes back up in the controller hierarchy, it assigns unused parts of $c->req->path into $c->req->args. We can demonstrate this with a little test application. Let's start a new application with catalyst.pl DispatchTest.

Rather than going through the nitty-gritty of which controller action hits when, let's look at how to work it out by example. The kind of technique we're going to use here is useful for figuring out for yourself how the Catalyst dispatcher works. We'll use this same technique for explaining the Chained dispatch type shortly. First, we'll replace the generated Controller::Root with the following:

```
package DispatchTest::Controller::Root;

use strict;
use warnings;

use parent 'Catalyst::Controller';

use YAML;
__PACKAGE__->config->{namespace} = '';

sub catchall : Path {
    my ( $self, $c ) = @_;
    push @{$c->stash->{matches}},
        { 'Root' . ' -> ' . $c->action => $c->req->args };
}

#   sub begin : Private {
#       my ($self, $c) = @_;
#       push @{$c->stash->{matches}},
#           { 'Root' . ' -> ' . 'begin' => $c->req->args };
#   }
```

```
#   sub auto : Private {
#       my ($self, $c) = @_;
#       push @{$c->stash->{matches}},
#           { 'Root' . ' -> ' . 'auto'  => $c->req->args };
#   }

sub end : ActionClass('RenderView') {
    my ($self, $c) = @_;
    push @{$c->stash->{matches}}, 'Root' . ' -> ' . "end";
    $c->res->body("<pre>\n" . Dump ($c->stash->{matches}) . "</pre>");
}

1;
```

Note that when we use catalyst.pl, the action that catches all other unmatched actions is named default : Path. In this example, we've called it catchall : Path instead, and because we're not going to use an index action in this mini-application, so we haven't included it at all. We also have a begin and an auto action that are commented out at the moment, and an end action that provides us with a very minimal view. We are going to explore what the begin and auto actions do shortly, but for now we'll leave them commented out.

All the end action does is serialize an array reference stored in $c->stash->{matches} using YAML to display the text. So long as we put sensible data in this stash key for each match, we can see what's called when during the dispatcher run. Our code puts information about the current controller, the current action, and $c->req->args in each of these assignments.

Now we can request the top-level page of our application with the test script:

```
$ CATALYST_DEBUG=0 script/dispatchtest_test.pl /
```

This request outputs the following:

```
<pre>
---
- Root -> catchall: []
- Root -> end
</pre>
```

In this code, we have a convention that each element of $c->stash->{matches} contains information about a particular point of the dispatch cycle. The fact that it's an array and we always push onto the end of the array in each action means that we can easily see the order in which different controller actions are called. In the catchall action, we add a hash reference to matches. The key of the hash reference is the base name of the controller (i.e., Root), an arrow symbol (->), and the name of the action, which we can obtain from $c->action. The value of the hash reference is the array reference obtained in $c->req->args. You can see that when we call the test script, the catchall action in Controller::Root is called, and $c->req->args is empty. After this, all that is called is the end action. We don't bother making the end action record as sophisticated data in the matches stash key, because by the time we get to end, we've explored all the data we're interested in for this application.

Next, if we request /dwarfs/grumpy/bashful/sneezy with the test script:

```
$ CATALYST_DEBUG=0 script/dispatchtest_test.pl /dwarfs/grumpy/bashful/sneezy
```

we get the following output:

```
<pre>
---
- Root -> catchall:
    - dwarfs
    - grumpy
    - bashful
    - sneezy
- Root -> end
</pre>
```

Now you can see that $c->req->args is full of the trailing arguments from the request.

Moving on, we can make a separate Dwarfs controller as part of the same application. Again, we'll comment out the begin and auto actions until we're going to use them.

```perl
package DispatchTest::Controller::Dwarfs;

use strict;
use warnings;

use parent 'Catalyst::Controller';

sub catchall : Path {
    my ( $self, $c ) = @_;
    push @{$c->stash->{matches}},
        { 'Dwarfs' . ' -> ' . $c->action => $c->req->args };
}

#    sub begin : Private {
#       my ($self, $c) = @_;
#       push @{$c->stash->{matches}},
#                   { 'Dwarfs' . ' -> ' . 'begin' => $c->req->args },
#    }

#    sub auto : Private {
#       my ($self, $c) = @_;
#       push @{$c->stash->{matches}},
#           { 'Dwarfs' . ' -> ' . 'auto'  => $c->req->args };
#    }

1;
```

Then we can make the same request for /dwarfs/grumpy/bashful/sneezy, which gives the
following output from the test script:

```
<pre>
---
- Dwarfs -> dwarfs/catchall:
    - grumpy
    - bashful
    - sneezy
- Root -> end
</pre>
```

Dwarfs is no longer in $c->req->args, as it matches the catchall action in Controller::
Dwarfs. Also see how $c->action contains the fully qualified request path for the request, not
just the terminal part of the request.

Now let's uncomment the begin action in each of the controllers and make the same
request. The output from the test script after we do this is as follows:

```
<pre>
---
- Dwarfs -> begin:
    - grumpy
    - bashful
    - sneezy
- Dwarfs -> dwarfs/catchall:
    - grumpy
    - bashful
    - sneezy
- Root -> end
</pre>
```

As you can see, only the most specific begin is being called. Catalyst::Controller::REST
uses this technique to set up the deserialization rules.

THE END ACTION

The most specific end action is also called as part of the request cycle. In almost all circumstances, you'll
want a single end action that is placed in Controller::Root. However, overriding end in a particular controller
is occasionally useful. For example, Catalyst::Controller::REST provides its own end action that does intel-
ligent data serialization. The job end performs is to do things like delegate to the view, set response headers,
and do anything else that needs to be finalized before the request body is sent across the wire.

Next, we can uncomment the two `auto` actions and make the same request again. The output now is

```
<pre>
---
- Dwarfs -> begin:
    - grumpy
    - bashful
    - sneezy
- Root -> auto: &1
    - grumpy
    - bashful
    - sneezy
- Dwarfs -> auto: *1
- Dwarfs -> dwarfs/catchall:
    - grumpy
    - bashful
    - sneezy
- Root -> end
</pre>
```

You can see that the most specific `begin` is called, and then the least specific `auto` followed by all other `auto` actions down the controller hierarchy. `$c->req->args` is the same (the `&1` and `*1` notation is YAML indicating that one reference is the exact same reference as the other). The common use for `auto` is setting up a chain of authentication and authorization rules.

LocalRegex and Regex Actions

You're generally discouraged from using `LocalRegex` and `Regex` actions, but occasionally you'll need them. In almost all cases, the `Chained` dispatch type obsoletes `Regex` actions, so feel free to skip this section and move straight on to the next section, "Internal Request Flow Control."

There are two types of `Regex` (regular expression) actions: `LocalRegex` and `Regex`. These both take quote-delimited regular expressions, and the grouped parts of the expression are available in `$c->req->captures`. Note that the `Regex` dispatch type was the initial implementation of a way of getting requests of the form `/items/list/1/delete` to work, but now in 99% of cases it's better to use `Chained`.

Let's add the following into our Dwarfs controller:

```
sub answer_phone :LocalRegex('(.*?\.mp3)') {
    my ($self, $c) = @_;
    push @{$c->stash->{matches}},
        { 'Dwarfs' . ' -> ' .
          $c->action  => [{ args => $c->req->args} ,
          {captures => $c->req->captures}] };
}
```

The preceding code will match a request of the form `dwarfs/answer_phone/anything.mp3` with what is presumably the name of an MP3 file, which you can access from `$c->captures`. Here's the result from the request for `/dwarfs/answer_phone/sneezy.mp3`:

```
<pre>
---
- Dwarfs -> begin: []
- Root -> auto: &1 []
- Dwarfs -> auto: *1
- Dwarfs -> dwarfs/answer_phone:
    - args: []
    - captures:
        - answer_phone/sneezy.mp3
- Root -> end
</pre>
```

If we change the type of action from `LocalRegex` to `Regex` and make the same request, we see the following output:

```
<pre>
---
- Dwarfs -> begin: []
- Root -> auto: &1 []
- Dwarfs -> auto: *1
- Dwarfs -> dwarfs/answer_phone:
    - args: []
    - captures:
        - dwarfs/answer_phone/sneezy.mp3
- Root -> end
</pre>
```

As you can see, the namespace of the controller is stored in `$c->req->captures`. This means that we can potentially call the `Regex` using a different leading path—for example, let's request `/answer_phone/sneezy.mp3`. If it's a `LocalRegex` in the Dwarfs controller, the `LocalRegex` action is not hit:

```
<pre>
---
- Dwarfs -> dwarfs/catchall:
    - answer_phone
    - sneezy.mp3
- Root -> end
</pre>
```

If, on the other hand, we use the Regex attribute, it *is* called:

```
<pre>
---
- Dwarfs -> begin: []
- Root -> auto: &1 []
- Dwarfs -> auto: *1
- Dwarfs -> dwarfs/answer_phone:
    - args: []
    - captures:
        - answer_phone/sneezy.mp3
- Root -> end
</pre>
```

With the Regex dispatch type, we could also call the path /shout_really_loud/sneezy. mp3?volume=11:

```
<pre>
---
- Dwarfs -> begin: []
- Root -> auto: &1 []
- Dwarfs -> auto: *1
- Dwarfs -> dwarfs/answer_phone:
    - args: []
    - captures:
        - shout_really_loud/sneezy.mp3
- Root -> end
</pre>
```

However, this requires a lot of manual error trapping and is hard to maintain. For almost all cases where you have parts of the URL that you want to match, you should use the Chained dispatch type. We'll discuss this in the upcoming "The Chained Dispatch Type" section.

Internal Request Flow Control: $c->forward, $c->detach, $c->go, and $c->visit

The dispatch rules map from the URL to the code that Catalyst runs. You also need a way to alter the chain of dispatch from inside an action. You will routinely want to do this for a number of reasons, including adding more data to an authorized request, but providing minimal data for an unauthorized request; and serving a login form for unauthorized users. In this section, we'll use our small-scale Catalyst application to demonstrate what happens here. First we'll discuss $c->forward and $c->detach, and then we'll look at the "full request" equivalents, $c->visit and $c->go.

forward and detach

Figure 7-2 shows the difference between flow control for forward and detach. Once a chain of actions is completed during a forward, the request continues from where forward was called. On the other hand, detach does not return to complete the request.

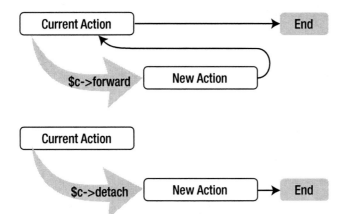

Figure 7-2. *Flow control logic for $c->forward and $c->detach. $c->forward returns to the calling action and completes the request, while $c->detach proceeds to the end action after the called actions are completed.*

We can illustrate how to use these two functions with code. We remove the catchall, begin, and auto subs in DispatchTest::Controller::Root and add the following code:

```perl
sub index : Path Args(0) {
    my ($self, $c) = @_;
    push @{ $c->stash->{matches} }, "index before";
    $c->forward('private_action');
    push @{ $c->stash->{matches} }, "index after";
}

sub private_action : Private {
    my ( $self, $c ) = @_;
    push @{ $c->stash->{matches} }, "private_action";
}
```

Then if we request the application root with the test script, we get the following output:

```
$ CATALYST_DEBUG=0 script/dispatchtest_test.pl /

- index before
- private_action
- index after
- Root -> end
```

We arrive at the index action, this runs some code, and then it forwards to the private action, where more code is run. The action then automatically returns back to the forwarding private action. detach is like forward, but it doesn't return to the calling action. So if we change our code in the index action to $c->detach('private_action') instead of forward and make the same request, we see that detach doesn't return from the calling action.

```
<pre>
---
- index before
- private_action
- Root -> end
</pre>
```

While the public actions are for defining what URL maps to what code, the private actions are for processing business logic internal to the workflow. The arguments for forward and detach are the same. Called with one argument as just shown, they forward to the controller with a named action. You can also temporarily override the values of $c->req->args for a forward or detach. To demonstrate, let's add the following to our example code:

```perl
sub path1 : Path('one') Args {
    my ($self, $c) = @_;
    push @{ $c->stash->{matches} }, { "path1" => $c->req->args };
    $c->forward('Root', 'path2', [ qw/new set of args/ ]);
    push @{ $c->stash->{matches} }, { "path1" => $c->req->args };
}

sub path2 : Path('two') Args {
    my ($self, $c ) = @_;
    push @{ $c->stash->{matches} }, { "path2" => $c->req->args };
}
```

Next, we run the text script again:

```
$ CATALYST_DEBUG=0 script/dispatchtest_test.pl /one/two/three
```

and we get the following output:

```
<pre>
---
- path1: &1
    - two
    - three
- path2:
    - new
    - set
    - of
    - args
- path1: *1
- Root -> end
</pre>
```

Note the way we've called forward here. The first argument is the controller (not necessary in this case, because we're calling to the same controller, but it's included for illustration purposes). The second argument is the subroutine name for the action, and the third is the array reference that will replace $c->req->args for this part of the request. You can omit the namespace or the action name, but not both. Note how the arguments revert back to the callers once the forward is over. However, if we forwarded to another action in the path2 action once it's called from path1, the modified $c->req->args are passed down the chain until that portion of the request is finished.

Use forward and detach when you want to process a few rules, maybe as part of a conditional statement. A typical use for detach is to move an action over to a login form once it's been established that the user is not yet logged in. You can also use detach to abort a forward if you call it with no arguments, as in $c->detach(), as it will just proceed to the relevant end action.

You might use forward to separate out the setting of stash items for information for the model and stash items relating to the view, so that you can keep controller code that obtains logic information from the view separate from controller code that corrals information together specifically for the use for the view. This is indeed what we did in the original LolCatalyst::Lite::Controller::Translate in Chapter 3.

visit and go

Figure 7-3 illustrates visit and go, which are analogues to forward and detach, and complete a whole request.

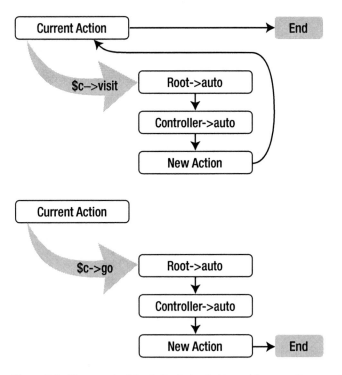

Figure 7-3. *Flow control logic for $c->visit and $c->go. Comparing this diagram to Figure 7-2 should illustrate how $c->visit is the full-request analog of $c->forward, and $c->go of $c->detach.*

To recap, forward returns to the original calling action after the last forward in the chain of dispatch. detach returns to the relevant end action after completion of the request flow for an action. If we want to pretend that we have a complete request but use the same pattern to do so, then $c->visit, the "whole request" version of forward or $c->go, is equivalent to detach. Both accept the same parameters as their counterparts, and both follow the same rules.

One use for visit and go is to get the template set properly for the Template Toolkit view. With the TT view, you don't need to set your template name manually if it is named after the first called action. So, for example, the following subroutine implicitly sets the Template Toolkit template to catchall.tt (assuming your application has the TT view as its default view, with default configuration):

```
path catchall : Path {
    my ($self, $c) = @_;
    $c->forward('an_action');
    $c->forward('some_other_action');
}
```

Sometimes this is not desirable behavior, though, and we want some_other_action to be in charge of setting the template. While we can set the template explicitly, this can become a maintenance headache in complex applications. It's better to use $c->visit('an_action') to get the template set to an_action.tt. If we use go, it works like forward, except it completes the request first before coming back to the caller (therefore then calling some_other_action). If we use visit instead, it is the equivalent of detach and some_other_action is never called, but an_action.tt is still the correct template.

Catalyst::View::Component::Subinclude is somewhat different from $c->visit or $c->go, as it enables you to render the template for a full request and returns the rendered template to the calling action. See Chapter 11 for details.

The Chained Dispatch Type

Previously, we mentioned the Chained dispatch type when we discussed the two Regex dispatch types. The Regex dispatch types were Catalyst's initial implementation of a way of dispatching to URLs with variables embedded in them, such as /thing/id/4/related/3, where the digits are variables that might be used in a database query or similar. Since then, the Chained dispatch type has been developed as a more flexible and robust solution to the same problem. Broadly speaking, Chained can be described as automatic, configurable, cascading forwards.

Chained is the preferred dispatch type of the experienced Catalyst developer. Catalyst developers working in other web frameworks frequently state that they really miss this dispatch type. That said, Chained is a step up in complexity from the other dispatch types that we covered in this chapter, and it takes a bit of mental effort to understand it properly (hopefully, this chapter will alleviate this effort somewhat). However, we think that learning how to use Chained is like learning to ride a bike: once you've learned it, you won't forget, and you'll have trouble remembering why it was a struggle to learn in the first place.

We'll use the same technique of pushing each called action onto a key in the stash in order to demonstrate how Chained works. First, let's create a new application with catalyst.pl DwarfChains and replace the Controller::Root with the following code:

```perl
package DwarfChains::Controller::Root;

use strict;
use warnings;

use parent 'Catalyst::Controller';
use YAML;

__PACKAGE__->config->{namespace} = '';

sub index :Path :Args(0) {
    my ( $self, $c ) = @_;
    $c->res->redirect( 'people' );
}

sub default :Path {
    my ( $self, $c ) = @_;
    $c->response->body( 'Page not found' );
    $c->response->status(404);
}

sub end : ActionClass('RenderView') {
    my ($self, $c) = @_;
    push @{$c->stash->{matches}}, 'Root' . ' -> ' . "end";
    $c->res->body("<pre>\n" . Dump ($c->stash->{matches}) . "</pre>");
}

1;
```

All this does is set up the index action to redirect to the People controller, and all other requests will return a "Not found" status and a suitable response body.

We're going to use the same technique implemented previously to illustrate what happens in the dispatch cycle, but because the information we want to display is a fair bit more complex than earlier, we can place the following subroutine in lib/DwarfChains.pm (*not* the root controller but in the top level namespace for the application).

```perl
sub push_stack {
    my ($self, $caller) = @_;

    # A hack to get the calling action using Catalyst internals
    my $action_name = $self->stack->[-1]->name;

    # Grab a Catalyst::Action object
    my $action = $self->controller->action_for($action_name);

    # Grab a URI from the action object if we can
    my $uri =
        $action ? $self->uri_for($action) : undef;
```

```
    # Add data to the stash
    push @{ $self->stash->{matches}},
        { ref($caller) => {
            $action_name => $uri,
        },
    }
}
```

This code adds the $c->push_stack() helper method into our application so we can add data for display to the matches stash key, which is then displayed in the end action. Don't worry about the $self->stack->[-1] line, this is a hack on Catalyst's internals to display the name of the calling action without passing it in explicitly.

To illustrate our first chained action, we will create DwarfChains::Controller::People as follows:

```
package DwarfChains::Controller::People;

use strict;
use warnings;

use parent 'Catalyst::Controller';

sub get_ready :Chained("/") :PathPart("name") :CaptureArgs(0) {
    my ($self, $c) = @_;
    $c->push_stack($self );
}

sub get_root :Chained("get_ready") :PathPart("") :Args(0) {
    my ($self, $c) = @_;
    $c->push_stack($self );
}

1;
```

The use of PathPart is analogous to the Path attribute encountered earlier, except rather than being a relative path to where the action matches, it's the part of the path in the current section of the chain. So if we use the test script to request /name, as follows:

```
$ CATALYST_DEBUG=0 script/dwarfchains_test.pl /name
```

we get the following output:

```
<pre>
---
- People:
    get_ready: ~
- People:
    get_root: !!perl/scalar:URI::http http://localhost/name
- Root: end
</pre>
```

You can see that the get_ready action is called initially, but it has no URI associated with it. This is because only chained actions with an endpoint are associated with publicly accessible parts of the web application, and these are defined by having an :Args([number]) attribute. In contrast, the CaptureArgs([number]) attribute indicates that this is a midpoint for the chained dispatch.

Another thing that's important to note is that we've decoupled the controller namespace from the publicly accessible URL, similar to the way we used the : Path attribute previously. Again, this means that our code declarations are independent of the namespace structure of the application, which makes code reuse easier and decreases maintenance overhead.

Let's next look at chaining across namespaces. Now that we've created a basic example of Chained dispatch, we can use a separate namespace to continue the dispatch. We'll create a new controller, DwarfChains::People::Info, with the following code:

```perl
package DwarfChains::Controller::People::Info;

use strict;
use warnings;

use parent 'Catalyst::Controller';

sub get_info_ready :Chained("/people/get_ready") :PathPart("who") :CaptureArgs(0) {
    my ($self, $c) = @_;
    $c->push_stack($self);
}

sub list :Chained("get_info_ready") :PathPart("") :Args(0) {
    my ($self, $c) = @_;
    $c->push_stack($self);
}

sub create :Chained("get_info_ready") : PathPart('add') : Args(0) {
    my ($self, $c) = @_;
    $c->push_stack($self);
}

1;
```

We should probably mention at this point that the debug output is particularly useful for chained actions. If we start the test server after adding the preceding code, we get a very useful table showing the mapping of public URLs to the method names.

```
[debug] Loaded Chained actions:
.-------------------------+--------------------------------------------------.
| Path Spec               | Private                                          |
|                         |                                                  |
+-------------------------+--------------------------------------------------+
| /name                   | /people/get_ready (0)                            |
|                         | => /people/get_root                              |
| /name/who/add           | /people/get_ready (0)                            |
|                         | ->/people/info/get_info_ready (0)                |
|                         | => /people/info/create                           |
| /name/who               | /people/get_ready (0)                            |
|                         | -> /people/info/get_info_ready (0)               |
|                         | => /people/info/list                             |
'-------------------------+--------------------------------------------------'
```

This table tells us that the /name action we already called calls the get_ready method in the People controller, and then the get_root method in the People controller.

Next, we'll call name/who. If this were a real application, the output would probably be a list of the residents of the dwarfs' house in the woods. However, we'll just have to settle for our ultrathin dispatch microviewer instead:

```
$ CATALYST_DEBUG=0 script/dwarfchains_test.pl /name/who

<pre>
---
- DwarfChains::Controller::People:
    get_ready: ~
- DwarfChains::Controller::People::Info:
    get_info_ready: ~
- DwarfChains::Controller::People::Info:
    list: !!perl/scalar:URI::http http://localhost/name/who
- Root: end
</pre>
```

We can see that the dispatch chain works as advertised by the debug table and that the list action is the endpoint of the chain. When Snow White meets a new arrival at the house in the woods, we can call /name/who/add to update the database of residents. The only difference between the two subroutine declarations is that for list, the PathPart attribute is the empty string, and for create, it's add.

We want to be able to browse information about specific dwarfs (and Snow White), so we want to implement URLs that take a specific ID. Thinking about the four most common actions—create, review (but only for listing many records in this case; the principle for reviewing a single record is the same as for the next two, though), update, and delete—we have the first two, but we need to provide actions for the second two. Both actions require that we get the individual's data, so we need an identifier for them. Thus, we'll want to get URLs like /name/who/[name]/review and /name/who/[name]/evict. First, we'll add the action that captures the name into $c->req->args (we'll set it to the stash there). Seeing as it doesn't make sense to leave the chain dangling, we'll code the two endpoints at the same time.

Here's the code to go in DwarfChains::Controller::Info:

```
sub get_id :Chained("get_info_ready") :PathPart("") :CaptureArgs(1) {
    my ($self, $c, $capture) = @_;
    $c->stash(capture => $capture);
    push @{ $c->stash->{matches} }, { CapturedArg => $capture };
    $c->push_stack($self);
}

sub delete :Chained("get_id") :PathPart("evict") :Args(0) {
    my ($self, $c) = @_;
    $c->push_stack($self, $c->stash->{capture});
}

sub edit :Chained("get_id") :PathPart("") :Args(0) {
    my ($self, $c) = @_;
    $c->push_stack($self, $c->stash->{capture});
}
```

At this point, note that to get the URI right for items with captured arguments, we need to pass them into our little view subroutine as well. This means we have to change our push_ stack subroutine in DwarfChains.pm. The first line that deals with the sub's arguments needs to change to

```
my ($self, $caller, $capture) = @_;
```

and the call to uri_for needs to be the following:

```
$self->uri_for($action, [$capture])
```

If we don't do this, uri_for will return undef. Again, it's recommended that you look at the debug output to work out what's going to happen when we call /name/who/sneezy. The mini-view invoked by the test script outputs the following:

```
---
- DwarfChains::Controller::People:
    get_ready: ~
- DwarfChains::Controller::People::Info:
    get_info_ready: ~
- CapturedArg: sneezy
- DwarfChains::Controller::People::Info:
    get_id: ~
- DwarfChains::Controller::People::Info:
    edit: !!perl/scalar:URI::http http://127.0.0.1:3000/name/who/sneezy
- Root: end
```

which illustrates what's called when quite nicely. The output for /name/who/impostor/evict will be very similar.

Our application chains from one namespace to another. In practice, we can chain across arbitrary numbers of namespaces. This approach can help us by providing a single point of entry across multiple controllers, which can be useful when organizing access control or setting common data across different parts of the application.

Overriding the Public Dispatch Paths with Configuration

The final thing to do in this chapter is show how the public URLs called by actions can be overridden with configuration. This is usually done to translate the URL scheme into a different language, although it can also be used for "white boxing" applications for different hosts. In this case, we'll translate our URL dispatch path for DwarfChains to Bahasa Indonesia (the official language of the Indonesian archipelago).

If we start with the People controller, we simply add the public parts of the URL to the configuration. We'll do this in dwarfchains.conf in the application root. Here's the addition to the configuration file:

```
<Controller People>
<action get_ready>
 PathPart nama
</action>
</Controller>

<Controller People::Info>
<action get_info_ready>
 PathPart siapa
</action >
<action create>
 PathPart lagi
</action >
<action delete>
 PathPart mengusir
</action >
</Controller>
```

Here's the corresponding dispatch table from the debug output of the test server:

```
.----------------------------+----------------------------------------.
| Path Spec                  | Private                                |
+----------------------------+----------------------------------------+
| /nama                      | /people/get_ready (0)                  |
|                            | => /people/get_root                    |
| /nama/siapa/lagi           | /people/get_ready (0)                  |
|                            | -> /people/info/get_info_ready (0)     |
|                            | => /people/info/create                 |
| /nama/siapa/*/mengusir     | /people/get_ready (0)                  |
|                            | -> /people/info/get_info_ready (0)     |
|                            | -> /people/info/get_id (1)             |
|                            | => /people/info/delete                 |
| /nama/siapa/*              | /people/get_ready (0)                  |
|                            | -> /people/info/get_info_ready (0)     |
|                            | -> /people/info/get_id (1)             |
|                            | => /people/info/edit                   |
| /nama/siapa                | /people/get_ready (0)                  |
|                            | -> /people/info/get_info_ready (0)     |
|                            | => /people/info/list                   |
'----------------------------+----------------------------------------'
```

Yet another way we can use this is to set up custom public dispatch points for URLs where we're inheriting from base controllers, with the public path part overridden in __PACKAGE__ ->config. We'll discuss this in Chapter 11.

Summary

In this chapter, we examined all of the dispatch types covered by Catalyst. First, we looked at the Private, Local, Path (and its Args modifier), Regex, and LocalRegex dispatch types. Following this, we discussed the special private actions begin and auto for automatically calling particular code during the beginning of the request cycle, and the use of the forward, detach, visit, and go methods for affecting flow control during the request cycle. Finally, we looked at one of Catalyst's most distinctive and powerful features, the Chained dispatch type which, while initially tricky to understand, has become the preferred way for performing URL dispatch for experienced Catalyst developers.

In the next chapter, we'll cover user access control in Catalyst applications with authentication and authorization.

CHAPTER 8

■■■

Authentication and Authorization

For many years, websites were primarily public access. A handful had HTTP authorization controls on certain files, but that was about it. In recent years, however, with the explosion of the interactive web and real web applications, the need for user identification has become one of the most pervasive parts of the web experience.

User access control has remained, however, one of the least understood and standardized portions of web application development. When switching from one application to another, you had to figure out how the new application handled the login process, how people stayed logged in, and so on.

Some application frameworks have addressed this issue by providing a unified authentication model. Unfortunately, this usually means sticking to a very particular model of authentication, and if your application doesn't fit that, you have to break out of the "standard" authentication model, and you are back to rolling your own authentication system.

Thankfully, Catalyst is not one of those frameworks. Catalyst has a very robust authentication system that allows you great freedom in how you handle authentication. At the same time, Catalyst provides a unified interface to work with authentication and authenticated users.

We've touched on authentication before in this book, but in this chapter we will cover the topic in full detail. We'll show you the most common type of authentication used in web applications as well as a more advanced configuration involving multiple sources of authentication data. We'll then talk briefly about working with data that directly relates to the authenticated user. First, though, we'll discuss what exactly it is that we want from authentication in a web application.

The Three Parts of Authentication

When we are working with authentication in a web application, we are really looking for three things: authentication, persistence, and authorization. *Authentication* covers figuring out if the user is who she says she is, *persistence* retains the user information from request to request, and *authorization* answers the question "Is this person allowed to do this?"

Catalyst's authentication system provides a standardized way of dealing with these three parts from the application perspective, while retaining the flexibility to change how each portion is handled behind the scenes. That's a long way of saying you can use what you need now, and when your application needs to grow, you can switch to new modules without rewriting all of your application code.

The way Catalyst accomplishes this is by providing a core authentication module that handles the application interaction and by delegating the three portions of authentication to other modules. Many of these modules are available for free on CPAN to interface with just about any source of authentication information you can think of. There are also detailed instructions on how to write your own, in the rare case where none of the available modules meets your needs (see Catalyst::Plugin::Authentication::Internals for details).

As you might guess, Catalyst's authentication system delegates each part of the authentication to a different module or set of modules. This allows each piece of the system to focus on doing its one very particular job.

In the sections that follow, we'll cover authentication realms: the system that determines the identity of the user, the use of browser sessions to achieve persistent state in the application (see Chapter 2 on the HTTP protocol for the background to this), and role-based authorization for finer-grained access control (e.g., adding an administrator user with more power than a regular user).

Authentication Realms

The first part of the authentication triad is the authentication realm. In Catalyst, it is the realm class that is responsible for answering the question "Is this user who he says he is?"

For the most part when you are asking about a given user in your Catalyst application, you are interacting with the realm object. The realm object is in many ways the central switching point for authentication. Anything to do with retrieving the user, inquiring if there is a user to retrieve, handling persistence, and so forth, all channels through the realm object. This makes the realm object very powerful and allows you to completely customize the authentication process, should you need to. (We'll touch on custom realms a bit later.)

That said, however, most people never use anything but the default realm class that is distributed with the Catalyst authentication modules. That's because the default realm class has very sensible default behavior. It uses the Catalyst Session plugin to persist users across requests, and it splits the user verification process into two pieces.

Before we delve too deeply into realms, it would help to see a sample of what the Catalyst authentication check looks like in its natural habitat.

```
if ( $c->authenticate({
                        username => $c->req->params->{'username'},
                        password => $c->req->params->{'password'}
                    }) )
{
    ## $c->user now contains the information related to the user
} else {
    ## authentication failed.
}
```

You can read this code and figure out immediately what it's doing. Let's talk a bit now about *how* it's doing what it's doing. When you think about how to do username/password authentication, there is a pretty ingrained pattern of how to handle it. First, you look up the user being requested somewhere, and then you compare the password for the user you found with the password that was provided. Pretty straightforward, really.

Catalyst's default realm class agrees, and it splits its duty across exactly those lines. A submodule called, appropriately, a user Store is used to find the user being requested, and then a submodule called a Credential (short for *credential verifier*) is responsible for comparing the user's credentials with those provided in the authenticate call. If a user is found, and the credentials provided match up with those required, then the user is verified and made available via $c->user.

Persistence

Once the user has been loaded and verified, you want to keep the user information available on the requests that follow. The Catalyst authentication system handles this via the Catalyst Session plugin. Once the $c->authenticate() call succeeds, the user information is stored in the session, and the user is automatically available on each request after that.

From that point on, you don't need to think too much about user persistence; the default authentication realm class handles the details for you. Each subsequent request will have $c->user automatically populated for you when you request it. You can test whether there is a user available by calling $c->user_exists(). This is good because in your action you can decide what to do based on whether or not you have an authenticated user. A common use of this ability would be to respond to a request with generic information when an unregistered user is accessing the page, but respond with personalized information when the user requesting the page is logged in, for example:

```
if ( $c->user_exists() ) {
    @interests = $c->user->interests->all();
    ## show customized information based on the user's interests
}
else {
    @interests = $items->most_popular(10);
    ## show top ten items to unknown users
}
## do stuff with @interests
```

Often, though, you'll want to go beyond answering the question "Do I know who is requesting this action?" in your application. If you wanted, for example, to determine whether the user requesting the action is allowed to do so, you could certainly look at the user object, check the contents of the user_type field, and so on. It's likely not the first time you've done that type of authorization checking. Thankfully, Catalyst makes that process a lot easier as well, using the concept of *roles*.

Authorization with Roles

Generally speaking, the goal when using authentication in a web application is to have a way to answer the question "Is the person making this request allowed to do so?" Everything up until that point in the process is overhead. Catalyst has a few options for authorization available, but by far the most common is the Roles plugin.

The Roles plugin allows you to define named roles for a given user, and then it allows your application code to verify that a user has those roles before performing a certain action. Many people name these roles after the class of user being referred to, such as registered or admin. Others name the roles after permissions, such as can_edit_articles or can_comment. We find the latter method to be more useful, as it allows flexible control over who can do what in your application.

Using roles is easy. Much like the $c->user_exists() check we did earlier, you can at any time check the user's roles. There are several methods to do this, and you can select the one that best fits your style. By far the simplest is the $c->check_user_roles() method, which simply returns true or false based on whether the authenticated user is in the roles specified. An example of using it this way would be something like the following:

```
if ( $c->user_exists() && $c->check_user_roles( qw/ can_edit / ) ) {
    ## do the edit
}
else {
    ## Tell them no, they are not allowed and send them on their way
}
```

You can also check for any of a set of roles. For example, if you wanted to say those with can_edit or is_superuser can perform a particular action, you'd use $c->check_any_user_role() like so:

```
if ( $c->user_exists() &&
    $c->check_any_user_role( qw/ can_edit is_superuser/ ) ) {
    ## proceed with edit
}
else {
    ## tell them to go away
}
```

As we've shown, interfacing with the Catalyst authentication system is quite simple. Authenticating a user, accessing the user's information, and setting up access control for your actions is straightforward and easy to understand. Knowing this will make it easy for you to understand what is going on when you encounter a Catalyst application in the wild. Setting up authentication initially in your own application, however, requires a little more effort, but not a lot. We'll cover that process in the next section.

Installing the Required Modules

Now that you've had a peek at what authentication looks like in a Catalyst application, it's time to move on to something a bit more substantial. In Chapter 3, we created an application that included authentication using Catalyst::Helper::AuthDBIC. In this chapter, we'll set up authentication manually through the application configuration and demonstrate how authentication is likely to appear in your own applications. We'll do this via an example application called SneakyCat in the next section. In preparation for that application, in this section we'll install the necessary modules.

To add authentication to your application, you first need to ensure that you have all the modules required. For this example, you will only need a handful:

```
Catalyst::Plugin::Authentication
Catalyst::Authentication::Store::DBIx::Class
Catalyst::Plugin::Authorization::Roles
Catalyst::Plugin::Session
Catalyst::Plugin::Session::State::Cookie
Catalyst::Plugin::Session::Store::FastMmap
```

If you have been following along with the examples in previous chapters, you will have already installed these. Before we create our application, let's briefly discuss what each of these modules does.

Catalyst::Plugin::Authentication

In keeping with Catalyst's modular nature, the authentication system is not actually included in the base Catalyst packages. It's an additional component that comes in the form of a plugin module. The Catalyst::Plugin::Authentication module, or C::P::Auth as it is sometimes called, provides the base authentication functionality as well as the simpler user data stores and the base realm. It also contains the most commonly used credential: the Password credential.

Catalyst::Authentication::Store::DBIx::Class

This is probably the second most commonly used authentication-related module for Catalyst. This user store is used to retrieve user information from a database using the DBIx::Class ORM, which, as you saw earlier in the book, is one of the more favored database interfaces. The Catalyst::Authentication::Store::DBIx::Class module also provides support for authentication role storage in the database.

In addition, this module provides the SimpleDB realm class. The price of the flexibility that the Catalyst authentication system provides is that the configuration can be somewhat complex and daunting to the newcomer. In modern web applications, the most common way to store user information is in a SQL database, and the most common way to authenticate users is by using a password. Catalyst::Authentication::Realm::SimpleDB makes that extremely common case very easy to configure. In this chapter we will show the full authentication process first, then later on in the chapter we will show the easier configuration for SimpleDB.

Catalyst::Plugin::Authorization::Roles

The Roles plugin, as it is commonly called, is responsible for providing permission-like information and access controls for your application. In other words, the Roles plugin is used to answer the question "Does the user have permission to perform this task?"

Catalyst::Plugin::Session

The last three modules on our list are session related, and some variation of these three will be loaded in any application where you use persistent session storage. The first module, Catalyst::Plugin::Session, contains the core of the session system. Like Catalyst's authentication system, however, the session module delegates much of its functionality to additional modules.

There are two parts to session management: one is *state*, which is responsible for associating session data with the site visitor it belongs to, and the other is *storage*, which is used to actually hold the session data between requests. The session system splits the work along these lines and expects you to choose the submodules to use. By far the most common modules for session storage are the ones we use. They are Catalyst::Plugin::Session::State::Cookie, which stores state information in the visitor's browser via cookies, and Catalyst::Plugin::Session::Store::FastMmap, which stores the data for a session in a file that is accessed via Mmap.

Catalyst::Plugin::Session::Store::FastMmap is a good module to use on a stand-alone server. However, because Mmap works only on the local server, it cannot be used when you have multiple servers running your site. When running multiple servers, you need to pick a session storage module that will be consistent no matter which machine the request is coming into. A number of session storage modules are available that fit this description, the most common being Catalyst::Plugin::Session::Store::DBIC, which stores session data in a database, and Catalyst::Plugin::Session::Store::Memcached, which stores the session data in a network-accessible memcached server. For simplicity's sake, however, in this example we will use the Mmap session storage module.

Our Example Application: SneakyCat

You've seen that there are a lot of pieces to authentication in a modern web application. As such, the best way to demonstrate the way all of these pieces fit together is to create a complete application.

The application we are going to build is called SneakyCat. The SneakyCat application gives you a view into the mind of a SneakyCat. SneakyCat thinks about things, and when you visit the SneakyCat main page, you will see what SneakyCat has been thinking about lately. If you are an unregistered user, that's about the end of the functionality. If you are registered, however, you will be able to see SneakyCat's more private thoughts. Finally, if you are SneakyCat's friend, you have elevated access and you can whisper to SneakyCat, giving him new things to think about.

SneakyCat is a simple application that demonstrates all of the basic authentication-related behavior including registered/unregistered access, login and logout processes, and elevated levels of access within the group of registered users.

Creating and Configuring SneakyCat

We create SneakyCat the same way we create any Catalyst application:

```
$ catalyst.pl SneakyCat
$ cd SneakyCat
$ script/sneakycat_create.pl View TT TT
$ script/sneakycat_create.pl Controller Ideas
$ script/sneakycat_create.pl Controller People
```

As you can see, our application will have two controllers. The first, Ideas, will contain the majority of the general application functionality, including displaying ideas and accepting new ones. The other controller, People, will contain the login-related routines. We recommend separating the login and registration processes into their own controllers in your own applications. As your web applications grow in size and complexity, access controls are likely to become more pervasive throughout the system. Having a single controller related to the actual authentication-related processes gives you a single place to verify authentication-related functionality and can save you a lot of headaches later on.

The next step in our application setup is to load the database schema and data we will be using in our SneakyCat application. You can find the SneakyCat.sql file, along with the rest of the code for this chapter, in the Source Code area of the Apress website (http://www.apress.com). The SQL for this file is as follows:

```
BEGIN TRANSACTION;
CREATE TABLE users (
  id INTEGER PRIMARY KEY,
  username char(32) NOT NULL DEFAULT '',
  password char(64) NOT NULL,
  status char(16) NOT NULL DEFAULT 'active',
  last_whisper char(20)
);
INSERT INTO "users" VALUES(1,'friend','foDCGe8hfTtg.',
                                 'active', NULL);
INSERT INTO "users" VALUES(2,'neighbor','baxXrXtQlOc6Y',
                                 'active', NULL);


CREATE TABLE users_to_roles (
  user int(11) NOT NULL,
  role int(11) NOT NULL,
  PRIMARY KEY (user,role),
  FOREIGN KEY(user) REFERENCES users(id),
  FOREIGN KEY(role) REFERENCES roles(id)
);
INSERT INTO "users_to_roles" VALUES(1,1);


CREATE TABLE roles (
id INTEGER PRIMARY KEY,
role char(32) DEFAULT NULL);
INSERT INTO "roles" VALUES(1,'can_whisper');
```

```
CREATE TABLE ideas (
  id INTEGER PRIMARY KEY,
  text text NOT NULL,
  secret char(3) NOT NULL DEFAULT 'no',
  added char(20) NOT NULL DEFAULT 'unknown',
  added_by char(32) NOT NULL DEFAULT 'unknown'
);
INSERT INTO "ideas" VALUES(1,'I like food','no',
        'Sun Apr 19 09:19:04 2009','SneakyCat');
INSERT INTO "ideas" VALUES(2,'I only eat salmon.','no',
        'Sun Apr 19 10:55:53 2009','friend');
INSERT INTO "ideas" VALUES(3,'I like milk too.','yes',
        'Sun Apr 19 10:56:02 2009', 'SneakyCat');
INSERT INTO "ideas" VALUES(4,'I hear a twitter.','no',
        'Sun Apr 19 11:26:08 2009', 'SneakyCat');
INSERT INTO "ideas" VALUES(5,'I think I will eat it.','yes',
        'Sun Apr 19 11:26:20 2009', 'SneakyCat');
COMMIT;
```

Now that we have our database file, let's load it into SQLite by entering the following:

```
$ mkdir db
$ sqlite3 db/sneakycat.db < db/SneakyCat.sql
```

Next, we need to let Catalyst know about the file by calling sneakycat_create.pl as follows (recall that Catalyst::Helper::Model::DBIC::Schema was covered in Chapter 6):

```
$ script/sneakycat_create.pl model SneakyCat DBIC::Schema \
    SneakyCat::Schema create=static dbi:SQLite:db/sneakycat.db
```

The main portion of the application has now been created. We created our TT view and the Controller and Schema classes we will need. While the Catalyst helper routines are very smart and save a lot of time, there are things they can't figure out. In order to have a fully functioning system, we need to make some minor adjustments.

Because in this case we didn't specify relationships in our database definitions, first we have to add a relationship to our User schema. In our application, we store the permissions that we will have in a table called roles. We then have another table called users_to_roles that links users to the roles they have. As you saw in Chapter 5, DBIx::Class has a powerful relationship system, and we take advantage of this to make our roles easy to work with. The DBIx::Class helper that created our schema files did most of the work for us already, creating the has_many relationships that link our users table to our users_to_roles table and our users_to_roles table to our roles table.

The type of relationship we have between users and roles in our database is generally called a *many-to-many relationship*, and while the DBIx::Class helper is smart enough to recognize our has_many relationships on its own, it needs some help with the many_to_many definition. We can add the many_to_many relationship by opening up our SneakyCat::Schema::Users schema class file and looking for the has_many definition, which will look something like this:

```
__PACKAGE__->has_many('users_to_roles',
'SneakyCat::Schema::Result::UsersToRoles', { 'foreign.user' => 'self.id'});
```

Below it, after the DO NOT MODIFY line, we need to add a similar line defining our many_to_ many relationship:

```
__PACKAGE__->many_to_many( roles => 'users_to_roles', 'role');
```

This creates a relationship we can access via the roles accessor on our user objects, which will allow us to retrieve all the roles a given user has. This will be important later.

We are almost ready to start writing code, but before we do, we need to do some configuration. The first step is getting all the important modules loaded. Some of the modules we covered earlier are plugins, so we need to edit lib/SneakyCat.pm and add them to the use Catalyst section:

```
use Catalyst qw/
                -Debug
                ConfigLoader
                Static::Simple

                ## We must add the following lines:
                Authentication
                Authorization::Roles
                Session
                Session::State::Cookie
                Session::Store::FastMmap
                /;
```

This enables authentication, authorization, and sessions, all of which are needed for normal authentication. You may have noticed that the Catalyst::Authentication::Store::DBIx::Class module from our earlier list is missing. This is not a mistake. Only Catalyst plugins need to be placed in the use Catalyst section. The Authentication store modules are not plugins and are loaded automatically by the Authentication module once it is initialized. The next step for us is to create our Authentication configuration. As mentioned in Chapter 3, configuration data that doesn't change per deployment should be placed in the lib/SneakyCat.pm file, and since we already have it open, we should add our Authentication configuration.

```
__PACKAGE__->config( name => 'SneakyCat',
                'View::TT' => {
                    INCLUDE_PATH => [
                        __PACKAGE__->path_to('root', 'src'),
                        __PACKAGE__->path_to('root', 'lib')
                    ],
                    TEMPLATE_EXTENSION => '.tt',
                    CATALYST_VAR       => 'c',
                    TIMER             => 0,
                    WRAPPER           => 'site/wrapper'
                },
```

```
                        'Plugin::Authentication' => {
                            default => {
                                credential => {
                                    class => 'Password',
                                    password_type => 'crypted'
                                },
                                store => {
                                    class => 'DBIx::Class',
                                    user_model => 'SneakyCat::Users',
                                    role_relation => 'roles',
                                    role_field => 'role',
                                    use_userdata_from_session => '1'
                                }
                            }
                        } );
```

That's quite a bit of configuration. Let's go over it to understand what it's doing. First, we are setting up our view. This isn't part of the Authentication configuration, but we need it nonetheless to create a functioning application using the TT view. Here we are telling the TT view it should look in the root/src and root/lib directories for template files, the template extension is .tt, and the context variable $c should be called c in the templates as well. We also tell it that every template it uses should be wrapped by the content provided in site/wrapper. This allows us to create a standard look and feel that is included into every page without us having to explicitly include it in each of our templates. Our site/wrapper includes the HTML setup, the navigational items, and the footer. Often the wrapper will include other files that cover different parts of the page, such as navigation and the footer. In our case, though, we have a very simple site, so we keep it all in one file.

Let's move on to the authentication portion of the configuration. The Plugin::Authentication line indicates that the entire hash that follows is configuration for the Authentication plugin. The Plugin::Authentication hash should contain one or more realm definitions. As we mentioned earlier, a realm is the workhorse of the Catalyst authentication system, and the default realm class does its job by deferring to a credential and a store. Not surprisingly, both credentials and stores require their own configuration.

The first key in the credential and store hashes is class. This tells the main authentication module which credential and store classes to use. Remember that we mentioned the Authentication module loads the Store class automatically? This is where it happens. The string you see here is automatically prefixed with Catalyst::Authentication::Credential:: or Catalyst::Authentication::Store:: respectively. After that, the corresponding Perl module is loaded and initialized with the contents of the appropriate configuration hash.

The Password Credential

The credential we are using is the one that comes with the core Catalyst::Plugin::Authentication module, Catalyst::Authentication::Credential::Password. The Password credential's job is to compare the password the user provided to the password stored in the database.

You might wonder why we need a password credential at all, if the password data is stored in the database. Can't we just pull it out and compare the two? Unfortunately, we can't. The proper way to store passwords securely is to encrypt or hash them prior to insertion into the database. This means that while the password being provided is almost certainly plain text, the password coming from the database is an encrypted string. If there is no module to handle this, no one would ever be able to log in. This is what the Password credential does: it hashes the password provided by the user and then compares it to the data it received from the user store.

In order to do this, however, the Password credential needs to be told what format the passwords are stored in. The Password credential understands a number of hashing formats— everything that can be created using the Digest module, in fact. If you want to use one of the other hashing algorithms, you can tell the Password credential to do so by using setting password_type to 'hashed' and setting password_hash_type to the hash type you want to use. However, to keep things easy to understand, we will use the simplest secure option available to us, the standard crypt algorithm. We do this by setting the password_type configuration option to 'crypted', like so:

```
credential => {
    class => 'Password',
    password_type => 'crypted'
}
```

Once we have done this, the Password credential has everything it needs to do its job. We can now proceed to the larger of the configuration options, the store.

The DBIx::Class Store

The Catalyst::Authentication::Store::DBIx::Class is a much more complex module than our simple Password credential. Database structures are one of the most variable components of web applications, and of all the tables in a database, the one most likely to vary from application to application is the users table and, by proxy, the permissions-related tables. The DBIx::Class store must be able to cope with all that variation. Thankfully, it's also very capable and allows you the full flexibility of DBIx::Class to find your users. Again, however, the cost of this flexibility is a fair amount of configuration. Let's examine the Store portion of the Authentication configuration:

```
store => {
    class => 'DBIx::Class',
    user_model => 'SneakyCat::Users',
    role_relation => 'roles',
    role_field => 'role',
    use_userdata_from_session => '1',
}
```

We know that class tells the Auth module which storage module it should load, but what about the rest of it? The first line after class is user_model. This tells the DBIx::Class store that user data is accessible through the SneakyCat::Users schema. This string is what you would pass to $c->model(...) to get to your user storage table. That is all the store needs to find your user data, and we could stop here, but we would be missing some key pieces of information.

The role_relation and role_field configuration options are extremely important in that they indicate how to find role-related information. As we discussed before, roles can most easily be thought of as permissions, and without the role options, our access control options would be limited to logged in or not logged in. Thankfully, once again the DBIx::Class store is smart enough to handle most of the complexities of role retrieval for us.

Recall that we created a many_to_many relationship when we were first setting up our application—this is why we needed it. The DBIx::Class authentication store determines what roles a user has by using the relationship defined by the role_relation configuration option. Doing this, it receives a set of role records from the database. Each role record will have a field that contains the name of the role; in our case, the field is role. We tell the DBIx::Class store which field contains the name by setting the role_field configuration option to role.

Now that we have all our database and role configuration in place, there is only one additional option to explain: use_userdata_from_session. This option tells the DBIx::Class store to keep the user data in the session from request to request. Without this option, the data would be re-retrieved from the database on each request. This is something you need to consider in your own applications because there is a trade-off here.

With use_userdata_from_session turned on, the user data can become stale over the course of a user's session because the user data is loaded into the session only when the user authenticates and not on subsequent requests. This means that if any changes are made to the user (e.g., new permissions) the user will have to log out and log back in to load the new data. Note that strictly speaking, it is possible to force a reload of the data by calling $c->persist_user(), but this is useful only if the changes are made in the current session. If they are made, for example, by another user in an admin tool, there is no way to know whether new user data is available. For this reason, it is wise to think carefully before enabling this setting.

The SimpleDB Option

Now that we have shown you what is involved in setting up authentication in a Catalyst application, we can quickly cover the SimpleDB alternative. The SimpleDB realm acts as a configuration filter, and for a simple database authentication it makes the configuration extremely simple. How simple? To create the same configuration that we had previously, with SimpleDB the configuration would look like this:

```
__PACKAGE__->config( name => 'SneakyCat',
                'Plugin::Authentication' => {
                    default => {
                        class => 'SimpleDB',
                        user_model => 'SneakyCat::Users'
                    }
                });
```

That is quite a bit more straightforward, and in the case of a small application with a straightforward specification, it makes sense. After some development, though, especially on a public site, you begin to realize that authentication often requires more than just a single realm or a simple database. When this happens, knowing the standard configuration options will make it much easier to adjust to the complexity your application will require.

A Side Trip into Application Setup

Since we are trying to create a complete application, we need to take a short side trip away from authentication for a moment. Catalyst has already handled the heavy lifting with the work we did earlier. We now have the full application structure, but there is still a bit of setup to do. Since we are building a web application, we need to create the overall web page structure our various forms and pages will fit into.

As we mentioned earlier, we do this by creating a WRAPPER file that will be wrapped around all the other content we provide in our templates. We configured the TT view to look for this wrapper in lib/site/wrapper. Let's edit that now and add the following:

```
<!DOCTYPE HTML PUBLIC "-//W3C//DTD HTML 4.01 Transitional//EN"
    "http://www.w3.org/TR/html4/loose.dtd">
<html>
<head>
    <meta http-equiv="Content-type" content="text/html; charset=utf-8">
    <title>SneakyCat</title>
    <link rel="stylesheet"
          href="/static/css/sneakycat.css" type="text/css"
          media="screen" title="no title" charset="utf-8">
</head>
<body id="SneakyCatBody">
<div id="header">
<h1>SneakyCat</h1>
  <img id='powered' src="/static/images/btn_88x31_built.png"/>
    <div id="navbar">
        <a href="[% c.uri_for('/ideas/share') %]">Home</a>
    </div>
</div>
    <div id="contentarea">
    [% IF message %]
    <div class="messageblock">[% message %]</div>
    [% END %]
    [% content %]
    </div>
</body>
```

This is a pretty standard HTML wrapper. It loads the style sheet, sets the title, and creates the HTML structure that our content will fit into. Predictably, our template content will be included in place of the [% content %] tag in the preceding code. Something to notice in the file is the message block. This gives us an easy way to display informative messages to our users, no matter what page they are viewing. We will use this later.

Of course, we also need to style our HTML. To do this we use Cascading Style Sheets (CSS). We could put the CSS in the wrapper file directly, but it's cleaner and easier to maintain if we put it in an external file. We will place it in a file called sneakycat.css in the root/static/css directory:

```
body {
    margin: 0px;
    padding: 0px;
    font-family: arial;
}
```

```css
#header {
    background-color: #990000;
    color: #ffffff;
    margin: 0px;
    padding: 1px;
    border-bottom: 3px solid red;
    height: 100px;
    width: 99%;
}
#header h1 {
    padding: 5px;
}
#navbar {
    position: absolute;
    background-color: #660000;
    border-top: 1px solid white;
    top: 74px;
    height: 24px;
    width: 99%;
}
#navbar a {
    color: white;
    padding-left: 10px;
    padding-right: 10px;
    text-decoration: none;
    font-weight: bold;
    font-size: 16px;
}
#navbar a:hover {
    background-color: #330000;
}
#powered {
    position: absolute;
    top: 20px;
    left: 600px;
}
#contentarea {
    background-color: #ffffff;
    color: black;
    padding: 5px;
    padding-top: 20px;
}
label {
    padding: 5px;
}
```

```
input {
    margin: 5px;
    border: 1px solid black;
}
.messageblock {
    background-color: #dddddd;
    margin: 20px;
    padding: 10px;
    border: 1px solid #009900;
    width: 500px;
    font-size: 1.2em;
}
.thought {
    margin: 10px;
    margin-bottom: 20px;
    width: 500px;
    font-size: 24px;
}
.secret_yes {
    font-style: italic;
}
.when {
    position: relative;
    color: #999999;
    left: 120px;
    font-size: 10px;
}
```

Explaining CSS is beyond the scope of this book, but suffice it to say that the CSS in our sneakycat.css file makes our sample application look a lot prettier. Note that the placement of this file in the filesystem is important. The default configuration of Catalyst's Static::Simple plugin recognizes that any request that starts with /static/ should be served directly out of the root/static directory, so any files you want to serve directly to the browser should be placed there. In production, you'll usually want your web server serving these files directly, as there is some overhead to Catalyst handling each request for static content. During development, however, the Static::Simple plugin makes your job a lot easier. See Chapter 5 on deployment for more details on serving static content.

Using Authentication

Now that we have our application all set up, we can begin to use the various authentication-related methods in our application. The first thing that we need to handle for any site that requires authentication is the actual authentication process. Most often this involves a login page and a login action. Our login action will go in the People controller we created earlier. Let's start, though, by creating our actual login page. Remember that our wrapper is handling most of our page, so our login template can be quite simple.

```
[% IF ! c.user_exists %]
<form action="[% c.uri_for('/people/login') %]"
  method="post" accept-charset="utf-8">
    <label for="username">Username</label>
    <input type="text" name="username" value="" id="username"/>
    <br/><br/>
    <label for="password">Password</label>
    <input type="password" name="password" value="" id="password"/>
    <p><input type="submit" value="Login &rarr;"></p>
</form>
[% ELSE %]
<p>You are already logged in.</p>
[% END %]
```

We will place this code in a file called root/src/people/login.tt. Again, the path is important. We configured our TT view to expect to find its templates in root/src. When we create a template for an action, our view expects to find it in a directory named after the controller it is in, in this case People. It then uses the action name, in this case login, and appends .tt to it to find the appropriate template. Stringing all of those together we get root/src/people/login.tt.

While the preceding logic works in most cases, it should be noted that the template chosen is based on the original action requested. This means that if your system calls $c->forward(...) or $c->detach(...), or otherwise triggers a different action than the one originally requested, the wrong template may be chosen. For this reason, it is a good idea to always explicitly define what template you want to use rather than relying on the built-in logic. You can do this easily by placing the directory and filename in $c->stash->{'template'}. We will do this in all of our actions going forward.

Now that we have our form, we can proceed to our login action. We will place our login action in lib/SneakyCat/Controller/People.pm:

```
sub login :Local :Args(0) {
    my ( $self, $c ) = @_;
    $c->stash->{'template'} = 'people/login.tt';
    if ( exists($c->req->params->{'username'}) ) {
        if ($c->authenticate( {
                            username => $c->req->params->{'username'},
                            password => $c->req->params->{'password'}
                        }) )
        {
            ## user is signed in
            $c->stash->{'message'} = "You are now logged in.";
            $c->response->redirect(
              $c->uri_for($c->controller('Ideas')->action_for('share') )
            );
            $c->detach();
            return;
        }
```

```
        else {
            $c->stash->{'message'} = "Invalid login.";
        }
    }
}
```

This routine is fairly straightforward. It's a combination form display and submit action, and it decides what to do based on whether a username parameter was provided. If it was, the action calls $c->authenticate() with the username and password as provided from the web browser. If the call succeeds, it will return true, and you can perform actions based on successful authentication. In this case, we set a nice "logged in" message and redirect users to the idea-sharing page. If the call fails, it returns false and we set an "invalid login" message to be displayed on the page, where we display the form again.

While the function of the authenticate call is fairly obvious, there is something about it that is not obvious: every field provided is being passed directly to the database for retrieval. This means that if the username field in your user table is actually called "login," then your authentication call would need to look like this:

```
$c->authenticate( {
                    login => $c->req->params->{'username'},
                    password => $c->req->params->{'password'}
                })
```

The password field is special because, as we mentioned before, it is usually encrypted. If your password field is called something else, say "pass," then you will need to update your configuration as well to tell the Password credential that it needs to look for a different field name. The credential portion of the configuration would need to look like this:

```
credential => {
    class => 'Password',
    password_type => 'crypted',
    password_field => 'pass'
}
```

Again, the authenticate call would also need to be modified to use 'pass' as the key instead of 'password'. This is all fairly straightforward, but it still belies the power that lives under the hood of the Authentication module with the DBIx::Class store. Let's examine a slightly more complex authentication scenario.

Suppose that your users have a status associated with them that is stored in the database. This status indicates whether their account is still active, if it's a trial, or if it has expired or been deleted. If a user's status is 'active' or 'trial', the user should be allowed access to the site. If the status is anything else, the user should not be able to access the site. This could be a complex piece of logic to add to your login process, but using the Catalyst authentication system, it's easy. You just alter the $c->authenticate() call to reflect your new requirements:

```
$c->authenticate( {
                    username => $c->req->params->{'username'},
                    password => $c->req->params->{'password'},
                    status => ['active', 'trial']
                })
```

All you have to do is add your new constraint to the `authenticate` call and you are done. What's actually happening is interesting. Generally speaking, the authentication store module uses all the information available to it to find the user being authenticated. In this case, the DBIx::Class store looks for a user with a status of either `'active'` or `'trial'`. If the user has a status of `'deleted'`, no user will be found matching the information provided. Thus authentication will fail, just as surely as if the user entered a username that did not exist.

With Catalyst::Authentication::Store::DBIx::Class, you can use any simple DBIx::Class argument directly in the `authenticate` call. The problem with the previous status method is that it requires that something sweep the database and change all users' status fields when their accounts are set to expire. You can get rid of this step by forgoing the status field and working with an expiration date field instead. If you put the date of the user's account expiration in the database, you can use that during the `authenticate` call:

```
## $today is set to the current date in the code preceding this
$c->authenticate( {
                    username => $c->req->params->{'username'},
                    password => $c->req->params->{'password'},
                    expiration => { '>=' => $today }
# The above is equivalent       => { '>=' ,  $today }
                  })
```

You can now avoid the scheduled process and still rely on the fact that your user access will be managed based on whether the account is active or expired. The DBIx::Class user store has facilities to handle much more complex authentication requests than the one just shown, though we will not cover them here. If you have requirements more complex than the preceding example, look at the documentation for Catalyst::Authentication::Store::DBIx::Class.

Since authentication in Catalyst is persistent, the user will remain logged in once he is authenticated. Sometimes perpetual login is good; however, you almost always want to give the user the option to log out of the system. Thankfully, that's probably the easiest action possible. To deauthenticate a user, you call the `$c->logout()` method. Once you do that, all authentication elements are removed and the next request will be exactly identical to a request from a user who never logged in. In our SneakyCat application, we created a `logout` action that does exactly that. Again, we place the following in `lib/SneakyCat/Controller/People.pm`:

```perl
sub logout :Local :Args(0) {
    my ( $self, $c ) = @_;
    $c->stash->{'template'} = 'people/logout.tt';
    $c->logout();
    $c->stash->{'message'} = "You have been logged out.";
}
```

Unlike our `login` action, we don't need a form on logout, but we do need something to let users know their logout was successful, so we will create a very simple logout template that we will place in `root/src/people/logout.tt`:

```
<h3>You are logged out</h3>
```

It doesn't get much simpler than that. Our users can now log out of the SneakyCat application.

Working with Authentication After Login

When working with authentication, our job never ends with the login process. In our applications, we commonly want to do a number of things relating to authentication. The first is to simply answer the question "Do we have a logged-in user?"

Once authentication succeeds, you have a new method available to you on your request context object $c: the $c->user() method. Calling this method will return the current user, or undef if there isn't one. You will get very familiar with $c->user as you develop applications, as it is the way you obtain information about the current user.

Unfortunately, there is a drawback to calling $c->user in some cases, and that is that calling $c->user triggers the restoration of the user from the session. Depending on the complexity of your application and user object, this can be an expensive operation. If, for example, the use_userdata_from_session option were off, the call to $c->user would trigger a load of data from the database.

Note Only the first call to $c->user in a request triggers restoration from the session. All subsequent calls to $c->user within the same request use the restored data, and thus do not come with the penalty just described.

While this is necessary if you intend to use some piece of data from the user record, in many cases all you want to do is figure out if there is a user present. For this reason, Catalyst's authentication system provides an alternative if all you want to do is find out if there is a user.

The call to determine if there is a user is simply $c->user_exists(). The $c->user_exists() call will return true if a user has logged in and false otherwise, but it does not trigger the re-creation of the user object from the session. This means that it is much more lightweight and is a much better option when trying to simply answer the question "Do we have a logged-in user?"

This question will need to be answered on the page that displays SneakyCat's ideas, since we will want to show secret ideas only to people SneakyCat knows. Let's create our idea-sharing page. First up is the template, root/src/ideas/share.tt:

```
<h3>SneakyCat is thinking....</h3>
[% FOREACH idea IN ideas %]
<p class="thought secret_[% idea.secret %]">[% idea.text %]<br/>
<span class="when">
 -- added by [% idea.added_by %] on [% idea.added %]
</span>
</p>
[% END %]
```

and now the action, which we will add to lib/SneakyCat/Controller/Ideas.pm:

```
sub share :Local :Args(0) {
    my ( $self, $c ) = @_;
    $c->stash->{'template'} = 'ideas/share.tt';
    my $idea_rs;
```

```
    if ( $c->user_exists() ) {
        ## SneakyCat knows you, and will share his secrets, so we make
        ## our $idea_rs a resultset that loads all of SneakyCat's ideas
        $idea_rs = $c->model('SneakyCat::Ideas')->search(
                        undef,
                        { order_by => 'id DESC'} );
    }
    else {
    ## If SneakyCat doesn't know you, we only want to load ideas
    ## that are not secret, so we set up our  resultset accordingly
        $idea_rs = $c->model('SneakyCat::Ideas')->search(
                        { 'secret' => 'no'},
                        { order_by => 'id DESC' });
        }
    @{$c->stash->{'ideas'}} = $idea_rs->all();
}
```

In this example, we want to know whether there is a user present, but we don't actually use any user-specific data. So rather than using $c->user and potentially incurring the user restoration overhead, we simply verify that we do have a user. This may not seem like a big deal now, but when your application is under production load, you will be thankful you chose the right approach.

Now that we have created our share action, we should make sure anyone coming to the site goes straight there. We do that by editing our Root controller in lib/SneakyCat/ Controller/Root.pm and editing the index action to detach to our newly created share action:

```
sub index :Path :Args(0) {
    my ( $self, $c ) = @_;
    $c->detach('/ideas/share');
}
```

That's it. Now anyone visiting the root of our web application will see SneakyCat's ideas.

Another common activity is checking user status within your template, in order to show or not show a portion of navigation, for example. You can use the $c->user_exists() call from within Template Toolkit just as easily.

Since we have already created our login and logout processes, we should add them to our navigation. We don't, however, want to show both options at the same time. Instead, we want to display the correct option for whatever state the user is in. Let's edit the navigation in our root/lib/site/wrapper file to add our login and logout options, using the $c->user_exists() call to determine which to show:

```
<div id="navbar">
    <a href="[% c.uri_for('/ideas/share') %]">Home</a>
    [% IF c.user_exists() %]
        <a href="[% c.uri_for('/people/logout') %]">Logout</a>
    [% ELSE %]
        <a href="[% c.uri_for('/people/login') %]">Login</a>
    [% END %]
</div>
```

Trying Out the Application

We've come a long way—we've created the majority of the SneakyCat application. Let's take our application for a spin. Let's start the development server and see what we can see. At a command prompt, issue the following commands:

```
$ cd SneakyCat
$ script/sneakycat_server.pl -r -d
```

You will see the SneakyCat application server start up and display the normal dev server debugging information. Toward the end, you will see a box that looks similar to the following:

```
[debug] Loaded Path actions:
.--------------------------------+-------------------------------------.
| Path                           | Private                             |
+--------------------------------+-------------------------------------+
| /                              | /default                            |
| /                              | /index                              |
| /ideas                         | /ideas/index                        |
| /ideas/share                   | /ideas/share                        |
| /people                        | /people/index                       |
| /people/login                  | /people/login                       |
| /people/logout                 | /people/logout                      |
'--------------------------------+-------------------------------------'

You can connect to your server at http://mylocalserver:3000
```

Note that this displays all the actions we defined and tells us how to connect to the dev server. If we cut and paste this URL into our browser, we will see something like Figure 8-1.

Figure 8-1. *Front page for the SneakyCat application*

You are, for the first time, seeing what SneakyCat looks like. There is not a lot to see here, mainly because SneakyCat does not know who you are. Let's change that—click the Login link in the navigation bar and sign in. You will be SneakyCat's neighbor, so log in with the username **neighbor** and the password **bar123**. Upon login, you will be directed back to the screen you saw before, only now it looks a bit different, as shown in Figure 8-2.

Notice now that you can see the more secret thoughts of SneakyCat. Notice also that the Login link in the navigation bar has disappeared, replaced by a Logout link. If you click Logout, you will see a page telling you your logout was successful. If you go back to the ideas page by clicking Home in the navigation bar, you will go back to seeing only SneakyCat's public thoughts.

Congratulations, you now have a complete functioning web application with basic authentication! In the next section, we will explore another important aspect of authentication in web applications: authorization.

Figure 8-2. *Front page for the SneakyCat application for a logged in user*

Adding Finer-Grained Access Control to SneakyCat with Authorization

Often when you are developing an application, simply knowing whether or not the user is logged in is not enough. It is very common in modern applications to have multiple levels of access for different types of users. These access permissions can be used to control actions and generally manage the things a user can do.

If you have worked with web applications for any period of time, you have probably seen numerous ways of controlling access to portions of an application. Most often, you'll see an account type such as "admin" used. Catalyst's authorization system supports this, but we find it better to use the roles system as a permissions system. Using roles this way makes it easy to coherently manage who can perform each discrete action.

As an example, in our SneakyCat application, we want certain users to be able to tell SneakyCat something to think about. We will do this by adding a whisper action in the Ideas controller. First, let's create the HTML form we will need in root/src/ideas/whisper.tt:

```
<form action="whisper" method="post" accept-charset="utf-8">
    <label for="secret">Tell SneakyCat</label>
    <select name="secret" id="type" size="1">
        <option value="no">an idea</option>
        <option value="yes">a secret</option>
    </select>
    <br/>
    <input type="text" name="whisper" value="" id="whisper"/>
    <br/>
    <p><input type="submit" value="Continue &rarr;"></p>
</form>
```

Remember, though, that we don't want everyone to have the ability to tell SneakyCat what to think about. So we will create a role called can_whisper and require that role in our whisper action. Let's add our whisper action to the lib/SneakyCat/Controller/Ideas.pm file now:

```
sub whisper :Local :Args(0) {
    my ( $self, $c ) = @_;
    if ($c->user_exists() && $c->check_user_roles( qw/ can_whisper /) ) {
        ## do whispery things
        my $current_time = scalar localtime();
        if (exists($c->req->params->{'whisper'}) &&
          length($c->req->params->{'whisper'}) > 1) {
            $c->model('Ideas')->create( {
                                text => $c->req->params->{'whisper'},
                                secret => $c->req->params->{'secret'},
                                added_by =>
                                        $c->user->get('username'),
                                added => $current_time
                            } );
            ## Now we update the user
            ## First we get the underlying DBIx::Class object
            ## then we set the value and save it
            my $user = $c->user->get_object();
            $user->last_whisper($current_time);
            $user->update();
            $c->stash->{'message'} = "SneakyCat heard you.";
            $c->detach('share');
        }
    }
    else {
        $c->detach("access_denied")
    }
}
```

In the preceding example, we do two checks. First, we verify that there is a user available using $c->user_exists(), and then we verify that the user has the role can_whisper by calling $c->check_user_roles(qw/ can_whisper/). The $c->check_user_roles() call will return false if the user does not have all of the roles specified. In this case, we are checking only a single role, can_whisper.

■**Note** Both the $c->check_user_roles() method and the $c->check_any_user_role() method are simply true/false checks on those conditions. Two other calls are used to check roles: $c->assert_user_roles() and $c->assert_any_user_role(). If you are an exception-minded programmer, these two calls are probably right up your alley. They perform the same test as their check_ counterparts, but they indicate failure by throwing an exception rather than returning false. If you are used to working with exceptions, this can make your code much cleaner by avoiding all the if/else checks. However, if you don't know how exceptions are handled in Catalyst, it can be confusing to get it right. They are mentioned here only for completeness.

In some cases, we might want to let the action proceed if the user is a member of any one of a set of roles. For example, you might have a superuser permission that overrides all others and provides full access to do everything available in the application. In that case, you would want to use $c->check_any_user_role(). $c->check_any_user_role() works like $c->check_user_roles(), except that rather than requiring all the specified roles, $c->check_any_user_role() will return true if the user is a member of any of the specified roles, for example:

```
if ($c->user_exists() &&
    $c->check_any_user_role( qw/ can_whisper is_superuser /) ) {
    #  do whispery things
    #  ...
}
```

This code will allow a user with either the can_whisper or the is_superuser permission to perform the whisper action.

There are a few things to note in the whisper action. First, though we define a template for the whisper action, that template is only used to display the form. If the user is allowed to tell SneakyCat something, after the data is stored in the database, we call $c->detach('share'), which transfers control to the share action. Since the share action defines its own template, it essentially takes over the display.

Next, notice that we used $c->stash->{'message'} to define a message to be displayed to the user. Even though we transfer control to the share action, our message is still displayed for the end user on the share page. This is because the contents of $c->stash remain intact when we call $c->forward() or $c->detach() to transfer control to another action.

Finally, if we determine that the user either doesn't exist or doesn't have the required permissions, we send the user to the access_denied action. Let's create that now. First, we create the template in root/src/ideas/accessdenied.tt:

```
<h3>Access Denied</h3>
```

Again, it doesn't get much simpler than that. Now we add the access_denied action to lib/SneakyCat/Controller/Ideas.pm:

```
sub access_denied :Local :Args(0) {
    my ( $self, $c ) = @_;
    $c->stash->{'template'} = 'ideas/accessdenied.tt';
    ## tell the user SneakyCat is ignoring them
    $c->stash(
      message => "SneakyCat has ideas of his own and is ignoring you."
    );
```

You might be wondering why we go through all this trouble simply to show an access denied message. The reason is simple: in a real-world web application, you almost always want to do something additional when a user tries to do something he is not allowed to do. If you are writing a back-office application, for example, you probably want to log that someone tried to do something he wasn't supposed to. If you are writing a public, user-facing application, you might want to attempt an upsell to give the user access to the feature he was trying to use. In other situations, you probably want to send a note to the debug log indicating that the user got to a section of the site he shouldn't have been able to see.

Getting back to our roles discussion, like the $c->user_exists() call, the $c->check_user_roles() call can be and often is made from within a template. Again, the most common occurrence is when building navigation to indicate the actions the user is allowed to take. Let's modify our navigation in root/lib/site/wrapper to take into account our permissions check:

```
<div id="navbar">
    <a href="[% c.uri_for('/ideas/share') %]">Home</a>
    [% IF c.user_exists() %]
        [% IF c.check_user_roles( 'can_whisper' ) %]
            <a href="[% c.uri_for('/ideas/whisper') %]">Tell</a>
        [% END %]
        <a href="[% c.uri_for('/people/logout') %]">Logout</a>
    [% ELSE %]
        <a href="[% c.uri_for('/people/login') %]">Login</a>
    [% END %]
</div>
```

Now, in addition to showing Login or Logout as appropriate in the navigation, if the user has the role can_whisper, she will see a link to the Tell page, which contains the form for telling SneakyCat something.

Let's try it. Make sure your Catalyst dev server is running, and then access your main SneakyCat page. You will see the share page for an unauthorized user. Click Login and log in with the username **neighbor** and the password **bar123**. You will again see the SneakyCat share page, as shown in Figure 8-3.

Figure 8-3. *The* ideas/share *page for SneakyCat's neighbor with finer-grained access control*

What's going on here? We just added the Tell link to the navigation menu, so why can't we see it? The answer is simple: SneakyCat doesn't listen to his neighbor, so the neighbor account doesn't get to see the Tell link. Let's log out and log back in as a user that SneakyCat listens to. Click Logout and then click Login. This time, use the username **friend** and the password **foo123**. Now you see the Tell link in the navigation menu, as shown in Figure 8-4.

Go ahead and click Tell and give SneakyCat something to think about. You can choose whether you are telling SneakyCat a secret or something he can share with everyone. Enter your thought and click the Continue button. You will now see that SneakyCat is sharing the thought you told him.

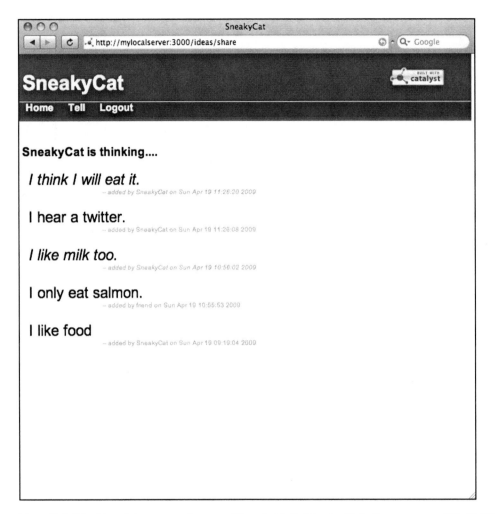

Figure 8-4. *The* ideas/share *page for one of SneakyCat's friends. Note the presence of the Tell link for a friend.*

Working with the Authenticated User

Up until now we have shown how to authenticate the user and how to verify the user is authorized to perform certain actions. This is a substantial part of working with authentication in a web application, but we still haven't covered a very important part of this process. In all but the simplest cases, after you have authenticated the user, you will want to work with the authenticated user's data.

In Catalyst, once authentication has completed successfully, you will have a user object available to you as $c->user(), which represents the authenticated user. The information available through $c->user varies depending on the source of the user information. In our case, using the DBIx::Class user store, all the information available in the users table will be available. You can see this type of access in our SneakyCat application when we are storing a new piece of data and we want to retain who added it:

```
## in the Ideas controller
sub whisper :Local :Args(0) {
    ## ...
    $c->model('Ideas')->create( {
                        text => $c->req->params->{'whisper'},
                        secret => $c->req->params->{'secret'},
                        added_by => $c->user->get('username'),
                        added => $current_time
                    } );
    ## ...
}
```

It is important to be aware that $c->user is the Catalyst authentication system's concept of a user. It is built to function within the authentication system and to allow basic retrieval of the user's data. You can access this user data by calling $c->user->get('fieldname'), which will retrieve fieldname from the user object and return its value. If all you need is to read the fields, this is the best way to work with authenticated user data. The reason for this is that $c->user->get() is guaranteed to work regardless of where the user data came from. This is important, because if you later change the store you use for your user data (e.g., from a SQL database to an LDAP server), your code will continue to work unmodified.

If, however, you need to do more than read the user's fields, you will need to get hold of the underlying user object originally retrieved from the user storage system. Thankfully, Catalyst's authentication system makes it easy to do that. If you call $c->user->get_object(), the underlying object will be returned to you.

The underlying object is needed whenever you are performing more advanced actions on the user data. It is required when you need access to user-related data that is not in the primary user table, for example. The underlying object is also needed when you need to update the user's data because each storage module will have a different method for updating data. In our SneakyCat application, we want to record the last time a user posted an idea, so we use the $c->user->get_object() method to get a DBIx::Class object for the user. You can see this in the whisper action in lib/SneakyCat/Controller/Ideas.pm:

```
# in the Ideas Controller
sub whisper :Local :Args(0) {
    my ( $self, $c ) = @_;
    # ...
    ## Now we update the user - first we get the underlying DBIx::Class object
    ## then we set the value and save it
    my $user = $c->user->get_object();
    $user->last_whisper($current_time);
    $user->update();
    # ...
}
```

As we mentioned before, it's a good idea to use `$c->user->get()` where possible, as it is guaranteed to remain compatible with future changes you may make to your application. After you've worked with authenticated users for a while, however, you will likely find yourself accessing the underlying object fairly often. Thankfully, there is a slightly shorter version of the get_object method: `$c->user->obj`. Because it is so much shorter, you are likely to see the extra variable creation avoided in favor of calling it directly. Using the `$c->user->obj` method, the preceding example looks like this:

```
sub whisper :Local :Args(0) {
    my ( $self, $c ) = @_;


    # ...
    $c->user->obj->last_whisper($current_time);
    $c->user->obj->update();
    # ...
}
```

This example is a bit more succinct than the previous option, but just a bit. Ultimately, the two samples provide identical functionality, so it's really a matter of personal preference.

Summary

By now, you should have a very solid grasp of Catalyst's authentication system. In this chapter, we covered the three aspects of access control in web applications: authentication, persistence, and authorization, and how Catalyst's authentication system handles each one.

We've shown that Catalyst's authentication system is capable of dealing with almost any authentication requirement. The SneakyCat application we developed demonstrates how authentication is most likely to be handled in a web application and how you are most likely to use it in your own applications. If you have not done so already, we encourage you to explore the SneakyCat application to see how all the pieces fit together in a running application. It is worth noting that the Cookbook also contains some examples of other authentication-related functionality you are likely to be interested in.

In the next chapter we cover using Catalyst to consume and produce web services. We show how to use an existing CPAN module to consume a web service, create our own REST service, and as a side effect of this, we show how to interrogate a REST web service if no existing CPAN module is available for it. Finally, we describe the options available if you want to use XML-based web services with Catalyst.

Interacting with Web Services in Your Applications

This chapter describes the use of web services within Catalyst, both for the consumption of external web services and for the provision of web services to other clients. The W3C, the Web's standards consortium, describes web services as "a software system designed to support interoperable machine-to-machine interaction over a network."

Essentially, web services come in two flavors: RESTful web services and XML-based web services. In Representational State Transfer (REST), logic underlying how the server processes the received data is governed by the HTTP request type (i.e., GET, POST, PUT, or DELETE), and the data returned to the client can be in a variety of formats. With XML-based services, this logic is contained in an XML payload contained within a POST request. Data is also returned as XML. XML web services come in two varieties, XMLRPC (XML remote procedure call) and its more complex sibling, SOAP (Simple object access protocol).

In this chapter, we'll cover how to consume a (REST-based) web service using an existing CPAN module that already exposes the web service API to Perl. Then we'll move on to produce our own REST base web service. As part of building the tests for this service, we'll also illustrate how to write code that makes REST requests to a server. Finally, we'll look at the other alternatives for producing and consuming other web services, in particular the recommended modules for consuming some XML-based web services (however, as this is a big topic that requires substantial knowledge of XML, we won't cover it in detail).

Consuming a Simple REST Service

The main purported advantage of SOAP is that in conjunction with Web Services Definition Language (WSDL), it is supposedly self-documenting (but only if you know XML well and understand what it all means). REST, on the other hand, is a simple ideology to retrieve and modify web services. This ideology is as follows:

GET request: Retrieve a resource.

POST request: Modify a resource.

PUT request: Create a resource.

DELETE request: Remove a resource.

Generally, an API that takes this approach is called a RESTful web service (and an over-zealous advocate of REST web services is called a RESTafarian). So to consume a web service in the raw, it's just a matter of using LWP::UserAgent with HTTP::Request::Common, as in Chapter 2 (we'll also cover this when testing our own REST service). If you have to consume a REST web service that doesn't have API bindings published on CPAN, this is the correct approach to take, along with an appropriate deserialization module.

Setting Up OpenCalais in a Catalyst Application

We're going to use Thomson Reuters' OpenCalais web service (http://www.opencalais.com/) as an example. OpenCalais provides an API service to some code that attempts to find named entities within text. *Named entities* are things like people, places, and organizations. We're using OpenCalais because it's a nice, simple web service with only a couple of functions. We are going to write our own module, which is mainly a Moose wrapper around Net::Calais. Taking this approach makes it easy to provide your own extensions to the web service.

This approach provides a scaffolding module for you to add your own output-processing functions very easily. The web service's interface is nice and simple, so it's perfect for illustrative purposes. Net::Calais will return data in XML or JavaScript Object Notation (JSON) format, but we're going to use only the JSON part of the web service, because as a rule JSON is much easier to work with than XML.

■**Note** JSON deserializes (almost) deterministically to Perl data structures. There have been minor differences in output between different JSON implementations on CPAN, but to the best of our knowledge at the time of this writing, some JSON implementations on CPAN are deprecated and others are now consistent with each other. JSON is, in fact, a variety of YAML without the whitespace sensitivity. It would be the perfect configuration format, except that it has the critical limitation that the JSON specification has no facility for comments. We came across YAML in Chapter 7 when demonstrating Catalyst's dispatcher.

Net::Calais has an API against the REST service provided by the CPAN module Net::Calais. Note that web service APIs are generally contained in the top-level namespaces Net::, Webservice::, and WWW:: on CPAN. A few web services modules (especially those owned by the big guys, such as eBay and Amazon) are generally contained in the top-level namespace of the company, such as Amazon::S3 or Ebay::API.

Net::Calais itself uses the modules HTTP::Request::Common, LWP::UserAgent, and XML::Writer to hook into the web service. The XML::Writer support is required to construct the input parameters to the web service. Its source code is generally pretty good, so we recommend this as a simple bit of source code to read in order to work out how to provide bindings to REST-based web services.

For the current example, if you want to follow along from here, you should obtain an API key from http://www.opencalais.com/user/register. Next, create a new Catalyst application with catalyst.pl MyCalais. Then you can modify the Root controller to have a single action. Here's the controller in its entirety:

```perl
package MyCalais::Controller::Root;


use strict;
use warnings;
use parent 'Catalyst::Controller';
use YAML;


__PACKAGE__->config->{namespace} = '';


sub default :Path {
    my ( $self, $c ) = @_;
    my $url = $c->req->query_parameters->{url};
    eval {
        $c->stash(response => $c->model('Calais')->url_as_data( $url) );
    };
    if ($@) {
        $c->stash(response => {
        error => qq(The OpenCalais service is experiencing
        problems.  Please retry after a few seconds), error_text => "$@" });
    }
}

sub end : ActionClass('RenderView') {
    my ($self, $c) = @_;
    $c->res->body('<pre>' . Dump ($c->stash->{response}) .  '</pre>');
}


1;
```

Note the error-trapping code in the eval and if ($@) blocks. While writing this code, we discovered that the semanticproxy service (a part of the OpenCalais infrastructure) was being a little unreliable, so if an error occurred, we could trap it from the value returned from the call to the Catalyst model.

Next, we can glue our actual model into MyCalais::Model::Calais with Catalyst::Model:: Adaptor, as used in Chapter 4. (Replace your_api_key with the API key you obtain on registration, as Catalyst will throw an exception about a missing default view if you forget this step.)

```perl
package MyCalais::Model::Calais;
use strict;
use warnings;
use parent 'Catalyst::Model::Adaptor';
```

```
__PACKAGE__->config(
    class => 'MyCalais::Processor',
    args => { apikey =>  'your_api_key'},
);

sub mangle_arguments {
    my ($self, $args) = @_;
    return %$args;
}


1;
```

In fact, as the API key will change on a per-deployment basis, we should probably remove the args { ... line from the code and add the following to mycalais.conf in the application root instead:

```
<Model Calais> <args> apikey your_api_key </args> </Model>
```

This keeps the information that will vary per deployment in an easily user-editable place, whereas the name of the class providing the interface to the API won't change.

Now we have to write a MyCalais::Processor class that will do the actual work of querying the API. The reason we're not using Net::Calais directly is that we want more flexibility than that module provides. Net::Calais won't return a native data structure, which is what we want. It's better to encapsulate the code in our model rather than do JSON-to-Perl data serialization in our controller (remember the thin controller pattern!). We put MyCalais::Processor in the lib/MyCalais directory below the application root:

```
package MyCalais::Processor;
use Moose;
use JSON::Any;
use Net::Calais;

has 'apikey'    => (is => 'ro', isa => 'Str',            required => 1  );
has 'json_data' => (is => 'rw', isa => 'Str'                            );
has 'api'       => (is => 'ro', isa => 'Net::Calais', lazy_build =>1 );

# provides the Net::Calais API object, and builds it only the first time it's
# called.
sub _build_api {
    my ($self) = @_;
    return Net::Calais->new(apikey => $self->apikey);
}


# provides the data returned from the semanticproxy web service in the
# requested format, defaulting to JSON.  Note we set the accessor
# $self->json_data as we get Moose's error trapping for free if we do it this
# way.
```

```perl
sub url_serialised {
    my ($self, $url, $format) = @_;
    $format ||= 'json';
    $self->json_data( $self->api->semanticproxy($url, output => $format) );
}


# provides the data from url_serialised in a perl data structure
sub url_as_data {
    my ($self, $url) = @_;
    my $format = 'json';
    my $j = JSON::Any->new;
    $self->url_serialised($url);
    return $j->jsonToObj( $self->json_data );
}


# send it some text and a content-type and return the requested format.
sub text_serialised {
    my ($self, $txt, $args) = @_;
    $args->{format} ||='application/json';
    $args->{content_type} ||= 'text/txt';
    return $self->api->enlighten($txt, %$args);
}


# as text_serialised but as a perl data structure
sub text_as_data {
    my ($self, $txt, $args) = @_;
    $args->{content_type} ||= 'text/txt';
    delete $args->{format} if $args->{format};
    my $json = $self->text_serialised($txt, %$args);
    my $j = JSON::Any->new;
    return $j->jsonToObj($json);
}


1;
```

Now we can fire up the text server and make a request for http://localhost:3000/?url=
http://dev.catalystframework.org/snow_white. If the web service is working properly, we
should receive a JSON data structure back with the content of the file and a representation
of all the named entities that could be found in the file. The data structure output from the
OpenCalais web service is quite complicated, and a successful response will start with the
string {"doc":{"info":{"document":". If that doesn't happen, make sure you used a correct
API key and be persistent in case the web service is having problems. In fact, the data structure
returned by OpenCalais isn't too useful by itself, and it's likely that you'll want to start adding
a variety of methods to the MyCalais::Processor class (or more likely, refactor the preceding
code to be more closely aligned to your goals).

Next we'll extend this web service to create our own web service. We'll write a method to
obtain some useful data from the structure returned by the web service and integrate that into
our own REST service.

Creating Web Services with REST

REST has four simple rules that govern how the GET, PUT, POST, and DELETE methods from HTTP are dealt with. Data is sent and received in a serialized data format (i.e., a textual representation of data structures). Authentication for API keys is sent in the HTTP header using standard HTTP authentication and authorization headers. Fortunately, the excellent Catalyst::Controller::REST exists to make providing REST services very simple.

Implementing the REST Controller

We'll make a REST layer by continuing with the code in the previous section. First, we need to add a persistent storage layer into our application. Under normal circumstances, you'll probably want this to be some kind of database, likely using DBIx::Class as described in Chapter 6. Because we're writing this code for illustrative purposes, we're going to keep the data in memory just for the duration of the server process. This means we'll add the following line to the MyCalais::Processor class:

```
has 'storage'=> (is => 'rw', isa => 'HashRef', default => sub { {} });
```

Note that to create an empty hashref for the starting value of storage, we wrap it in a subroutine reference to keep Moose happy. If we were going to do this properly, we would add our DBIC schema instead. Assuming our database schema is called MyCalais::Schema, the line would look something like this:

```
has 'schema'    => (is => 'ro', isa => 'MyCalais::Schema', lazy_build => 1);
```

We would also have to provide a _build_schema method to actually create and return the DBIC schema object the first time we accessed it in code.

First up with any REST service that we want to implement, we should sketch out the dispatch rules we want for our REST controller. We'll do that now:

./ (shorthand for local controller index action): Lists all available URLs that we've already processed with the semanticproxy method.

./ (PUT request with URL as a parameter): Adds a new URL's information into the database. The data is delivered to the server by passing a JSON string representing a hash reference with a single key of URL, with the address to be translated. This goes in the Content header. We'll show how this is implemented in the test script we write for the controller later on in this section.

./$encoded_url (DELETE request with URL as a parameter): Deletes a URL's information from the database. There's no request body—all of the information required to delete the resource is contained within the request string. However, because the primary key to access is a URI and this will always contain a forward slash (as in http://), the argument to this request should be URI escaped. Therefore, a DELETE request to remove the http://example.com key from our database should be requested as http%3A%2F%2Fexample. com. Note that you'd usually hide this part (or all) of the API behind an authentication wall. The simplest way to implement this is with the Catalyst::Authentication::Credential:: HTTP credential.

./$encoded_url GET request: Returns all available data for a particular URL or returns "404 Page not found" if the URL is not in the database. Again, you have to URI-escape the request as for the DELETE request.

Now that we've defined our dispatch logic, the next thing we do is install Catalyst:: Controller::REST from CPAN. This controller makes a new attribute ActionClass('REST') available that provides rules for serialization of data. We'll illustrate how it works with the code that follows. Note that during development, if you forget to put ActionClass('REST') in your base action, yet you make a REST-style request, you will get serialization errors and the method with the request type appended will not be called. That is, if you start to get nonobvious error messages, check that you've added the ActionClass('REST') attribute.

First we'll install Catalyst::Controller::REST from CPAN (don't worry about the optional dependencies), and then we'll make a new controller for our application with the command script/mycalais_create.pl controller REST. After that, we can modify our own REST controller to provide normal Catalyst actions.

```
package MyCalais::Controller::REST;

use strict;
use warnings;
use base 'Catalyst::Controller::REST';

sub index : Path Args(0) ActionClass('REST') {
    my ($self, $c) = @_;
}

sub record :Path Args(1) ActionClass('REST') {
    my ($self, $c) = @_;
}

1;
```

So far it's just like a normal Catalyst controller, except for the extra attribute and the fact that none of the actions actually do anything. This is where the magic of Catalyst::Controller:: REST comes in. The ActionClass('REST') attribute means that you can "magically" add subroutines of the following form into your controller, and the controller will dispatch to each action depending on whether the request is for GET, POST, PUT, DELETE, or HEAD. So for our PUT request (adding another URL to the database), we'll add the following code:

```
sub index_PUT {
    my ($self, $c) = @_;
    my $url = $c->req->data->{url};
    my $model = $c->model('Calais');
    my $data;
    eval { $data = $model->url_as_data($url) };
    if (! $@ ) {
```

```perl
            $model->storage->{$url} = $data;
            $self->status_created($c,
                            location => $c->req->uri->as_string,
                            entity => { $url => $data } );
    }
    else { # there was an error with the web service
            $c->res->status(502);
            $c->stash( rest => {
                error =>
                'Error with the upstream web service, please retry shortly'
            } );
    }
}
```

Next, we can start sketching out what we expect the code to do by creating some tests. Create or modify the test file in t/controller_rest.t to be as follows. Note that as HTTP::Request::Common does not export the DELETE method by default, you need to export all the methods that you're going to use in HTTP::Request::Common explicitly.

```perl
use strict;
use warnings;
use Test::More qw/no_plan/;

BEGIN { use_ok 'Catalyst::Test', 'MyCalais' }
BEGIN { use_ok 'MyCalais::Controller::REST' }

use HTTP::Request::Common qw/GET POST PUT DELETE/;
use JSON::Any;
my $j = JSON::Any->new;

my $resp;
my $req_data;

diag 'Add a resource';
$req_data = { url => 'http://dev.catalystframework.org/snow_white'};
$resp = request( PUT '/rest', 'Content-Type' => 'application/json',
                Content => $j->objToJson($req_data) );
diag $resp->status_line;
diag $resp->content;

$req_data = { url => 'http://dev.catalystframework.org'};

$resp = request( PUT '/rest', 'Content-Type' => 'application/json',
                    Content => $j->objToJson($req_data) );
diag $resp->status_line;
diag $resp->content;
```

Aside from making sure that our code compiles, we haven't bothered to put any other tests in. We just set up our REST request and print out the response with the call to diag. Recall from previous chapters how to run our test—we run prove against our test file:

```
CATALYST_DEBUG=0 prove -l t/controller_rest.t
```

If we're lucky and the web service is up, we'll see a 200 status and a lot of JSON data about the named entities from the Snow White story. If we're unlucky, we'll see a 502 error code and the error message telling us to try again shortly.

So with a controller based on Catalyst::Controller::REST, we don't need to set the stash and the HTTP status code manually (the returned HTTP status code is part of the REST web services specification). We can use the status helpers from the controllers to deal with the common case.

However, what we have next is not a common case. If our external web service fails, we'll want to return a 502 (bad gateway) response code and return some informative error message. While we could write a status_bad_gateway method in our own controller, it's probably easier to just set the response status manually, and set the response in $c->stash->{rest} to an informative error message, as demonstrated in the else block in the index_PUT method.

In this case, a PUT and a POST request will be identical, so we can alias the index_POST subroutine to the index_PUT subroutine by adding the following line to Controller::REST:

```
*index_POST = *index_PUT;
```

What's happening in this code is that we use the helper subroutines provided by Catalyst::Controller::REST to return data and the appropriate response code. We set the serialized data type using the request header, but we can override this all manually by setting $c->stash->{rest} and $c->response->status. Note that our class has no end action because this is taken care of by Catalyst::Controller::REST for us, and we don't have to worry about the end action that we had in the Root controller interfering with this controller.

The second part of our specification is where we retrieve the data for a URL that already exists in the system. This time we'll make a request to our controller with one argument, which will be the URL-encoded address of the resource that we want to run through the Calais service. Here are the controller methods that we want:

```
sub record_GET {
    my ($self, $c, $uri) = @_;
    # see how $uri is automatically unescaped by Catalyst.
    my $model = $c->model('Calais');
    if (exists $model->storage->{$uri}) {
        $self->status_ok( $c,
                            entity => { $uri => $model->storage->{$uri} },
                        );
    }
    else {
        $self->status_not_found($c, {message => "$uri is not in the database"});
    }
}
```

We also need to add to our test code in t/controller_rest.t here:

```
use URI::Escape;
diag 'Retrieve a resource';
my $uri = uri_escape('http://dev.catalystframework.org/snow_white');
my $path = "/rest/$uri";
$resp = request( GET $path , 'Content-Type' => 'application/json');
diag $resp->status_line;
diag $resp->content;
```

The final thing is to make the DELETE request, which is very similar to the GET request.

```
sub record_DELETE {
    my ($self, $c, $uri) = @_;
    my $model = $c->model('Calais');
    if (defined $model->storage->{$uri}) {
        my %rec = %{$model->storage->{$uri}}; # copy resource before deletion
        delete $model->storage->{$uri};
        $self->status_ok( $c,
                        entity => {
                            $uri =>  \%rec },
                    );
    }
    else {
        $self->status_not_found($c,
                            message =>
                            "$uri is not in the database, can't be deleted" );
    }
}
```

We can also add the test code in t/controller_rest.t:

```
diag 'Delete a resource';
$resp = request( DELETE $path, 'Content-Type' => 'application/json');
diag $resp->status_line;
diag $resp->content;
```

Finally, we can run the test code with the command CATALYST_DEBUG=0 prove -l t/controller_rest.t, but because the web service is a little unreliable, we can't guarantee that it's going to work every time, which is why we haven't made formal tests for this code.

Changing the Data Type for Serialization

Catalyst::Controller::REST can serialize to and deserialize from a number of formats. So far, we've used the JSON format by providing the Content-Type => 'application/json' header. We can change this by using a different format—we could use YAML, Config::General, the Perl module Storable's format, or even raw Perl or PHP data structures, by changing the content header. For example, to indicate that our request body is YAML or the response we require is YAML, we change the Content-Type header as follows:

```
Content-Type => 'text/x-yaml'
```

In t/controller_rest.t, we can change the last test as follows:

```
use YAML; # provides Dump
diag 'Add a resource';
$req_data = { url => 'http://dev.catalystframework.org/snow_white'};
$resp = request( PUT '/rest', 'Content-Type' => 'text/x-yaml',
                    Content => Dump ($req_data) );
diag $resp->status_line;
diag $resp->content;
```

We can also change the default content type for responses by providing the configuration key in our REST controller:

```
__PACKAGE__->config->{'default'} => 'application/json';
```

Additionally, we can change the Perl modules to provide serialization and deserialization by setting the config->{serialize} key if required, as well as the stash key used in serialization. For example, the following will set the serialized stash key to $c-stash->{response} and the JSON processor to JSON::Any.

```
__PACKAGE__->config(
    serialize => {
        'stash_key' => 'response',
        map         => {
            'application/json'  => 'JSON::Any',
            }
        };
```

Parts of this (the bits you want to vary on a per-deployment basis) can be altered in the configuration file for your application, for example:

```
<Controller REST >
 <serialize>
  <map>
    application/json => JSON::Any
  </map>
 </serialize>
</Controller>
```

Note it wouldn't make sense to alter the stash_key configuration item in the configuration file under most circumstances. The documentation for Catalyst::Controller::REST is excellent and should be referenced for further details.

Remaining Options for Web Services

We recommend consuming web services with the relevant CPAN module if one exists for your web service. If such a module doesn't exist, we have demonstrated via our MyCalais::Processor class and the tests for the REST controller how to consume your own REST service. Producing code to query existing REST services is a straightforward matter of creating requests according to the API documentation with LWP::UserAgent and HTTP::Request::Common qw/ GET POST PUT DELETE/.

We've gone through what is by far the easiest way to produce and consume web services using Catalyst, but there are three other options: XML-RPC, JSON-RPC, and SOAP. With one exception, they require significant knowledge of XML and are best left to experienced developers with expertise in XML processing.

XML-RPC

XML-RPC (remote procedure calls using XML) is the grandfather of XML-based web services, and it is actually quite simple, though its toolchain is a little fragile. Catalyst provides Catalyst::Plugin::Server::XMLRPC, which does data serialization and deserialization in a similar manner to Catalyst::Controller::REST. However, because the dispatch rules for XML-RPC are different from straight HTTP dispatch rules, the plugin needs to hook into the Catalyst request and response cycle. XML-RPC servers receive POST requests to a particular URL, by default /rpc with the Catalyst plugin. The equivalent of $c->req->path is contained within the XML payload. The server responds with a standard HTTP response with XML in the response body.

In addition, while it has many production users, Catalyst::Server::XMLRPC can be tricky to get working. If you want to use this plugin for your work, read through the tutorial provided in Catalyst::Plugin::Server::XMLRPC::Tutorial. There's a very good chance the plugin will work as advertised, but the XML processing infrastructure used can be fragile, and the configuration varies widely across platforms. If you have problems with installation, contact the usual support channels (i.e., the catalyst-users mailing list or the #catalyst IRC channel).

JSON-RPC

JSON-RPC is pretty similar to XML-RPC, except the request and response payloads are contained in JSON rather than XML. In fact, JSON-RPC is probably slightly easier than XML-RPC, as JSON is easier to parse than XML. This, and the direct correspondence between JSON data and Perl data structures, makes it easier to work with than XML-RPC. JSON-RPC also has better browser support for working with JavaScript in standard Ajax web pages. The Catalyst plugin to use is (not surprisingly) Catalyst::Plugin::Server::JSONRPC.

SOAP

SOAP is an extension of XML-RPC, much used in "enterprise" web applications. It's difficult to use and requires much more knowledge of enterprise architecture solutions than the other methods we've looked at in this chapter. It also requires very detailed knowledge of XML. Your options for consuming SOAP services, in order of preference, are to use existing API bindings available from CPAN if they exist, or to use XML::Compile or Catalyst::Model::SOAP depending on how likely it is you want to reuse your SOAP consumption code outside of Catalyst.

To provide SOAP, you'll want to use Catalyst::Controller::SOAP and provide a WSDL file to make your service self-documenting. Be aware that SOAP is complicated and confusing, so make sure that you budget your time for implementing SOAP consumers and services appropriately and that you are getting paid properly for the job. While creating web services for noncommercial purposes using REST or maybe XML/JSON-RPC may be a sensible thing to do, using SOAP for recreational purposes is probably the haunt of the insane (although some people would say that statement is a little extreme).

Summary

In this chapter, we covered producing and consuming REST web services, explicitly via using a pre-existing CPAN module and implicitly by showing the type of code written in the test script for the REST module. We also briefly examined the other major options for implementing web services in Catalyst.

In the next chapter, we'll look at extending Catalyst. We'll first discuss how to create your own base controllers and views, and then we'll look at the various methods with which you can create your own subroutine attributes.

■ ■ ■

## CHAPTER 10

Extending Catalyst

So you want to extend Catalyst. Well, that's what it's for. Actually, it's for getting out of your way and letting you operate on your problem, while unobtrusively handing you the scalpel, forceps, clamps, suction, and surgical drills. However, as with any skilled surgeon on the cutting edge of your craft (sorry), there may be times that you need to machine your own instruments. In this chapter, we introduce you to the dies and casts to help you get that little extra out of your trade.

Many people think that programmers are more like plumbers than surgeons, in which case you want to know about and be able to use flexible faucet fittings rather than having to solder rigid copper pipe to the sink fixtures, as it will make your job quicker and easier.

Recall that in the Chapter 7, we looked at the request cycle, specifically the flow of control from the engine to the dispatcher, through to the controllers (where flow control goes in and out of Catalyst::Models, and finally output is rendered in a view), and then finally back to the engine, where the data is sent to the client for display. Catalyst's architecture allows you to hook into the request cycle throughout this process.

After creating models (which have been discussed thoroughly already in this book), we'll move on to base controllers, then we'll cover a quick Catalyst::View, and finally we'll take a detailed look at different ways of creating new dispatcher attributes.

Base Controllers

Most of the time for extension work, what you in fact want is a new base controller. For example, if we want a common auto action across a number of controllers, all we have to do is create a BaseController directory in lib/MyApp from the application root, and then create a new Catalyst::Controller there, for example, Startup:

```
package MyApp::BaseController::Startup;
use Moose;
extends 'Catalyst::Controller';
use namespace::clean -except => 'meta';
```

```
sub auto : Private {
    my ($self, $c) = @_;
    $c->stash( some_data =>
      'available in every controller that uses this base controller');
}

1;
```

Then in our main controllers in MyApp, when we want this auto action we replace the line

```
extends 'Catalyst::Controller';
```

with

```
extends 'MyApp::BaseController::Startup';
```

▌**Note** use base 'Catalyst::Controller' and use Moose; extends 'Catalyst::Controller'
are essentially the same. In some circumstances if you use the second version, you'll need to wrap it in a
BEGIN block. See the "Cleaning Up Multiple Attributes with Roles" section of this chapter for details.

We could also add multiple base controllers:

```
extends qw/MyApp::BaseController::Startup
           MyApp::BaseController::AnotherOne/;
```

And that's pretty much it. All the base controller has to do is inherit from Catalyst::
Controller or from another module that does so—it doesn't have to live in our application's
namespace or even the Catalyst namespace.

An example using a base controller for the Chained dispatch type is given in Catalyst::
Manual::ExtendingCatalyst. Catalyst::Controller::REST, as covered in the previous chapter
showcases pretty much the entire set of features that can be used in base controllers. However,
note that much of the work is done elsewhere: in Catalyst::Action::REST, Catalyst::Request::
REST, and Catalyst::Action::Serialize/Deserialize. This is because Catalyst's REST infrastructure makes deep hooks into the controller functionality, as well as some hooks into Catalyst's
processing of requests. Hopefully by the end of this chapter, you'll start to develop an appre-
ciation of how this works. However, first we should touch on a neglected topic: views.

A Simple SerialiseStashKey View

In Chapter 7, we used an absolutely minimal "view" in our application's Root controller, which
receives selected data from the stash and renders it in YAML wrapped in <pre> tags. To recap,
the code for this is as follows:

```
sub end : ActionClass('RenderView') {
    my ($self, $c) = @_;
    $c->res->body('<pre>' . Dump ($c->stash->{matches}) . '</pre>')
        unless $c->res->body;
}
```

Let's demonstrate how to make a new Catalyst::View by taking this idiom and turning it into a configurable view. First, we want this to be a new module, so with the help of Module:: Starter (which can be installed from CPAN), we can issue the following command in a suitable location on our filesystem:

```
$ module-starter --mi --module=Catalyst::View::SerialiseStashKey \
  --author="Me" --email=you@example.com
```

This will create the directory Catalyst-View-SerialiseStashKey, which contains everything needed to start programming. Note that CatalystX::Starter is an alternative to Module::Starter, and which you use is basically a matter of preference, depending on whether you want more or less boilerplate code. Of course, there's nothing wrong with writing out your material by hand, either.

We'll start by creating the class declarations in lib/Catalyst/View/SerialiseStashKey:

```
package Catalyst::View::SerialiseStashKey;

use Moose;
use YAML;
use namespace::autoclean;
extends 'Catalyst::View';
```

Next we want to make sure that we can override the stash key to be serialized into YAML with application configuration. We'll make the default stash key response, as that's consistent with what we had earlier:

```
has stash_key => ( is => 'ro',
                   isa => 'Str',
                   required => 1,
                   default  => matches );
```

Our view needs to implement two methods, process and render. The process method sets the response body, which can then be picked up by the Catalyst engine in use, while render just returns the content itself.

```
sub process {
    my ($self, $c) = @_;
    my $content = $self->render($c);
    $c->response->body($content);
}
```

```
sub render {
    my ($self, $c) = @_;
    my $data = Load( $c->stash->{ $self->stash_key } );
    my $content = "<pre>\n$data</pre>";
    return $content;
}
```

Finally, we need to add the true value to return from our package.

```
1;
```

Now we can demonstrate how this will work by folding it into our DwarfChains example from Chapter 7. First, we can change the end in the Root controller back to the original:

```
sub end :ActionClass('RenderView) { }
```

Next, we can either install our new Catalyst view via cpan . or, because this code is a bit trivial, copy the SerialiseStashKey.pm file into lib/Catalyst/View/ from our application root (although actually we could dispense with that as well as the block of code immediately below and just put the code straight into MyApp::View::Serialise, changing the package name appropriately). We create a Catalyst view by adding the following into lib/DwarfChains/View/Serialise.pm:

```
package DwarfChains::View::Serialise;


use strict;
use warnings;
use parent 'Catalyst::View::SerialiseStashKey';
1;
```

If we run through the DwarfChains examples again with the new Catalyst view instead of the old end action, the output will be identical to what it was before. If we run CATALYST_ DEBUG=0 script/dwarfchains_test.pl /name, we get the following output:

```
<pre>
---
- People:
    get_ready: ~
- People:
    get_root: !!perl/scalar:URI::http http://localhost/name
- Root: end
</pre>
```

There's a fairly rich vein of Catalyst::View modules on CPAN, from the simple, such as Catalyst::View::Download, to the sophisticated, such as Catalyst::View::Graphics::Primitive and Catalyst::View::ContentNegotiation::XHTML (although this last one is a bit different; it's a Moose::Role to extend other Catalyst views).

Action Classes

An *action class* is a type of Catalyst::Controller that uses the bottom-level namespace of the class as an argument to the ActionClass attribute. This means that the execute method from Catalyst::Action::MyAction will be called if you have a controller action with ActionClass('MyAction'). In most circumstances, you will want code execution to then proceed up the call stack back to Catalyst::Action and then to Catalyst.pm itself. So our most basic possible custom action would look something like this:

```
package Catalyst::Action::MyAction;
use MRO::Compat; # ensures that inheritance works properly for all
                 # versions of perl supported by Catalyst
extends 'Catalyst::Action';

sub execute {
    my $self = shift;
    my ($controller, $c)  = @_;

    # do stuff before parent class's processing here
    # ...

    # call the parent class's execute method
    $self->next::method(@_);

    # do stuff after  parent class's processing here
    # ...

    return $c->state; # not required if only processing before parent
}
```

Catalyst::Action::RenderView and Catalyst::Action::REST are worth studying before you implement your own Catalyst::Action classes. For a complete, simple example of Catalyst::Action, Catalyst::Action::Firebug available on CPAN is a good bet. This may also be something you can add to your debugging toolkit.

Adding Attributes to Controller Actions

Now that we've covered controllers, views, and ActionClass extensions, we can look at how to go about adding our own attributes. We'll look at three ways to add custom attributes in this section: first, a simple but nonextendible way that hard-codes the behavior to a specific auto action; second, a slightly more sophisticated way that will work application wide; and third, a way that allows us to add new attributes in a generic fashion without hard-coding into a specific application.

A Simple Example

The most basic way to add a new action to our application is to check for it in the relevant controller method. For example, if we want to make sure that our application redirects to a welcome page unless the request is encrypted (i.e., https), then we can make the following base controller:

```
package MyApp::Controller::Root;
use parent 'Catalyst::Controller';

sub auto : Private {
    my ($self, $c) = @_;

    # redirect unless the called action has the C< Unsecure > attribute.
    return 1 if exists $c->action->attributes->{Unsecure};
    $c->res->redirect('/welcome') unless $c->secure;
    return 1;
}
```

Now if we have a subroutine like the following:

```
sub thing : Path : Args(1) {
    my ($self, $c, $args) = @_;
}
```

the application will die unless it's requested over a secure port. However, we can also call a method that won't redirect as follows:

```
sub welcome_page : Path('welcome') Unsecure {
    my ($self, $c) = @_;
}
```

A More Sophisticated Example

The preceding example is not great, because our code isn't terribly reusable and it requires the execution of the correct auto action. We'd like to keep the attribute independent from particular actions in the controller. In the example in this section, we'll do the opposite to the previous example—that is, if we request a page that hits an attribute with a : Secure action from an unsecure page (i.e., not https), we'll redirect to an informative page. Here's the class we create in lib/MyApp/Action/EnsureEncryption.pm:

```
package MyApp::Action::EnsureEncryption;

use Moose;
use MRO::Compat;
use namespace::clean -except => 'meta';

extends 'Catalyst::Action';
```

```
around execute => sub {
    my self = shift;
    my ($controller, $c) = @_;

    if ( !$c->request->secure && !exists $self->attributes->{Secure} ) {
        $c->res->redirect($c->uri_for('/welcome_page') );
        # this time we use detach rather than return
        # this avoids repeatedly running the test for later chain parts
        $c->detach; # safe since we're in execute rather than dispatch
    }

    # actually execute the action if we got this far
    return $self->next::method->(@_);
};


1;
```

Note that with MRO::Compat and $self->next::method(@_), we're setting up for the code to be able to be used in multiple inheritance later on. At this stage, if we ignore the inheritance issues, it doesn't make any difference, but omitting the $self->next::method(@_) call would lead to an explosion later on.

We don't actually have to do much to ensure that the new ActionClass is loaded into our application—we just provide the correctly named attribute in our code. Unfortunately, now that we've factored out of our main code, the syntax becomes more complicated than it was previously:

```
sub login : Path('login')
           ActionClass('+MyApp::Action::EnsureEncryption')
                                                           { # ...
```

The + symbol in the preceding code means that Catalyst::Action should look at the fully qualified namespace to get the attribute definition rather than checking in the Catalyst::Action namespace.

To fix this inconveniently verbose call to our custom action and simultaneously turn it into a custom attribute instead, we can put the following in a base controller and use extends 'MyApp::ControllerBase::Secure'; instead of extends 'Catalyst::Controller';:

```
sub _parse_Secure_attr {
    return ActionClass => 'MyApp::Action::EnsureEncryption';
}
```

We don't need the + symbol this time, as we're inside a method that isn't expecting anything other than a fully qualified namespace. Finally, we can define a method that needs to be accessed only over https:

```
sub secret : Path('quiet') Secure { # ...
```

Adding More Than One New Attribute

Let's create an ActionClass to serialize the stash to the response body:

```
package MyApp::Action::SerializeStash;

use Moose;
use MRO::Compat;
use JSON::Any;
use namespace::clean -except => 'meta';

extends 'Catalyst::Action';

has json_emitter => (
    is      => 'ro',
    default => sub { JSON::Any->new },
    handles => {
        encode_json => 'to_json',
    },
);

after execute => sub {
    my ($self) =shift;
    my ($controller, $c) = @_;
    $c->response->body( $self->encode_json($c->stash) );
};

1;
```

We can also add the attribute parsing code into the base controller:

```
sub _parse_Serialize_attr {
    return ActionClass => 'MyApp::Action::SerializeStash';
}
```

So now we can have actions that are either ActionClass('Secure') or
ActionClass('Serialize'), but not both. There are two ways of getting around this. The first
is a pretty horrible hack using multiple inheritance. We can make a new action class that
creates a new MyApp::Action::SecureSerializeStash:

```
package MyApp::Action::SecureSerializeStash;

use Moose;
use namespace::autoclean;
extends qw/MyApp::Action::EnsureEncryption
           MyApp::Action::SerializeStash/;

1;
```

and then in our base controller:

```
sub _parse_SecureSerialize_attr {
    return ActionClass => 'MyApp::Action::SecureSerializeStash':
}
```

The trouble with this is that once we start breeding new action classes, and we start wanting to use them together, we'll end up with lots of useless subclasses just to combine all the actions together. The more actions you add, the more subclasses that you need. Fortunately, a solution exists with Catalyst::Controller::ActionRole on CPAN. Eventually, we intend to avoid needing action classes at all through a combination of roles, modifiers, and custom method metaclasses, but that's still a little way down the Catalyst 5.8 road.

Cleaning Up Multiple Attributes with Roles

Next, for both examples of an ActionClass (the Serialize and Secure ones), we can substitute use Moose with use Moose::Role. The functionality will remain the same, but as a role it is not inherited in the normal way that inheritance works (it's more like bolted-on functionality, whereas in inheritance, if A inherits from B, B is a superset of A), we don't have the limitations caused by the multiple inheritance model described earlier. However, we do need to move the namespace for the two attribute modules. Previously we had MyApp::Action::SerializeStash and MyApp::Action::EnsureEncryption; now we need to move the module namespace to MyApp::Action::Role::SerializeStash and MyApp::Action::Role:: EnsureEncryption, respectively.

We change the line in the Controller classes where we want access to our custom attributes from extends 'Catalyst::Controller'; to BEGIN {extends 'Catalyst::Controller:: ActionRole'; }. Note that we have to use the BEGIN block because the setup of subroutine attributes occurs at compile time, but under normal circumstances extends does processing at runtime. The need to create a BEGIN block will be removed in some future version of Catalyst:: Controller::ActionRole, but it is required for the time being.

Finally, we can call our code with multiple attributes. Catalyst::Controller::ActionRole provides us with the Does attribute. We can call each ActionRole together in the same subroutine:

```
sub for_coders : Path('l33t')
                 Args(0)
                 Does('EnsureEncryption')
                 Does('SerialiseStash') { # ...
```

Catalyst::Controller::ActionRole will look for action classes in the Action::Role namespace (relative to the current application's namespace). Early versions of ActionRole needed a tilde (~) symbol for this functionality, but this is no longer a requirement. If no suitable module is found there, the namespace search moves to Catalyst::Action::Role. If you're storing action classes outside either of these namespaces, you'll have to use a + symbol to denote a fully qualified namespace, as described previously.

Extending Catalyst with Plug-ins

In the early days of Catalyst, almost everything was extended via adding a new Catalyst::Plugin. Unfortunately, this resulted in a proliferation of silly plug-in modules that added little value and polluted the global Catalyst namespace on CPAN. Plug-ins do have a place, but only when what you're doing is intimately bound up with the request cycle.

Here's an example of what not to do with a plug-in, using the very old plug-in Catalyst::Plugin::Textile (for processing the Textile markup formatting to HTML):

```
package Catalyst::Plugin::Textile;
use strict;
use base 'Class::Data::Inheritable';
use Text::Textile;
__PACKAGE__->mk_classdata('textile');
__PACKAGE__->textile( Text::Textile->new );
```

This adds a $c->textile method into MyApp. Really, we would want to make this model code, for example:

```
package MyApp::Model::Textile
use base Catalyst::Model::Adaptor;
__PACKAGE__->config( class => 'Text::Textile');
1;
```

We can then call $c->model('Textile')->textile from controller code, or even better, with a bit of messing around with the view class, we could provide a helper method in the view for data (e.g., particular stash keys) to be processed as Textile markup. We could use our own Template::Plugin if we're using the Template Toolkit.

Having shown a more correct way to do things, we can focus on where plug-ins make sense. The purpose of showing you an incorrect plug-in and the corresponding correct model is so that when you're writing code, you can tell if you need a model or a plug-in. If you need information from $c in your model, one way of achieving this is with Catalyst::Model::Adaptor, Catalyst::Model::Factory, or Catalyst::Model::FactoryPerRequest. Each of these is described in Chapter 11.

Helper Methods in MyApp.pm

We can make an application-specific plug-in just by declaring a new subroutine in our application. In fact, you saw this with the DwarfChains example in Chapter 7. For example, we might want to change the way $c->uri_for works, depending on which Catalyst view is currently active. This could be very specific to our particular action. In the following code, we override uri_for to produce a URI with a different base depending on whether we want to publish a page or edit it:

```perl
use MRO::Compat; # normally for consistent style we put use statements
                 # at the top of the source file
use URI;

sub uri_for {
    my $self = shift;
    my $uri = $self->next::method(@_);
    $self->stash->{current_view} = 'Edit'
        unless $self->stash->{current_view}; # eliminate ugly undef warnings
    if ($self->stash->{current_view} eq 'Publish') {
        my $login = $self->stash->{site_config}->{username};
        my $path = "~$login".$uri->path;
        my $new_base;
        if ($self->stash->{site_config}->{root} ) {
            $new_base = $self->config->{publish_base}
                        . "/"
                        . $self->stash->{site_config}->{root};
        }
        else {
            $new_base = $self->config->{publish_base}
        }
        $DB::single=1;
        $uri = URI->new_abs( $path, $new_base);

        # the following two lines deal with some annoying Template
        # Toolkit behavior with respect to $c->uri_for

        $uri =~ s{//}{/}g;
        $uri=~ s{http:/}{http://}g;
    }

    return URI->new($uri)
}
```

Elsewhere in the controllers for this code, we do something like the following (both views are TT views with different configurations):

```perl
# publish the static view
$c->stash( current_view => 'Publish');
my $page = $c->view('Publish')->render($c, 'index.tt');

# render template as normal
$c->model('Publish')->store_page(@path, $file);
$c->stash( current_view => 'Edit');
```

This code solves specific logic to do with a specific application. It's not a very generalized solution, so it doesn't deserve status as a plug-in. A better solution that provides a generalizable behavior over multiple applications is Catalyst::Plugin::SmartURI, which we will discuss next.

Catalyst::Plugin::SmartURI

Catalyst::Plugin::SmartURI intercepts calls to $c->uri_for and $c->uri_with (i.e., it alters the current request's URI with different GET parameters, which is useful for paging and similar functions), so that depending on application wide configuration or the value sent to $c->uri_disposition provided by the plug-in, $c->uri_for will return either an absolute URL, a relative URL, or a URL returned by the value of the Host header in the HTTP request. Because Catalyst::Plugins import methods into the current application's namespace, using inheritance, the plug-in uses $c->next::method(@_) to ensure that the complete code is run when our extended method is called.

This is the same technique we used when overriding process in our own ActionClass definitions previously. There's not much to it apart from that. This plug-in overrides the two methods, uri_for and uri_with, as well as the internal process method that corrals information from the engine to the application (in order to intercept the Host HTTP header) and the setup method for extending Catalyst's existing infrastructure, which obtains values from configuration. It provides the new method uri_disposition to set the way that the URI should be generated. This plug-in is a good example of a nontrivial yet simple plug-in to study if you need to write your own.

Catalyst::Plugin::Static::Simple

At some point you may want to make a plug-in with deeper hooks into more than one part of the Catalyst request cycle. Catalyst::Plugin::Static::Simple is the grandfather of these types of plug-ins, and it has uses both in development and in production. Mostly, you'll want to use Catalyst::Plugin::Static::Simple during development to avoid using the Catalyst dispatcher to process requests that will hit a static file, and just serve them directly. To this end, it overrides the following methods from Catalyst.pm:

- setup: This code runs when your application is first set up. For this plug-in, all that happens is the configuration hash is obtained using Catalyst's existing infrastructure, and defaults are set, so you know what paths and file extensions correspond to static files and what their MIME type should be.

- prepare_action: This method checks if $c->req->path actually points to a static file and sets the response status to 404 and a "Page not found" message if it's a path covered under config but the file requested is not present. In versions of Static::Simple prior to 0.12, processing of the rest of the request would be short-circuited here, but this caused problems with other plug-ins that intercepted the prepare_action, so this is no longer the case.

- dispatch: Here the plug-in sets the (hopefully) correct MIME-type header for the static file to be served and sets the response body.

- finalize: This is where logging specific to Static::Simple's functionality is performed after the static file has been sent to the client.

One possible exercise to do for practicing writing plug-ins is to add functionality that does the display of directories for paths under Static::Simple's control, much in the same way that a "real" web server can do.

Catalyst::Plugin::Server

We mentioned Catalyst::Plugin::Server and its close relative Catalyst::Plugin::Server::XMLRPC in the previous chapter. We have another opportunity to mention it here. Should you find the need to make deep changes to Catalyst's internals, such as having different dispatch rules (e.g., from parsing XML data in the request body for XML-RPC, or JSON data in the request body for JSON-RPC), then you will need to intercept the prepare_action method. Doing so will defer to a new dispatch type (Catalyst::Plugin::Server::XMLRPC::DispatchType::XMLRPCPath, in this case). This means that our code no longer uses $c->req->path and $c->req->args to determine how Catalyst actions are called. It parses information from XML in the request body instead.

Once you're in this deep as far as extending Catalyst goes, the work becomes very detailed and requires substantial knowledge of Catalyst's internals. However, the techniques are the same as detailed previously. Moose, Moose::Role, and MRO::Compat (and Class::C3, where all the things like $self->next::method(@_) are documented) are your primary tools. The challenging part of this job is understanding the anatomy of your problem (remember the surgeon analogy from the start of the chapter) or the way the pipes are laid out for this particular building (recall the plumbing analogy). Extending Catalyst in this detailed fashion is an excellent way to understand Catalyst and, to a lesser extent, Perl's internal workings, more thoroughly.

Summary

In this chapter, we covered writing your own view and your own base controllers. We then described how to implement your own subroutine attributes using a variety of techniques. For maximum code reusability, we recommend that you use Catalyst::Controller::ActionRole for this. Finally, we looked at the appropriate use of Catalyst plug-ins and detailed what you should use them for and how they should be used.

In the next chapter, we present the Catalyst Cookbook, a range of programming techniques and other tricks that you may find useful, but that we couldn't fit into other bits of the book. Broadly speaking, the recipes are split into models, views, controllers, development process, and other miscellaneous topics.

CHAPTER 11

■ ■ ■

Catalyst Cookbook

This chapter presents a variety of short "recipes" that either demonstrate bits of Catalyst functionality or solve a small, specific problem. The recipes are divided into three categories as follows:

- *Model/View/Controller*: By this point in the book, you should be very familiar with the meaning of MVC. In this section, we'll look at models (mostly DBIx::Class), some different approaches to views, and a handful of the things that we can do with subrequest snippets and base controllers.

- *Miscellaneous*: This section contains recipes that don't fit particularly well into the MVC pattern category but have to do with the functionality of an application.

- *Development process*: In this section of the cookbook, we'll look at a number of useful tips and techniques for the development process. This stuff is here to make your life easier.

Many of the recipes assume that you're starting with a basic generated Catalyst application:

```
$ catalyst.pl MyApp
```

If we mention MyApp in a recipe, this is our starting point. If we want you to start with something else, we'll let you know. Some examples have a fair bit of setup overhead. In this case, we'll just show snippets of code that contain enough information for you to get working on your particular use case.

Model/View/Controller

These recipes present various aspects of MVC in Catalyst and how you can use them to provide specific functionality for your applications.

Import Existing Schemas to DBIx::Class

Sometimes you'll come across a big database schema that you need to fold straight into your application. Writing resultset classes for every table of a 50-table database would be tedious in the extreme. Fortunately, as we discussed in Chapter 6, DBIx::Class::Schema::Loader will do all the heavy lifting for you. But for complex databases, it's pretty likely that you'll need to use a code-tweak-recode cycle to get everything the way you want it. Where you're relying on the autogeneration facility of the Schema::Loader module to do much of the recoding for you, you'll need to be careful.

We'll handle the Zotero database as an example in this recipe. Zotero is a Firefox browser extension for document storage. It uses SQLite to store data, which means that it will interoperate with DBIx::Class nicely. The database schema contains around 50 tables, and crucially, the relationships are specified properly in the SQL table declarations, which means that DBIx::Class::Schema::Loader can pick up on them.

If you want to try this at home, you can grab Zotero from http://zotero.org and install the extension to Firefox. Then you'll want to add some collections and items to your library and close down Firefox. Next, you'll want to find the zotero.sqlite file in your Firefox profile directory (if you can't work out where this is, just search the filesystem for it).

Now we can write a script to use DBIx::Class::Schema::Loader that uses the same code to generate a set of DBIx::Class schema files as used by Catalyst::Helper::Model::DBIC::Schema, which we covered in much of Chapter 6. While we won't write a Catalyst application to demonstrate this, if you decide to do so, you should probably put it in script/make_zotero_schema. pl relative to the application root. Here's the script:

```perl
#!/usr/bin/perl
use warnings;
use strict;
use FindBin qw/$Bin/;
use DBIx::Class::Schema::Loader qw/ make_schema_at /;

my %options;
if (@ARGV) {
    my $table = shift @ARGV;
    %options = ( constraint => $table,
                 components => [@ARGV]);
}

make_schema_at("Zotero::Schema",
            {
                %options,
                debug => 1,
                relationships => 1,
                use_namespaces => 1,
                dump_directory => "$Bin/../lib" ,
            },
            ["dbi:SQLite:dbname=/path/to/your/copy/of/zotero.sqlite",
             "",""]);
```

```
=head1 make_zotero_schema.pl [table name] [components]

    Make the DBIC schema from the zotero db; optionally, limit it to a
    particular table and add specific components to the table.

=cut
```

You can run this script with `perl script/make_zotero_schema.pl`. Note that the options hash is unused as yet. You'll see a lot of debug output in this case, because we've set the debug option in the `make_schema_at` method to true.

Say we continue coding for a while, and then we realize that we want our database to reflect that the `collections` table contains a tree structure. Checking the documentation of DBIx::Class::Tree::AdjacencyList and the contents of the database table, we realize that it will work unmodified if we add it to the schema. This is where the trickery with the `%options` hash and the arguments to the script comes in. If we just run the script without any arguments, the options hash is empty, and we get a dump of the whole schema without any components being loaded. It's quite important with a large, complex database to load components only for tables that need them. This is where the script's original arguments come in. First, we specify the table that we want to regenerate, and then we specify the components that we want to have added to the table's class. In this case, we want the `collections` table to be regenerated, and we want to add the Tree::AdjacencyList component. We'll now run the script with arguments:

```
$ perl script/make_zotero_schema.pl collections Tree::AdjacencyList
```

This results in a lot less output, as we're only updating the Result class for the `collections` table, which now loads that component. However, we'll also need to specify the column that defines the tree structure, which indicates the parent of the tree (below the "do not modify" line, of course). So we add the following line to Zotero::Schema::Result::Collections:

```
__PACKAGE__->parent_column("parentcollectionID");
```

And now we have tree support in our application.

More generally, we can use this same script to add other DBIx::Class components to other tables in our database.

See Also

Refer to the many other DBIx::Class components on CPAN, notably DBIx::Class::DateTime, DBIx::Class::EncodedColumn, DBIx::Class::File, and DBIx::Class::ForceUTF8.

In the next recipe, we'll show how to use the JSON data structure to make a JavaScript-generated tree in our application.

Use DBIx::Class::Tree and Display with JavaScript and the Template Toolkit

It's often useful to display tree structures in web pages. Looking at the Collections class from the previous recipe, you can easily see how the relationships work for a tree class. Here's the code generated with our script from the previous recipe, with the edit after the "do not modify" line:

```
__PACKAGE__->load_components("Tree::AdjacencyList", "Core");
__PACKAGE__->table("collections");
__PACKAGE__->add_columns(
  "collectionid",
  { data_type => "INTEGER", is_nullable => 0, size => undef },
  "collectionname",
  { data_type => "TEXT", is_nullable => 0, size => undef },
  "parentcollectionid",
  { data_type => "INT", is_nullable => 0, size => undef },
);
__PACKAGE__->set_primary_key("collectionid");
__PACKAGE__->belongs_to(
  "parentcollectionid",
  "Zotero::Schema::Result::Collections",
  { collectionid => "parentcollectionid" },
);
__PACKAGE__->has_many(
  "collections",
  "Zotero::Schema::Result::Collections",
  { "foreign.parentcollectionid" => "self.collectionid" },
);

# Created by DBIx::Class::Schema::Loader v0.04005 @ 2009-04-26 01:13:03
# DO NOT MODIFY THIS OR ANYTHING ABOVE! md5sum:SHNC6dOLncXwqIkdPgDgKg

  __PACKAGE__->parent_column("parentcollectionID");


1;
```

While the relationships themselves contain sufficient information to reconstruct the tree structure, the Tree::AdjacencyList component makes doing so a lot more convenient. To illustrate this, we'll create the following class in Zotero::ResultSet::Collections (you'll have to create the ResultSet directory yourself). This code outputs a data structure that is suitable for serializing in JSON format, either from the bottom root of the tree (in get_collections_tree) or from a specific node (in get_children).

```
package Zotero::ResultSet::Collections;
use warnings;
use strict;

use base qw/DBIx::Class::ResultSet/;

sub get_collections_tree {
    my $self = shift;
    my @res;
    my $rs = $self->search( {parentcollectionid => undef},
                            {order_by => [ 'collectionname' ] },
                          );
```

```
      while (my $node = $rs->next) {
          push @res, $self->get_children($node);
      }
      return \@res;
  }


  sub get_children {
      my ($self, $node ) = @_;
      my $res = {};
      $res->{title} = $node->collectionname ;
      $res->{key} = $node->collectionid;
      my @kids = $node->children;
      $res->{expand} = 1;
      if (@kids) {
          my @children;
          foreach (@kids) {
              push @children, [$self->get_children($_)];
          }
          $res->{children} = \@children;
      }
      return $res;
  }


  1;
```

Note that the use of recursion in this recipe is safe because DBIx::Class::Tree already does constraint checking to ensure that there are no infinite loops in our tree structure already. You'll need to write your own component to cope with graph data structures (e.g., nodes with multiple parents) stored in a database (or check CPAN to see if anyone else has done so) if you need this.

You can see that we now have methods on our resultset to retrieve the whole tree (get_collections_tree) and another method to retrieve the tree from a particular node. To understand how these subroutines work, we suggest writing a test case and stepping through them with the Perl debugger.

Before we get this working in Catalyst, we have to make our Catalyst model and define the DSN. We can make the Catalyst model with Catalyst::Helper::Model::DBIC::Schema:

```
$ script/myapp_create.pl model Zotero::Schema DBIC::Schema \
  Zotero::Schema
```

We also have to remember to put the connection information into `myapp.conf`:

```
<Model Zotero::Schema>
connect_info dbi::SQLite:dbname=__path_to('zotero.sqlite')__
</Model>
```

Now let's look at how to use this in Catalyst controller code. If this method were in Controller::Root, it would run when we requested /collection:

```perl
use JSON;

sub list_collection : Path('collection') : Args(0) {
  my ($self, $c) = @_;
  my $tree = $c->
              model('Zotero::Schema::Collections')->
              get_collections_tree;

 $c->stash(
          tree => objToJson($tree),
          template => 'browse/collection.tt',
    );
}
```

If there were greater use of JSON in this application, we might forgo creating the JSON directly and use the subinclude method to grab the stash key illustrated later in this chapter.

Here's the template that displays the tree, which uses the jQuery JavaScript framework (http://jquery.com), the jQuery UI enhancements, and the jQuery Dynatree extension (http://code.google.com/p/dynatree/):

```
[% WRAPPER page.tt title = pagetitle  %]
<script type='text/javascript'
   src='[% c.uri_for('/static/js/jquery.js')%]'></script>
<script type='text/javascript'
   src='[% c.uri_for('/static/js/ui.core.js')%]'></script>
<script type='text/javascript'
   src='[% c.uri_for('/static/js/jquery.dynatree.js')%]'></script>
<link  href="[% c.uri_for('/static/css/ui.dynatree.css') %]"
   rel="stylesheet" type="text/css" />
<script type='text/javascript'>
  $(function(){
     // Attach the dynatree widget to an existing <div id="tree"> element
     // and pass the tree options as an argument to the dynatree() function:
     $("#tree").dynatree({
        onSelect: function(dtnode) {
        // A DynaTreeNode object is passed to the select handler
        var url = "[% c.uri_for('collection') %]" + '/' + dtnode.data.key;
        window.location.href = url;
      },
     children:
               [% tree # ***here's our JSON generated from the database*** %]
               })});
     </script>

  </head>
```

```
<body>

<h1> Viewing collection structure </h1>

<p> Click on the + symbol to expand the collection tree.  Click on the
collection name to review items in the collection. </p>

<div id="tree"></div>

[% END %]
```

If you don't want to mess around with the template, then you could just put
`$c->res->body($c->stash->template{tree})` at the end of the action we wrote.

Figure 11-1 presents a screenshot of the output that we expect here (although you won't
have all the style sheet stuff in the Template Toolkit wrapper that we have here—this is presented in the upcoming recipe, "A Way to Quickly Resolve Browser Compatibility Issues").

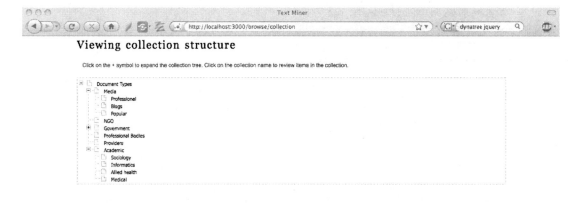

Figure 11-1. *Output of tree structure from JSON input using the DBIx::Class::Tree component, JSON, and the jQuery JavaScript library*

Catalyst::Model::Factory and Catalyst::Model:: Factory::PerRequest

---

■**Note** Thanks to Jonathan Rockway for his assistance with this recipe.

We've used Catalyst::Model::Adaptor elsewhere in this book to set up a plain class as a
Catalyst model at application startup time. This helps us to write models that will work
as well outside of Catalyst as inside Catalyst. If you need more flexibility than this, you
should use Catalyst::Model::Factory::PerRequest to instantiate your class once per Catalyst
request, or Catalyst::Model::Factory if you need a new object every time you call a particular
$c->model. Setup for either is the same as Catalyst::Model::Factory.

Here's a simple class that uses Catalyst::Model::Factory:

```
package MyApp::Model::Something;
use strict;
use warnings;
use parent 'Catalyst::Model::Factory';

__PACKAGE__->config(
    class => 'Some::Plain::Class',
    args => { arg =>  $self->arg},
);

1;
```

Say we needed access to Catalyst's path_to method in our model. We could easily set this
up within a Catalyst::Model::Adaptor model with the following inside our MyApp::Model::
Something class, by adding extra code above the 1;:

```
use Moose;
use namespace::autoclean;
sub ACCEPT_CONTEXT {
    my ($self, $c ) = @_;
    my $new = $self->meta->clone_object($self, arg => $c->path_to(''));
    return $new;
}
```

The ACCEPT_CONTEXT method is a special method documented in Catalyst::Component that
grabs relevant parts of the application's context object (what we usually call $c) during con-
struction of the Catalyst component.

However, if we needed information from the current Catalyst request object for our model to work, then we'd want to use use parent 'Catalyst::Model::Factory' instead of use parent 'Catalyst::Model::Adaptor', and our ACCEPT_CONTEXT might look like this:

```
use Moose;
use namespace::autoclean;
sub ACCEPT_CONTEXT {
    my ($self, $c ) = @_;
    # we can have path_to like before
    my $new = $self->meta->clone_object($self, arg => $c->path_to(''));
    # and also the request path
    $new = $self->meta->clone_object($self, arg => $c->req->path);
    return $new;
}
```

We have to use Catalyst::Model::Factory because models inheriting from this cause our model to be instantiated at runtime, not upon request, and so only in this instance do we have access to the current request path.

Finally, if our model depended on something to do with the current application state, we'd want to use use parent 'Catalyst:Model::Factory::PerRequest', and our ACCEPT_CONTEXT subroutine might be as follows:

```
use Moose;
use namespace::autoclean;
sub ACCEPT_CONTEXT {
    my ($self, $c ) = @_;
    my $new = $self->meta->clone_object($self, arg => $c->stash->{something});
    return $new;
}
```

Note that PerRequest means per time that it is requested in the code, not per request cycle, which is slightly unintuitive.

A Way to Quickly Resolve Browser Compatibility Issues

Browser compatibility is one of the most time-consuming and painful aspects of the web developer's job. If you have a separate designer on the team, this problem is somewhat less severe. In this recipe, we'll outline a few open source tools that can make your life substantially easier.

To follow along, after creating the MyApp application, obtain emastic (http://code. google.com/p/emastic/), a CSS framework. Download the ZIP file, put it in the root/static directory, and unzip it in there. Now change the name of the unzipped directory to something more sensible, for example, emastic. This provides you with the whole distribution, including the demos (HTML and image files). You'll want to keep these files around to check how to use emastic, but you'll probably want to delete all of this at the end of your development.

Let's create a TT view in MyApp with the command `script/myapp_create view Web TT` (recall that we did this in Chapter 3). We'll modify the Web view configuration to provide an automatic `WRAPPER` as well. We change the configuration line in MyApp::View::Web to be as follows:

```
__PACKAGE__->config(TEMPLATE_EXTENSION => '.tt',
                    WRAPPER            => 'page.tt',
              );
```

Before we start working on the template itself, we must note that while emastic deals with many (Internet Explorer) compatibility issues, it's not perfect. To fix most of the remaining issues, we can get the IE7 JavaScript library (available from `http://code.google.com/p/ie7-js/`), which provides us with a compatibility layer on top of Internet Explorer that we can insert with Microsoft's proprietary conditional comments in our template. Since it's very unlikely that we'll be doing primary development in Internet Explorer, it's probably fine for us to serve these files directly from Google's infrastructure rather than from a local file.

Note The IE7 library can slow down Internet Explorer a bit. If performance is important to your users (which we tend to consider likely), then don't use it. You'll have to work around problems manually instead.

Now for our `WRAPPER` template, which we put in `root/page.tt`. Note the inline comments in bold with some information about what's what in here.

```
<!DOCTYPE html PUBLIC "-//W3C//DTD XHTML 1.0 Strict//EN"
     "http://www.w3.org/TR/xhtml1/DTD/xhtml1-strict.dtd">
<html xmlns="http://www.w3.org/1999/xhtml" xml:lang="en" lang="en">
<head>
<title>[% title %]</title>
<meta http-equiv="content-type" content="text/html; charset=UTF-8" />

<!-- ***IE7 JavaScript library conditionals*** -->
<!--[if lt IE 7]>
<script src="http://ie7-js.googlecode.com/svn/version/2.0(beta3)/IE7.js"
     type="text/javascript"></script>
<![endif]-->
<!--[if lt IE 8]>
<script src="http://ie7-js.googlecode.com/svn/version/2.0(beta3)/IE8.js"
     type="text/javascript"></script>
<![endif]-->

<link rel="stylesheet" href="[% c.uri_for('/static/emastic/css/reset.css') %]"
     type="text/css" media="screen, projection">
<link rel="stylesheet" href="[% c.uri_for('/static/emastic/css/grid.css') %]"
     type="text/css" media="screen, projection">
<link rel="stylesheet" href="[% c.uri_for('/static/emastic/css/type.css') %]"
     type="text/css" media="screen, projection">
```

```
<link
   rel="stylesheet" href="[% c.uri_for('/static/emastic/css/gadgets.css') %]"
   type="text/css" media="screen, projection">

<!-- *** Emastic contains its own IE compatibility workarounds, but
      its coverage isn't as good as IE7 ***-->
<!--[if IE]>
<link rel="stylesheet" href="[% c.uri_for('/static/emastic/css/ie.css') %]"
      type="text/css" media="screen, projection">
<![endif]-->

<!-- *** your local styles go in this file in the root/static directory *** -->
<link rel=stylesheet" href="[% c.uri_for('/static/local-styles.css') %]"
   type="text/css" media="screen, projection">
</script>
</head>
[% content %]
</html>
```

Our index.tt template is as follows:

```
<body>
<div class="main gridlines">
<div class="clear"></div>

<div class="ml10 mr15 clearfix"><h1> Heading  </h1>
<p class="note">Menu here! (note style defined locally)</p>
</div>

<div class="dr15"> Right hand column
</div>

<div  class="dl10">
<p> Left hand column </p>
</div>

<div class="ml10 fluid mr15">

<p>
[% IF error %]
<p class="error"> c.stash.error goes here.  We define the error style in our
local css file</p>
[% END %]
<p> Main content goes here - Central column </p>
<div class="hp oldbook tc">

Footer goes here

</div>
</div>
```

Finally, we'll rewrite the generated index action in MyApp::Controller::Root so that we serve the template. We'll set the template implicitly from the name of the action, as we did in Chapter 3.

```
sub index :Path :Args(0) {
    my ( $self, $c ) = @_;
}
```

Now if you start the development server and visit http://localhost:3000, you have the beginnings of a decent cross-browser, pure-CSS, three-column layout.

Output CSV from a Controller Action

This simple recipe shows how to output a comma-separated variable (CSV) file from a controller action. Note that if you have a lot of different actions that output CSV, or lots of different content types that you want to be downloadable from your pages, you might want to use Catalyst::View::Download or Catalyst::View::Download::CSV (both available from CPAN) instead.

Here's the action we'll use:

```
sub action_name :Path('public_action_name') Args(0) {
    my ($self, $c) = @_;
    my $filename= $c->req->params->{filename} || 'data.csv';
    my $csv_data = $c->model('Something')->get_csv_data;
    $c->stash(data => $csv_data);
    $c->response->headers->header("Content-Type" => "text/csv")
    $c->res->headers->header( 'Content-Disposition' =>
                              "attachment; filename=$filename");
    $c->response->body($csv_data);
}
```

We obtain the filename from the filename parameter if it's available; otherwise, it defaults to data.csv. Following that, we obtain the CSV file contents from a Catalyst model, set the Content-Type header to reflect the CSV MIME type, and then set the Content-Disposition header to provide a default filename for the data file. Finally, we serve the content in the response body.

You can adjust this recipe for other content types as well, by setting the appropriate MIME_TYPE.

See Also

Refer to the Catalyst views already mentioned in this recipe. Also see the serve_static_file method in Catalyst::Plugin::Static::Simple for a way of serving files that have already been written to the computer's disk. In case you use this plug-in, if your file has an appropriate extension, the CPAN module MIME::Magic will set the Content-Disposition header for you.

Dynamically Generate Graphics with Catalyst::View::GD

GD (which stands for *graphics display*) is a versatile open source library for generating graphics. It is written in C. There's also a CPAN module called GD that is an interface to the C library. Finally, there's a Catalyst view that renders GD objects to images in the browser. It takes care of the logic of rendering the object into a displayable graphic and serving it up with the appropriate Content-Type header for you.

If you're on Linux, you can install the libgd package from your package manager. If you're on Windows, you can install GD from http://gnuwin32.sourceforge.net/packages/gd.htm. If you're on OS X, unfortunately installing GD is somewhat involved at the time of this writing, but there is no shortage of instructions available by searching the Internet if you have the patience to follow them.

Here we'll start our MyApp on an Ubuntu system with the packages libgd2-noxpm libgd2-noxpm-dev installed. Then we install Catalyst::View::GD. Starting with MyApp, we add the following subroutine to the file. In production code this belongs in a Catalyst::Model or even an independent model, but this code (which we took straight out of the test suite for Catalyst::View::GD) is fine for illustrative purposes.

```
sub create_image {
    my $self = shift;

    my $img   = GD::Image->new(100, 100);

    my $white = $img->colorAllocate(255, 255, 255);
    my $black = $img->colorAllocate(0, 0, 0);
    my $red   = $img->colorAllocate(255, 0, 0);

    $img->rectangle(0, 0, 20, 20, $black);
    $img->rectangle(20, 20, 50, 50, $red);

    return $img;
}
```

Now we'll change the generated index action to call this subroutine and set it to the stash:

```
sub index :Path Args(0) {
    my ($self, $c) = @_;
    $c->stash(gd_image => $self->create_image,
            current_view => 'Graphics',
        );
}
```

Strictly speaking, the current_view key isn't necessary here, as we're going to have only one view in this application. However, as we'll almost always be generating HTML along with images, we'll set current_view to illustrate best practices.

Now we need to create the view, which we'll call MyApp::View::Graphics. Here's the package:

```
package MyApp::View::Graphics;

use strict;
use warnings;

use base 'Catalyst::View::GD';

1;
```

When we start the development server and visit http://localhost:3000, we get the image shown in Figure 11-2 (except in color).

Figure 11-2. *Output from Catalyst::View::GD*

You can change the image type output by changing the configuration in the view. Catalyst::View::GD contains basic documentation that will get you started.

See Also

In addition to GD, you can create graphics with the Perl modules Imager or Image::Magick. Our preference for simple tasks such as resizing photos for thumbnails is Imager, as it's higher level than GD and, in our subjective opinion, has a nicer interface than Image::Magick.

Dynamically Generate Barcodes from Catalyst

There are two Catalyst views for generating barcodes: Catalyst::View::GD::Barcode and Catalyst::View::GD::Barcode::QRcode. We're doing to deal with the latter here because QRcode is slightly more interesting.

A QRcode is a 2D barcode capable of being read using mobile phone–quality cameras and special software. We'll produce one in Catalyst now.

To produce example QRcode output, we start with MyApp (or you can reuse the application from the previous recipe if you like). Then we install Catalyst::View::GD::Barcode::QRcode from CPAN (with the same caveat on support for different platforms as for the previous recipe).

Next, we add the QRcode view for our application. There is a helper provided, but at the time of this writing, it doesn't provide any useful extra functionality, so we write the class by hand:

```
package MyApp::View::QRcode;

use strict;
use warnings;
use base 'Catalyst::View::GD::Barcode::QRcode';
__PACKAGE__->config(
    ecc         => 'M',
    version     => 4,
    module_size => 4,
    img_type    => 'png'
    );

1;
```

Then we can make an action in our Root controller:

```
sub generate_qr_code :Path('qr') {
    my ($self, $c) = @_;
    $c->stash(qrcode => 'http://catalystframework.org',
             current_view => 'QRcode',
        );
}
```

When we visit http://localhost:3000, we get a QRcode glyph, as shown in Figure 11-3, that with the appropriate software can be decoded by a mobile phone camera into the url http://catalystframework.org.

Figure 11-3. *Output from Catalyst::View::GD::Barcode::QRcode*

▪Note Make sure your CPAN mirror is up to date when running this application. Only the most recent versions of C::V::GD::Barcode::QRcode (0.05 and later) work with Catalyst 5.8.

Produce Graphs with Chart::Clicker and Catalyst::View:: Graphics::Primitive

Chart::Clicker is a relatively new and pretty exciting module for producing your own device-independent graphics within Perl. It's based on Graphics::Primitive, which has a Catalyst view available for it. Graphics::Primitive in turn requires Cairo, a graphics display library available from http://cairographics.org. This package is available for all the major operating systems.

Starting with MyApp, first install Catalyst::View::Graphics::Primitive and Chart::Clicker from CPAN. This is a fairly heavy installation, and depending on your system, it may take some time.

As in the previous recipe, the Catalyst helper for this module doesn't really provide us with any benefits, so we'll write our view by hand.

```perl
package MyApp::View::Graphics;
use strict; use base 'Catalyst::View::Graphics::Primitive';
__PACKAGE__->config( driver => 'Cairo',
                    driver_args =>
                            { format => 'png' },
                    content_type => 'image/png' );
1;
```

We'll also create MyApp::Model::Chart:

```perl
sub make_chart {
    my $cc = Chart::Clicker->new(width => 300, height => 150);

    my @years = ( 1999 .. 2009);
    my @top = qw( 0 0 0 0 0 0 70 30 50 70 90);
    my @bottom = qw( -70 -50 -40 -90 -50 -70 -20 -10 0 0 0);

    my $series = Chart::Clicker::Data::Series->new(
        keys    => \@years,
        values  => \@bottom,
        name => 'Before Catalyst',
    );

    my $series2 = Chart::Clicker::Data::Series->new(
        keys    => \@years,
        values  => \@top,
        name => 'After Catalyst'
    );

    my $ds = Chart::Clicker::Data::DataSet->new(series => [ $series, $series2 ]);
    $cc->add_to_datasets($ds);

    my $defctx = $cc->get_context('default');
    my $grey = Graphics::Color::RGB->new(
        red => .36, green => .36, blue => .36, alpha => 1
    );
```

```perl
    my $red = Graphics::Color::RGB->new(
        red => .71, green => .71, blue => .71, alpha => 1
    );

    $cc->color_allocator->colors([ $grey, $red ]);
    $cc->border->width(0);

    $cc->plot->grid->visible(0);
    $cc->legend->visible(1);

    $defctx->renderer(Chart::Clicker::Renderer::Bar->new);
    $defctx->range_axis->baseline(0);

    $defctx->domain_axis->hidden(1);

    $defctx->range_axis->label('ΔWork');
    $defctx->range_axis->format('%d');
    $defctx->domain_axis->fudge_amount(.1);
    $defctx->renderer->brush->width(1);
    $defctx->domain_axis->tick_values([qw(2000 2002 2004 2006 2008)]);

    $cc->add_to_over_decorations(
        Chart::Clicker::Decoration::OverAxis->new(context => 'default'));

    return $cc;
}


1;
```

There's a lot of code here with no explanation. This is because code to produce charts like this is necessarily complex and is beyond the scope of this recipe. Hopefully, the preceding code will give you something to start playing with.

We can change the index method in our Root controller, which grabs the Chart::Clicker object from the model and sets it to Graphics::Primitive's special stash key. For completeness, we set the current_view stash key again, too.

```perl
sub index :Path :Args(0) {
    my ( $self, $c ) = @_;
    my %chart_data = $c->model('Chart')->make_chart;
    $DB::single=1;
    $c->stash( graphics_primitive => $cc ,
               current_view       => 'Graphics' );
}
```

We can now test our application by visiting http://localhost:3000. From this we get the chart shown in Figure 11-4.

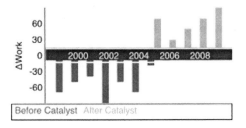

Figure 11-4. *Output from Catalyst::View::Graphics::Primitive and Chart::Clicker*

Note that code to generate graphs—and indeed many other image types—gets quite complex quickly. This is the ideal opportunity to practice the Catalyst independent fat model pattern advocated elsewhere in this book.

See Also

A couple of excellent examples are available at http://www.catalystframework.org/calendar/2008/3 and http://www.catalystframework.org/calendar/2008/9. Otherwise, the documentation for Chart::Clicker and Graphics::Primitive is fairly sparse at the time of this writing, and you'll need to read the source code. Further information is available at http://www.onemogin.com/clicker/.

Alternative Templating Systems

> ■**Note** Code for this recipe was contributed by Florian Ragwitz.

HTML::Mason is a popular templating system that predates the proliferation of web frameworks. It is almost a framework in its own right, but it also scales down well as a templating system. It's probably the most popular view for Catalyst after the Template Toolkit view. We should state that in general we prefer the Template Toolkit, as it is somewhat simpler to use and its limited syntax really helps prevent putting too much logic in templates. However, Mason is widely used inside and outside Catalyst.

Starting with a bare MyApp again, we first install Catalyst::View::Mason from CPAN. We also install namespace::autoclean from CPAN so we can show how to use the Moose extends in our view cleanly (see Chapters 2 and 10).

Next, we can create our view. Rather than use Catalyst::Helper to autogenerate it for us, we'll write it by hand in MyApp::View::HTML.

```
package MyApp::View::HTML;
use Moose;
__PACKAGE__->config(
    comp_root            => MyApp->path_to(qw/root templates/),
    default_escape_flags => 'h',
);

1;
```

Pausing to check that the development server still starts, we'll replace the modified Controller::Root with the following:

```
package MyApp::Controller::Root;

use Moose;
use namespace::autoclean;

BEGIN { extends 'Catalyst::Controller'; }

__PACKAGE__->config->{namespace} = '';

sub index : Path Args(0) {
  my ($self, $c) = @_;
  $c->stash(things => [qw/
      affe
      tiger
      loewe
      birne
  /]);

  # template name automatically inferred to be root/templates/index
}

sub default : Path {
    my ($self, $c) = @_;
    $c->response->body( 'Page not found' );
    $c->response->status(404);
}

sub end : ActionClass('RenderView') {}

1;
```

If we run the development server here (script/myapp_server.pl) and visit http://localhost:3000, we receive an error screen with the following message:

```
Couldn't render component "index" - error was
 "could not find component for initial path '/index'
 (component roots are: '[...]MyApp/root/templates')
```

which tells us that we haven't written the template yet.

While the Template Toolkit has the WRAPPER directive, Mason has the concept of an autohandler, which has the same function. So, in root/templates we can create the file autohandler as follows:

```
<html>
<body>
<h1>Mason Demo App</h1>
<div id="content">
% $m->call_next;
</div>
</body>
</html>
```

% $m-call_next is the equivalent of the [% content %] construct in a Template Toolkit WRAPPER.

After this, we create the index file in the same directory:

```
<%args>
$things
</%args>

<ul>
% for my $thing (@{ $things }) {
  <li><% $thing %></li>
% }
</ul>
```

Note that the beginning and end of a Mason block is delineated with a line beginning with a % sign. Also note that the template code itself looks much more like Perl code than the Template Toolkit code.

If we start the development server and visit http://localhost:3000, we'll find the following page source:

```
<html>
<body>
<h1>Mason Demo App</h1>
<div id="content">

<ul>
  <li>affe</li>
  <li>tiger</li>
  <li>loewe</li>
  <li>birne</li>

</ul>
</div>
</body>
</html>
```

At this point we're done—we have a very simple testbed for the Catalyst Mason view.

See Also

For more details on Mason, see http://www.masonhq.com/ and the book *Embedding Perl in HTML with Mason* by Dave Rolsky and Ken Williams (O'Reilly, 2002; http://www.masonbook.com/). Mason has a lot of features not covered here—for example, you can automatically nest the autohandler templates into a directory hierarchy for multiple controllers.

For yet more templating systems, see Catalyst::View::ClearSilver, Catalyst::View::PHP, Catalyst::View::Template::Declare, Catalyst::View::Text::Template, and many others on CPAN. As we demonstrated in Chapter 10, it's pretty easy to write your own Catalyst::View if you want to use a templating system for which no Catalyst view exists yet.

Easy Spam Protection with Catalyst::Controller::reCAPTCHA

The brilliant thing about reCAPTCHA is that you provide your website with some protection against comment spam or spurious registrations, while simultaneously contributing to the public good by digitizing scanned public domain books. Figure 11-5 shows what the reCAPTCHA service looks like in your browser.

Anit-spam validation (required):

Figure 11-5. *An example of what the reCAPTCHA service looks like. Note the reload, audio alternative, and help buttons to the right of the text input.*

Integrating Catalyst::Controller::reCAPTCHA into your application is easy. This base controller takes care of reCAPTCHA generation and checking for you by adding two private actions, captcha_get and captcha_check, to your controller.

We'll show minimal usage in a fresh MyApp. To start, we need to add the valid API keys before the __PACKAGE__->setup line in MyApp.pm to configure our API keys. You'll need to register at http://recaptcha.net/ to obtain these.

```
__PACKAGE__->config->{recaptcha}->{pub_key} = 'public_key_here';
__PACKAGE__->config->{recaptcha}->{priv_key} = 'private_key_here';
```

Next, we replace the generated Controller::Root with the following code:

```
package MyApp::Controller::Root;
use strict;
use warnings;

__PACKAGE__->config(namespace => '');

use parent 'Catalyst::Controller::reCAPTCHA';
```

```
sub index :Private {
    my ($self, $c) = @_;
    $c->forward('captcha_get');
    my $recaptcha       = $c->stash->{recaptcha};
    my $recaptcha_ok    = $c->stash->{recaptca_ok};
    my $recaptcha_error = $c->stash->{recaptcha_error} || "no error";
    my $check_uri       = $c->uri_for('/check');

    my $body = qq{
    <html><body>
     <p> recaptcha error:  $recaptcha_error </p>
     </p><form name="recaptcha" action="$check_uri"
         method="post"> $recaptcha <br/>
     <input type="submit" value="submit" /> </form>
     </body></html>
     }

    $c->res->body($body);
}

sub check : Local {
    my ($self, $c) = @_;
    if ($c->forward('captcha_check')) {
        $c->detach('ok')
    }
    else {
        $c->detach('index');
    }
}

sub ok : Private {
    my ($self, $c) = @_;
    $c->res->body('You appear to be human');
}
1;
```

Note that the $c->forward statement in check returns a value if the captcha was OK, and it returns undef otherwise. Once you have this code working, you should be presented with a reCAPTCHA to solve when you visit http://localhost:3000, and if you get it right, after you submit the form you should see the text "You appear to be human."

See Also

See HTML::FormFu::Element::reCAPTCHA in the HTML::FormFu distribution for use of reCAPTCHA with HTML::FormFu.

Catalyst::View::Component::SubInclude

This view provides a means to add snippets that are the results of complete controller actions within our template. We'll show how to do this using the Template Toolkit, but this should also work with any other templating system that will work with Catalyst.

Catalyst::View::Component::Subinclude is implemented as a Moose role, so the style with which we write the view is a little bit different from that presented elsewhere in the book. Starting with MyApp.pm, we can make the view:

```
package MyApp::View::Web;
use Moose;
use namespace::autoclean;

extends 'Catalyst::View::TT';
with 'Catalyst::View::Component::SubInclude';
__PACKAGE__->config( TEMPLATE_EXTENSION => '.tt',
                     WRAPPER => 'wrapper.tt',
                );

1;
```

Next, we change the use Catalyst qw/ ... lines in MyApp.pm to add Catalyst::Plugin::SubRequest (the default subrequest mechanism is Catalyst::Plugin::SubRequest):

```
use Catalyst qw/-Debug
                ConfigLoader
                Static::Simple
                SubRequest/;
```

We need the file wrapper.tt to reflect our configuration. We show one way of conditionally applying a different wrapper based on the presence of the subreq stash key here.

```
[% IF ! subreq %]
<html><body>
 <pre>
 #### BEGIN WRAPPER
  [% content %]
 #### END WRAPPER
 </pre>
[% ELSE; content; END %]
```

Then we'll make a snippet.tt template:

```
# here's our subrequest!
```

and an index.tt template:

```
## We'll include the subrequest below:
[% subinclude('/snippet') %]
```

Now we have to make a Root controller that will render these templates. We change the generated index action and add the snippet action as follows:

```
sub index :Path :Args(0) {
    my ( $self, $c ) = @_;
}

sub snippet :Local {
    my ($self, $c) = @_;
    if (ref($c->engine) =~ /SubRequest/ ) {
    $c->stash->{subreq} = 1 ;
    }
}
```

From here we can run the test server. If we request http://localhost:3000, we get the following output:

```
#### BEGIN WRAPPER
  ## We'll include the subrequest below:
    # here's our subrequest!
#### END WRAPPER
```

If we request http://localhost:3000/snippet, we get the following:

```
#### BEGIN WRAPPER
# here's our subrequest!
#### END WRAPPER
```

See Also

To use this mechanism with Edge Side Includes (ESI), see http://www.catalystframework.org/calendar/2008/17 and the CPAN module Catalyst::View::Component::SubInclude::ESI.

For another Catalyst view extension implemented as a Moose role, see Catalyst::View::ContentNegotiation::XHTML on CPAN.

Handle Legacy CGI Scripts in Catalyst

Catalyst::Controller::CGIBin and Catalyst::Controller::WrapCGI can handle existing CGI scripts written in Perl. Starting with MyApp, we add a cgi-bin directory into the root folder. We need to install Catalyst::Controller::CGIBin from CPAN, which will automatically install Catalyst::Controller::WrapCGI as well. Next, we can place our CGI script from Chapter 1 into the acgi.pl file in this folder:

```
#!/usr/bin/env perl

use warnings;
use strict;
use Template;
```

```perl
my $template = Template->new();
my @dwarfs = qw/Bashful Doc Dopey Grumpy Happy Sleepy Sneezy/;
my $cgi_stash = {
    title   => "Howdy!",
    message => "Hello World!",
    dwarfs  => \@dwarfs,
};

$template->process(\*DATA, $cgi_stash);

__DATA__
Content-Type: text/html; charset=ISO-8859-1

<!DOCTYPE html
        PUBLIC "-//W3C//DTD XHTML 1.0 Transitional//EN"
         "http://www.w3.org/TR/xhtml1/DTD/xhtml1-transitional.dtd">
<html xmlns="http://www.w3.org/1999/xhtml" lang="en-US" xml:lang="en-US">
<head>
<title>[% title %]</title>
<meta http-equiv="Content-Type" content="text/html; charset=iso-8859-1" />
</head>
<body>
<h1>[% message %]</h1>
<ul>
[%- FOREACH dwarf IN dwarfs -%]
<li>[% dwarf; IF dwarf != dwarfs.last %] and [% END -%]</li>
[%- END %].
</body>
</html>
```

Now we need a controller for it to run in. We create MyApp::Controller::CGIBin with the following contents:

```perl
package MyApp::Controller::CGIBin;

use strict;
use warnings;
use parent 'Catalyst::Controller::CGIBin';

1;
```

If you run the development server and visit http://localhost:3000/cgi-bin/acgi.pl, you should see the page source as it was when you ran the script in Chapter 1.

Catalyst::Controller::WrapCGI

This is a slightly lower-level module that is suitable if you can't put all your CGI scripts into a single directory. To demonstrate it, we create the following controller:

```perl
package MyApp::Controller::WrapCGI;

use strict;
use warnings;
use parent 'Catalyst::Controller::WrapCGI';

sub serve_cgi :Path :Args(1) {
    my ($self, $c, $file) = @_;

    $self->cgi_to_response($c, sub {
        system ($^X, $c->path_to("root/cgi-bin/$file") );
    });
}


1;
```

Note the strange $^X variable in the code. This provides the name of the command used to execute the currently running copy of Perl. As this is a rather ugly solution, it suggests that if at all possible you should use Catalyst::Controller::CGIBin.

Now if you visit http://localhost:3000/wrapcgi/acgi.pl, you will see the same page source yet again.

Intelligent Use of Base Controllers

Recall the LolCatalyst-Lite application from Chapter 4. We had two separate views, the Web (Template Toolkit) view and the Web Service (JSON) view. Originally, we called the translate_ service action in our Root controller, which is fine for the very simple original web service. However, if we wanted to extend the web service, things would become pretty unwieldy in short order. Fortunately, fixing this issue is fairly quick.

First, we can write the new controller:

```perl
package LolCatalyst::Lite::Controller::Translate::Service;

use strict;
use warnings;
use parent qw(LolCatalyst::Lite::Controller::Translate);

sub base :Chained('/') :PathPart('translate/service') :CaptureArgs(0) {
    my ($self, $c) = @_;
    $self->next::method($c);
    $c->stash(current_view => 'Service');
}


1;
```

This is pretty neat, but we can take it further, as we want identical dispatch logic for the public action /translate/service to the original controller but with just a different view. We can remove the action declaration and move everything into the package configuration:

```
package LolCatalyst::Lite::Controller::Translate::Service;

use strict;
use warnings;
use parent qw(LolCatalyst::Lite::Controller::Translate);

__PACKAGE__->config(
  current_view => 'Service',
  actions => {
    base => {
      PathPart => 'translate/service'
    },
  },
);


1;
```

We will want to write tests to cover this functionality in t/controller_Translate_Service.t as well. These tests are in fact very similar to the tests in t/controller_Translate.t, so we present the following patch in unified diff format to make the differences between the two test files clear:

```
--- t/controller_Translate.t    2009-04-26 00:51:37.000000000 +1000
+++ t/controller_Translate_Service.t    2009-04-26 00:51:37.000000000 +1000
@@ -9,7 +9,7 @@
 my ($request, $response);

 $request = POST(
-          'http://localhost/translate',
+          'http://localhost/translate/service',
          'Content-Type' => 'form-data',
          'Content'      => [
             'lol' => 'Can i have a cheese burger?',
@@ -17,11 +17,11 @@

 ok( $response = request($request), 'Request');
 ok( $response->is_success, 'Response Successful 2xx' );
-is( $response->content_type, 'text/html', 'Response Content-Type' );
+is( $response->content_type, 'application/json', 'Response Content-Type' );
 like( $response->content, qr/CHEEZ/, "contains translated string");
```

```
  ok(
-   $response = request(GET 'http://localhost/translate/1'),
+   $response = request(GET 'http://localhost/translate/service/1'),
    'Request for default translation type'
  );

@@ -30,14 +30,14 @@
  like( $response->content, qr/CHEEZ/, "contains translated string");

  ok(
-   $response = request(GET 'http://localhost/translate/100'),
+   $response = request(GET 'http://localhost/translate/service/100'),
    'Request for default translation type on nonexistent object'
  );

  cmp_ok( $response->code, '==', 404, '404 error returned');

  ok(
-   $response = request(GET 'http://localhost/translate/1/to/LOLCAT'),
+   $response = request(GET 'http://localhost/translate/service/1/to/LOLCAT'),
    'Request for specific translation type'
  );

@@ -46,7 +46,7 @@
  like( $response->content, qr/CHEEZ/, "contains translated string");

  ok(
-   $response = request(GET 'http://localhost/translate/1/to/NONEXISTENT'),
+   $response = request(GET 'http://localhost/translate/service/1/to/NONEXISTENT'),
    'Request for nonexistent translation type'
  );
```

Finally, we've made our original translate_service action in the Root controller redundant, so we can update this to provide backward compatibility:

```
sub translate_service : Local {
    my ($self, $c) = @_;
    $c->res_redirect($c->uri_for('/translate/service', $c->req->args);
}
```

Note how we use a redirect rather than $c->detach in order to signal to the end user that there has been some permanent change in our application's functionality.

See Also

Refer to Chapter 4 for the LolCatalyst-Lite application and the end of Chapter 7 for information on chaining public path dispatch through configuration.

Catalyst::View::Email::Template

Note Code in this recipe was provided by Alexander Hartmaier.

Sending e-mail is an integral part of most web applications. In this recipe, we'll show you how to send e-mail starting with the standard MyApp. You'll then want to install Catalyst::View:: Email::Template and Email::Send from CPAN.

First, we add a standard Template Toolkit view. For this we can use the helper:

```
$ script/myapp_create view TT TT
```

We then add an Email::Template view. We create lib/MyApp/View/Email/Template.pm and add the following:

```
package MyApp::View::Email::Template;

use strict;
use base 'Catalyst::View::Email::Template';

__PACKAGE__->config(
    stash_key       => 'email',
    template_prefix => ''
);
```

Along with this, we need to configure this view with system-specific data, which goes in myapp.conf.

```
name            MyApp
default_view    TT
# this is the Catalyst::View::Email config
<View::Email::Template>
    <sender>
        mailer SMTP
        <mailer_args>
            Host    127.0.0.1
        </mailer_args>
    </sender>
    <default>
        content_type    text/html
        charset         utf-8
    </default>
</View::Email::Template>
```

This code sets up the application to use an SMTP server running on the local machine, along with the content type. See the documentation for Email::Send for more complex configuration.

Now we add the following private action to the Root controller (put your own e-mail address in the to field if you want to see the results):

```
sub email : Private {
    my ( $self, $c ) = @_;

    $c->stash->{email} = {
        to          => 'user@example.com',
        from        => 'myapp@company.com',
        subject     => '[MyApp] notification',
        template    => 'email.tt',
    };

    $c->forward( $c->view('Email::Template') );
}
```

We also need to add the email.tt template into the application's root/ directory:

```
<?xml version="1.0" encoding="UTF-8" ?>
<!DOCTYPE html PUBLIC "-//W3C//DTD XHTML 1.0 Strict//EN"
        "http://www.w3.org/TR/xhtml1/DTD/xhtml1-strict.dtd">
<html xmlns="http://www.w3.org/1999/xhtml" xml:lang="en" lang="en">
<head>
    <meta http-equiv="Content-type" content="text/html; charset=UTF-8" />
</head>
<body>
MyApp sent you an email!
</body>
</html>
```

Next, we modify the index action in the Root controller to be as follows:

```
sub index :Path :Args(0) {
    my ( $self, $c ) = @_;
      $c->forward('/email');

    # then show the user a status page
    if ( scalar( @{ $c->error } ) ) {
        $c->error(0); # Reset the error condition if you need to
        $c->response->body('There was an error sending the email!');
    } else {
        $c->response->body('Email sent OK! (At least as far as we can tell)');
    }
}
```

Finally, we want to modify our code so we send both an HTML e-mail and a plain text e-mail. To do so, we have to change the content of the email stash key to the following:

```
$c->stash->{email} = {
    to              => 'user@example.com',
    from            => 'myapp@company.com',
    subject         => '[MyApp] notification',
    # if all of our mails contain plain text and html, we can
    # change the default content_type in myapp.conf,
    # if not, do it here per mail
    content_type    => 'multipart/alternative',
    templates   => [
        {
            template        => 'email.plain.tt',
            content_type    => 'text/plain',
            charset         => 'utf-8',
            # we might even specify a nondefault view here
            view            => 'TT',
        },
        {
            template        => 'email.html.tt',
            content_type    => 'text/html',
            charset         => 'utf-8',
        },
    ],
};
```

We now have an application capable of sending e-mail.

See Also

Refer to the documentation for Email::Send and Catalyst::View::Email::Template. See Chapter 12 for how to send an e-mail in Reaction, a more advanced framework based on Catalyst. This recipe provides a good point of comparison between Catalyst and Reaction.

Miscellaneous Recipes

These recipes present various aspects of Catalyst development that relate to the functionality of an application but don't fit neatly into the MVC design.

Run Parts of an Application As a Stand-Alone Script

One important thing about following the fat model design pattern (see Figure 1-2 in Chapter 1) is that it makes it easy to run parts of your application independently of Catalyst. Recall from Chapter 6 the discussion about not actually allowing a user to delete him- or herself, but marking the user as deleted for later deletion by an administrator. This is much better done without having to run your full application.

In this recipe, we'll consider a stand-alone script that lives in an application's script directory. Using the application itself to get the model, the script looks like this:

```
#!usr/bin/env perl
use warnings;
use strict;
use FindBin qw($Bin);
use lib "$Bin/../lib";
use MyApp;
my $schema = MyApp->model->('DB');
my $result = $schema->resultset('Users')->search({ marked_deleted => 1} );
# and so on ...
```

This creates substantial overhead and will really gum up system resources if it runs regularly. Depending on the architecture of the application, this script could cause other problems, too. It's much better to rely on the database schema alone in this instance.

```
#!usr/bin/env perl
use warnings;
use strict;
use FindBin qw($Bin);
use lib "$Bin/../lib";
use MyApp::DB;
my $dsn = get_dsn();
my $schema = MyApp::DB->connect($dsn);
my $result = $schema->resultset('Users')->search({ marked_deleted => 1} );
# and so on ...

use Config::General;
sub get_dsn {
    $config = ParseConfig("$Bin/../myapp.conf");
    return $config->{Model::DB}
}
```

It's good practice to make sure that you always write stand-alone scripts in the second way, with the independent model, rather than the first way, where you depend on MyApp.

MojoMojo: The Catalyst Wiki

Note Thanks to Mateu Hunter and other MojoMojo developers for the instructions in this recipe.

MojoMojo is a sophisticated web application that requires some effort to install and configure. Despite the extra work, MojoMojo has a number of features that make it an attractive proposition. It supports all of the popular wiki markup syntaxes (and Perl's POD format) with live markup. It doesn't require disambiguation pages like other wikis, as it stores data in a tree structure (e.g., /plants/Paris vs. cities/Paris), but it also supports tagging for entries that don't neatly fit into a hierarchy. MojoMojo's permission system is very flexible and powerful, with the ability to restrict who can view and edit pages separately. For more information on MojoMojo's features, see http://www.mojomojo.org/advocacy.

In this recipe, we'll step through the MojoMojo installation process to reap the benefits of a high-grade web page authoring system. From the command line, use the CPAN client to install MojoMojo:

```
cpan MojoMojo
```

Many Module Dependencies

MojoMojo has a long chain of CPAN dependencies. CPAN will ask if you want to install any modules MojoMojo relies on that you don't currently have installed. Respond "yes" to all mandatory modules, and decide for yourself if you want optional modules. Some Formatter modules are optional (e.g., DocBook), so respond "no" unless you want them. Not requiring installation of certain system packages (DocBook, XSLT, etc.) will make overall installation easier. This step is the most time-consuming part of installing MojoMojo. There may be a package available for your operating system, packaged for FreeBSD in the p5-MojoMojo port. By the time of this book's publication, there may also be packages for the Debian and Ubuntu Linux distributions.

If you have to install CPAN dependencies, this is the slowest part of the process.

Tests

MojoMojo requires some external libraries to be installed on your system. In particular it wants libxml (http://www.xmlsoft.org/downloads.html) and libjpeg (http://en.wikipedia. org/wiki/Libjpeg and http://www.ijg.org/). If one of these is not installed, you may see test failures like this:

```
t/schema_DBIC_Attachment.t .. 1/13 format 'jpeg' not supported -
formats bmp, ico, pnm, raw, sgi, tga available for
reading at /home/user/D/MojoMojo-0.999028/lib/MojoMojo/Schema/Result/
          Photo.pm line 177.
```

For Imager, you may need to force install Imager from the CPAN shell once you have installed libjpeg.

Setting Up the Wiki

Once all the necessary modules are installed, you need to configure MojoMojo. You will need to find the location where MojoMojo was installed and find the configuration file, mojomojo. conf. It lives in the same directory as MojoMojo/INSTALL, which should be just under wherever MojoMojo.pm ended up, for example, /usr/local/share/perl/5.10.0/MojoMojo/mojomojo.conf.

Another way to find the configuration file is to use the location of MojoMojo.pm. The mojomojo.conf file lives in the MojoMojo/ subdirectory of where MojoMojo.pm is found. You can find where MojoMojo.pm is as follows:

```
perl -MMojoMojo -le 'print $INC{"MojoMojo.pm"}'
```

This will print out something like the following:

```
/usr/local/share/perl/5.10.0/MojoMojo.pm
```

Once you've located your configuration file, it's time to make some edits to match your particular needs.

Database Configuration

The database connection information is very important. It is standard DBI connection information, and you can choose among PostgreSQL, MySQL, and SQLite. They are configured as follows:

- *PostgreSQL*: connect_info dbi:Pg:dbname=mojomojo;host=localhost;port=5432 connect_info user connect_info password

- *MySQL*: connect_info dbi:mysql:database=mojo_database;host=localhost connect_info user connect_info password

- *SQLite*: connect_info dbi:SQLite:/var/lib/mojomojo/mojomojo.db connect_info not_used connect_info not_used

---

▌Note SQLite does not require a username/password. Access privileges are based on the file permissions of mojomojo.db.

You can leave the default of

```
index_dir __path_to(index)__
```

which will cause the search engine (KinoSearch) to place its index/ directory under where mojomojo.conf was installed.

A custom directory path for MojoMojo search index files can be specified in mojomojo.conf as follows:

```
index_dir /var/lib/mojomojo/search_index
```

You can leave the default of

```
attachment_dir __path_to(uploads)__
```

which will cause the uploads to be placed in the uploads/ directory under where mojomojo.conf was installed.

A custom directory path for upload files can be specified in mojomojo.conf as follows:

```
attachment_dir /var/lib/mojomojo/uploads
```

You can simply use the mojomojo.conf file to configure MojoMojo for your needs, but a better idea is to copy mojomojo.conf over to mojomojo_local.conf after it's been configured. This local configuration file will override settings in mojomojo.conf and be preserved upon upgrades of your MojoMojo installation that create a new mojomojo.conf.

Initialize the Database

Now that you have database connection information, you can initialize the MojoMojo database. This process asks a few questions about your particular MojoMojo instance, such as the site name and admin account information. Run this from the directory where `mojomojo.conf` lives:

```
$ mojomojo_spawn_db.pl
```

and you will see the following set of questions, to which you can accept the default or type in something different:

```
It's time to set some default values:
Name of the wiki? [default MojoMojo]
Username of the admin user? [default admin]
Password of the admin user? [default admin]
Full name of the admin user? [default root]
E-Mail address of the admin user? [default root@localhost]
E-Mail address of the Anonymous user? [default anonymous.coward@localhost]
Deploying schema to dbi:SQLite:/var/www/db/mojomojo.db
Creating initial data
Success!
```

Start Up MojoMojo

Now you are ready to reap the rewards of installation. Start up the MojoMojo application as follows:

```
mojomojo_server.pl
```

This will start an instance on port 3000. You should see something like this:

```
You can connect to your server at http://localhost:3000
```

Go the URL you are presented with after you start MojoMojo and log in with the admin account you created, which defaults to a username and password of "admin."

See Also

For community support, you can use the MojoMojo IRC channel #mojomojo on server `irc.perl.org` or the project mailing list, which you can browse or subscribe to from `http://lists.scsys.co.uk/cgi-bin/mailman/listinfo/mojomojo`. If you require commercial support for MojoMojo, this is also the place to make inquiries.

Persistent Login and API Authentication

Most public-facing sites nowadays have some form of a persistent login system that allows users to return to the site days or even weeks after a visit and have the site continue to recognize who they are without their having to log in again.

In Chapter 8, you saw that Catalyst has a robust authentication system that allows for flexible authentication sources, user persistence, and permissions checking. By default, once a user is authenticated, that user remains authenticated for the duration of his or her session.

This session length can be anything from until the user closes the browser to weeks or months. Unfortunately, long-running sessions can produce difficult data management scenarios, not the least of which is additional storage requirements for each user of your site. For this reason, it is usually better to come up with a different way to handle persistent login that is going to last more than a day or two.

We've seen persistent login implemented in many different ways over the years, but rarely have we seen it done well. In this recipe, we'll show you how to create a long-term persistent login system that you can easily apply to any of your web applications.

Authentication Keys

The key to persistent login is a token, which we will call an *auth key*, that uniquely identifies a single user on your site. You relay this auth key to and from the browser in the form of a cookie.

Your auth key should *not* be guessable and should *not* be in any decodable form. Many times, we've seen an authentication key–type solution for persistent login, but because it was a known value, it was completely insecure. We've seen everything from just a user's e-mail address to a user's DB ID in Base64 encoding. The problem with this is obvious—if the auth key is guessable or decodable, someone who can figure it out can break into a user's account.

There are many options for generating an auth key, but in practice simpler is usually better. With that in mind, we will use the String::Random CPAN module to generate a 64-character string that we will place in the user's database record. The benefit of using the String::Random method is that it has nothing whatsoever to do with the user's information, so it is not guessable based on any data that an attacker might have about your user.

The easiest way to implement the preceding is just to add an auth_key column to your user table, and populate the column when the user registers or when the user logs in. We will do the latter here, since we need to send the cookie at the time of authentication anyway. Our addition to the login controller is as follows:

```perl
sub login : Path('login') {
    my ($self, $c) = @_;

    ## other login code here
    if ($c->authenticate( { username =>
            $c->request->params->{'username'},
                        password =>
            $c->request->params->{'password'}
        }) )
    {
        # authentication is successful
        if ( $c->request->params->{'keep_me_logged_in'} )
        {
            if ( !$c->user->get('auth_key') )
            {
                # we do not have a defined auth_key, let's create one.
                $c->user->obj->auth_key(
                    String::Random::random_string('.'x64) );
                $c->user->obj->update();
            }
```

```
            $c->response->cookies->{'auth_key'} = {
                            value => $c->user->get('auth_key'),
                            domain => '.yourdomain.com',
                            expires => '+2M',
                        };

            $c->response->cookies->{'username'} = {
                            value => $c->user->get('username'),
                            domain => '.yourdomain.com',
                            expires => "+2M",
                        };
        }

        ## do other post-login work here
    }
}
```

That's it. The preceding code adds both the generation of the auth_key if it doesn't exist and the passing of the auth key to the user's browser in the form of a cookie.

We do, however, have a problem. We have to come up with a way to use the auth key to authenticate users. Luckily for us, the Catalyst authentication system can be configured to have multiple authentication methods. These methods are referred to as *realms*, and it is very easy to add them to our application. In our application configuration, we simply add a new realm that we will use for auth key–based authentication. Within our lib/MyApp.pm file, we can add our new realm called authkeyusers:

```
__PACKAGE__->config(
    authentication => {
        default_realm => 'users',
        users => {
                credential => {
                    class => 'Password',
                    password_field => 'password',
                    password_type => 'crypted',
                },
                store => {
                    class => 'DBIx::Class',
                    user_class => 'MyApp::Users',
                }
        },
        authkeyusers => {
            credential => {
                class => 'Password',
                password_type => 'none',
            },
            store => {
                class => 'DBIx::Class',
                user_class => 'MyApp::Users',
            }
        }
    }
);
```

Adding the authkeyusers realm allows us to authenticate using only our auth key. Note that when we add a second realm, we need to tell the authentication system which one it should use by default. The easiest way to do this is to set default_realm to the name of our default authentication realm.

Now that we've added our new realm, we have a method to authenticate, but we are not quite finished. We must provide a nonintrusive way to authenticate using the auth key, and we must do this in a way that allows us to run the code before any other part of the page processing occurs. Again, luckily for us, Catalyst provides a way for us to add exactly this sort of code to our application. In the Root controller (lib/Controller/Root.pm), we can add a method called auto that will run at the start of each request. This is the perfect spot to add our auth key check:

```perl
sub auto : Private {
    my ($self, $c) = @_;

    ## let's do our auth key check.
    ## first we don't bother if the user is already logged in:
    if ( !$c->user_exists() )
    {
        if (exists($c->req->cookies->{'username'} &&
            exists($c->req->cookies->{'auth_key'} ))
        {
    ## we have both required cookies, let's do our authentication
    if ( !$c->authenticate({
                username => $c->req->cookies->{'username'},
                auth_key => $c->req->cookies->{'auth_key'}
        }, 'authkeyusers') ) {
    ## note that we are here only if authentication fails.
    ## if it fails, we want to destroy the cookies so that
    ## we don't waste time performing this check on every request

        $c->response->cookies->{'auth_key'} = { value => '',
                                                expires => '-1M' };
        $c->response->cookies->{'username'} = { value => '',
                                                expires => '-1M' };
            }
        }
    }
}
```

Adding this code to our Root controller's auto method will ensure that it is run every time a request is made; hence no matter what page the user visits on the site, the first request will trigger the automatic reauthentication.

The most important line in the preceding code is the call to $c->authenticate. The realm we set up does not do a check against the password field—instead, our new realm looks to find a user in the database that matches both the username and auth_key fields provided. If it finds a user matching those credentials, the user is authenticated. This happens transparently, and since auto runs before any other action, it will appear to your code elsewhere that the user has already signed in.

The code also ensures that we have the cookies we need before we attempt to authenticate. This is because the call to `$c->authenticate()` is potentially expensive in that it hits the database server. Adding this authentication process here without these safeguard checks in place could add an additional database call for every request to our application (potentially even static files). Needless to say, we would not want that on a busy public-facing site.

One additional thing to notice is that if authentication fails, we delete the username and auth_key cookies. This is to ensure that we do not wind up performing this check over and over with every web request. If they fail the first time, they are going to fail every time they are presented.

What About API Access?

API access within your application is easily accomplished using the exact same method described previously. The only change you need to make is to add the auth key as a parameter to your API calls. Then, instead of retrieving the auth key from the cookie, retrieve it from the query parameter. If you are using auth keys only for API access, you can also move the authentication check from your Root controller's auto method to the API controller's auto method (or the root of the API chain, if you are using chained dispatch).

Some Important Notes About Persistent Login

Adding the code in the previous section to your application gives you a quick and easy persistent login. There are, however, some important things to note about the code.

You probably noticed that we actually use two cookies to perform the auth check, auth_key and username. Strictly speaking, this is not necessary if the authentication key is unique across all users. For the sake of simplicity, we did not perform a uniqueness check on our auth key, so we must provide another piece of information that is unique. In this case, we used the username. If you add the code required to ensure uniqueness of the auth key, you can omit the username from the cookies and from the `$c->authenticate()` call.

Another thing to note is that since the auth key is not tied to the password, the auth key will permit authorized access to the site even if the user has changed his or her password. The primary reason users change their password is that someone learned it or they think that someone might have learned it. Since the auth key effectively bypasses the password once the user logs in, it is a good idea to either clear or regenerate the user's auth key whenever the user changes his or her password.

Finally, it should be noted that while it is difficult to obtain the auth key for a user, if someone does get physical access to the user's computer, the user's auth key could be copied down and then added on a different computer. Enabling persistent login also means that the computer the user uses will have full access to the user's account, no matter who is using it. For these reasons, *precautions should be taken to ensure that further verification of the user's identity is required when performing sensitive operations.* One example might be to require the original password before allowing the password to be changed. Another example would be to require complete reauthorization before using or allowing any stored credit card or other sensitive information on the site.

Multirealm and Progressive Authentication

There are a large number of different authentication interfaces on CPAN that allow Catalyst's authentication system to interface with a variety of systems. Kerberos, htpasswd, LDAP, and OpenID are just a few of the options available. It's not hard to find an interface that will plug right into the Catalyst authentication system and will do what you need it to do.

When you are building a new web application, you get to design how users will be stored and what method of authentication they will use. Often, though, you are in a position of replacing or adding to an existing system. Other times, you have to bring together users from multiple active systems within another system, or authenticate users from a third-party service. Fortunately, unlike many other frameworks, Catalyst allows as many sources for authentication as you like in any given application. These authentication sources are referred to as *realms.*

Setting up multirealm authentication is quite easy. You simply add a realm to your authentication configuration to the realm's configuration requirements. For example, if we were using one database for one set of users and a legacy admin table for site admins, our authentication configuration might look like this:

```
__PACKAGE__->config(
    'Plugin::Authentication' => {
        default_realm => 'dbusers',
        dbusers => {
            credential => {
                class => 'Password',
                password_field => 'secret',
                password_type  => 'hashed',
                password_hash_type => 'SHA-1',
            },
            store => {
                class       => 'DBIx::Class',
                user_class => 'Schema::Person::Identity',
            },
        },
        adminusers => {
            credential => {
                class => 'Password',
                password_field => 'secret',
                password_type  => 'hashed',
                password_hash_type => 'SHA-1',
            },
            store => {
                class       => 'DBIx::Class',
                user_class => 'Schema::Person::Identity',
            },
        },
    },
);
```

This is pretty straightforward. Now that we have both realms defined, we can choose which one to authenticate against in our login code. We would likely want to have separate login processes, one for site users and one for admins. Because we set the `default_realm` configuration option to `dbusers`, calls to `$c->authenticate` would access the `dbusers` realm. In order to log in our admin users, we need to specify that we want to authenticate against that group of users. We do this by adding an additional argument to the `$c->authenticate` call, like so:

```
sub adminlogin : Path('adminlogin') {
    my ($self, $c) = @_;

    ## do login stuff
    if ($c->authenticate({
                username => $c->req->params->{'username'},
                password => $c->req->params->{'password'}
                }, 'adminusers')) {
        ## do post-login stuff here.
    }
}
```

Note the `'adminusers'` argument to the authenticate call. This tells the authentication system to use the `adminusers` realm to perform the authentication. This is all fairly straight-forward, and our admin users are now able to use the `adminlogin` action to log into the site. For the most part, `$c->user` will respond normally, and the environment for the developer is exactly the same as if a user authenticated. We can tell if the authenticated user came from the `adminusers` realm by calling `$c->user_in_realm('adminusers' )`.

Everything we are used to in Catalyst authentication works in this configuration. It is, however, not as clean as we would like. We need to have two separate login pages, even though after login, apart from access controls, our users are essentially the same from the developer's perspective. There has to be a better way.

Unsurprisingly, there is: the Progressive realm. The Progressive realm provides an auto-matic way for us to call multiple authentication processes until one of them succeeds or they all fail. What this means is that our login action can be as simple in the multirealm authentica-tion configuration as in a single-realm configuration, and Catalyst will do the right thing.

Configuring the Progressive realm is actually quite simple. All we have to do is create a new realm in our authentication configuration, tell it to use the Progressive class, and indicate the order in which we want the other realms tried. Our previous example using the Progressive realm would look like this:

```
__PACKAGE__->config(
    'Plugin::Authentication' => {
        default_realm => 'do_in_order',
        do_in_order => {
            class => 'Progressive',
            realms => [ 'dbusers', 'adminusers' ],
        },
```

```
            dbusers => {
                credential => {
                    class => 'Password',
                    password_field => 'secret',
                    password_type   => 'hashed',
                    password_hash_type => 'SHA-1',
                },
                store => {
                    class        => 'DBIx::Class',
                    user_class => 'Schema::Person::Identity',
                },
            },

            adminusers => {
                credential => {
                    class => 'Password',
                    password_field => 'secret',
                    password_type   => 'hashed',
                    password_hash_type => 'SHA-1',
                },
                store => {
                    class        => 'DBIx::Class',
                    user_class => 'Schema::Person::Identity',
                },
            },
        },
    );
```

And that's it. We can get rid of the `adminlogin` action altogether. Since we set our `default_realm` to our new Progressive realm, when we call `$c->authenticate` in our main login action, Catalyst will attempt authentication in the order we defined in the `realms` portion of the Progressive configuration. In the example just shown, it would attempt authentication first using the `dbusers` realm and, failing that, it would try the `adminusers` realm with the same information. If one of them succeeds, the user will be authenticated and our code works as normal. If they both fail, then the user is denied access.

All of this happens behind the scenes, so our application code is as simple as if we had only a single source of authentication. `$c->user_in_realm('adminusers')` still works, and everything functions the same as if we still had two separate login processes, but we've simplified our code significantly.

The Catalyst authentication system combined with multiple-realm and progressive authentication methods provide an unprecedented amount of flexibility in how you authenticate your users, while offering a simple, standard way of interacting with the user postauthentication. In this example, we dealt with normal and admin class users. We could just as easily have had a system with both local users and remote users who were authenticating via an OpenID provider or their account on Facebook.

Deploy with a Cache

When you are building a public-facing site, there is little you can do to improve performance that is more effective than adding a cache. Adding a cache, however, buys you nothing if your application doesn't tell it what to do. Adding cache control to your Catalyst application is so easy that there is absolutely no reason not to do it.

The key to controlling caching, whether the cache is in the browser or in a cache server, is the Cache-Control header. This header tells the requesting cache or browser exactly what to do with the content that it is receiving.

This header has a lot of options that you can investigate in the HTTP 1.1 RFC, but only two are really important. The two forms of the Cache-Control header that we care about are max-age, which sets the amount of time a page can be cached, and no-cache, which indicates that the content cannot be cached at all. Examples of these headers are as follows:

```
B<Tells the cache not to cache the response.>
Cache-Control: no-cache

B<Tells the cache to cache the response for 5 minutes (300 seconds)>
Cache-Control: max-age=300
```

It doesn't get much simpler than that. Adding this to the response in Catalyst is a simple matter of adding the header to the response object:

```
# tell the requestor not to cache this item
$c->response->header('Cache-Control' => 'no-cache')

# tell the requestor it's ok to cache the response for 300 seconds
$c->response->header('Cache-Control' => 'max-age=300');
```

If you add these responses as appropriate in your Catalyst actions, your cache server or browser will obey the instructions you give it. Sprinkling these responses around your application code, though, is somewhat messy. It also gets extremely complicated when you start using chained actions, as different parts of the chain may require different caching.

Fortunately, there is an easy way to deal with this. We can create an entry in the stash that contains the time the response can be cached. Each action can then specify its own expiration time. Then, no matter how many actions we pass through, we will still know the cache time we should add to the response.

We could do this by extending Catalyst in some way, but it's actually much easier than that. We can add an entry to the stash that contains all the cache information. Let's call it $c->stash->{cachecontrol}. If we create an element under this for each action we pass through, we can later determine the correct cache time to use. Let's see what this would look like:

```
sub articleview : Path('view') {
    my ($self, $c) = @_;

    # Don't allow articleview to last more than 5 minutes
    $c->stash->{'cachecontrol'}{'articleview'} = 300;
```

```
        # do whatever else the articleview action does
        # ...
    }
```

This continues to work even if we use chained dispatch, as each element of the chain can have its own expiration. By the end of the request, all the information required to set our cache time is collected in one place. We still have to get it to the requesting server or browser, though.

Fortunately, Catalyst provides a way to handle something at the very end of the request. The end action in each controller runs after all the other actions are run. If the controller does not have an end action, Catalyst will fall back to the parent packages, eventually landing at the Root controller. Most of the time, final processing for the request (including triggering of the view) happens in the Root end action. This is where we will add our cache control logic.

If your application is like most, your Root end action looks something like this:

```
sub end : ActionClass('RenderView') {}
```

Obviously, this needs to be expanded to handle cache control logic. Remember that we have a stash variable that contains all of our expiration information. We have to boil this down to a single time to send to the client. The correct behavior in most cases is to use the shortest expiration time out of all the actions, so we need to boil down the cache time to a single value. Also, since we do not want the browser or cache to store an error, we need to ensure that if we experience an error, we set the cache time to zero. Let's change our Root end action to do that:

```
sub end : ActionClass('RenderView') {
    my ( $self, $c ) = @_;

    # $cachetime will be our final cache time
    # after processing the cachecontrol hash.
    # we start by setting it to the default cache
    # time in seconds. (20 minutes here)
    my $cachetime = 1200;

    # check to see if we have an uncacheable scenario.
    # if we do, force $cachetime to 0.
    if ( $c->req->method() eq 'POST' || $c->user_exists()
        || scalar @{ $c->error } ) {
            $cachetime = 0;
    }
    else {
        # otherwise we examine each element
        # of cachecontrol to find the shortest
        # cache time set.

        foreach my $section ( keys %{$c->stash->{'cachecontrol'}} ) {
```

```
            # if the currently selected cachecontrol value is lower
            # than the $cachetime value so far, we drop the $cachetime
            # to the new limit.
            if ($c->stash->{'cachecontrol'}{$section} < $cachetime) {
                $cachetime = $c->stash->{'cachecontrol'}{$section};
            }
        }
    }

    if ($cachetime == 0) {

        # if $cachetime is 0, then we can't cache the page and we
        # need to tell our requesting server/browser that.

        $c->response->header('Cache-Control' => 'no-cache')

    }
    else {
        # otherwise we set max-age to the cache time specified.
        $c->response->header('Cache-Control' =>
                             'max-age=' . $cachetime);
    }

}
```

Now our application will tell cache servers and browsers the right thing to do with our data.

You'll notice some additional uncacheable checks in the preceding code. That is because there are some things aside from errors that make our response uncacheable. Perhaps the most important is that we almost always do not want to cache data when a user is logged in, as it is likely to be tailored to the user in question. If you are talking to the browser directly, using the cache is fine, but if you are using a cache server, it's wise to include a check for an authenticated user. This is not a hard and fast rule, and it can be avoided when using things like Edge Side Includes (ESI), but it's important to be careful with authenticated users. There is nothing quite as alarming as visiting your profile page and seeing someone else's credit card information.

Which brings us to another point: you generally do not want to cache responses to form submissions. The preceding code will automatically force responses from POST requests to be uncachable. If you follow the good practice of making all form submissions use the POST method, the preceding code will ensure that no one is ever served a cached response from any form submission.

Controlling web caching is an extremely easy and worthwhile addition to your application, and it can increase your site's performance dramatically, sometimes by as much as over 100 times. Even if your data must be super-fresh, a cache time of one minute means that for any given piece of data, you have to perform the work to retrieve it/process it only once every 60 seconds. This can make all the difference in the world on a busy site.

See Also

See the following for more information:

- *Making Your Catalyst App Cache-Friendly:* `http://dev.catalyst.perl.org/wiki/adventcalendararticles/2007/11-Making_your_Catalyst_App_Cache-friendly`

- *Using the Varnish cache with Catalyst:* `http://www.catalystframework.org/calendar/2008/14`

- *Using Edge Side Includes with Catalyst:* `http://www.catalystframework.org/calendar/2008/17`

- *The SubInclude recipe in this chapter* (in the section titled "Catalyst::View::Component::SubInclude")

Development Process

The recipes in this section present various issues related to the Catalyst development process.

Enforce Coding Standards with Perl::Critic and Perl::Tidy

We think Perl is marvelous because of its rich expressive syntax and the fact that it's an excellent general-purpose programming language. However, some regard the expressivity of Perl as a drawback, as it can be difficult to implement a consistent programming style across multiple members of a team. Fortunately, two tools are available that go a long way toward allaying these concerns: Perl::Tidy and Perl::Critic.

The first, Perl::Tidy, is just a reformatter that deals with indentation issues. The second, Perl::Critic, is a static source code analyzer that will tell you if your Perl code is up to scratch. By default, it uses policies from the book *Perl Best Practices* by Damian Conway (O'Reilly, 2005), but you can write your own policies as well.

Most version-control programs provide some precommit utility that allows you to run code before it is committed into the repository. You could use this to ensure you don't commit anything that causes failing tests, or in this case, we're going to prevent the committing of code that doesn't pass Perl::Tidy and Perl::Critic tests. We'll show how to use this with the git version control software.

We place the following script in the file `.git/hooks/pre-commit` and ensure that it is executable (`chmod +x .git/hooks/pre-commit` on a Unix system):

```perl
#!/usr/bin/perl

use warnings;
use strict;
use Perl6::Slurp;
use Perl::Critic;
use Perl::Tidy; # dies if perltidy not installed

my $status = slurp '-|', 'git-status';
```

```perl
# only want what is going to be committed
$status =~ s/Changed but not updated.*$//s;

my @dirty =
grep { !file_is_tidy($_) }
grep { !file_meets_policy($_)} # critic violations
grep { /\.(pl|pod|pm|t)$/ } # perl file
map { /(?:modified|new file):\s+(\S+)/ } # to be commited
split "\n", $status;

exit 0 unless @dirty; # Alles gut

warn qq{
Something you tried to commit is not tidy or  violates Perl::Critic policy
Please fix before committing.
}

exit 1;

### utility functions #############################################

sub file_is_tidy {
    my $file = shift;

    my $original = slurp $file;
    my $tidied = slurp '-|', 'perltidy', $file, '-st';

    return $original eq $tidied;
}

sub file_meets_policy {
    my $file = shift;
    my $code = slurp $file;
    my $critic = Perl::Critic->new(-severity=> 'gentle');
    my @violations = $critic->critique(\$code);
    return @violations ? undef : 1 ;
}
```

Now if we try to commit a file that either Perl::Tidy or Perl::Critic doesn't like, we get the following error:

```
Something you tried to commit is not tidy or violates Perl::Critic policy
Please fix before committing.
```

This script is a proof of concept. You'll want to modify it appropriately before using it to get a sensible error message on failed commit, and likely so that you use your own preferred Perl::Critic policies. To work out how the script operates, you could use the debugger by modifying the shebang (first line of the script) to be #! /usr/bin/perl -d to drop into the debugger. Alternatively, you could use Carp::REPL as detailed in the section titled "Alternative to perl -d: Devel::REPL and CatalystX::REPL."

See Also

Refer to the documentation for Perl::Critic and Perl::Tidy. A useful article on Perl::Critic is available at http://perltraining.com.au/tips/2009-02-05.html.

Advanced Usage of Catalyst::Test

▐**Note** This recipe was written in collaboration with Jos Boumans.

When testing your application, in almost every case, you'll need to keep testing data separate from production data. This recipe shows you one way of doing so. We'll also touch on an exciting new feature of Catalyst::Test. Our code is based on an actual application.

Placing Configuration in a Constants File

We create a lib directory as a subdirectory of t ourselves. You'll usually want to start testing so that your application data is identical at the beginning of every test run. The best way of doing this is by including a file, as it simplifies configuration of your test suite and allows you to set up reasonable defaults (or scaffolding). The following is an example of such a script. A sensible name is inc.pl and a sensible location is inside the application's t/lib directory.

```perl
use strict;
use warnings;

# chdir to the dir the test directory. Now we always know where we are
# relative to other files.
BEGIN {
 use FindBin     qw/$Bin/;

 # test script dir
 chdir $Bin if -d $Bin;

 # Include our application dir and our own lib dir
 use lib "$Bin/../lib";
 use lib "$Bin/lib";

 # Set up the testing config.
 # Note, because this is included in the script in t/ FindBin finds the
 # location of the test script, not this inc.pl script.
 $ENV{CATALYST_CONFIG} = "$Bin/lib/myapp.conf";
}

# load the application in -- it's something we have to do for *every* test
use Catalyst::Test 'MyApp';
```

```
# make the Dump() sub available in every test for debugging output
use YAML qw/Dump/;

use vars qw/ $User $Passwd $Mech /; # a rare use of global variables in perl.

# Set up a ready to use TWMC
use Test::WWW::Mechanize::Catalyst;
$Mech    = Test::WWW::Mechanize::Catalyst->new( catalyst_app => 'MyApp' );

# login credentials for all testing code
$User    = 'test';
$Passwd  = 'test';

1;
```

Now in our regular test script, we'll have the following at the top of the file:

```
use strict;
use warnings;
use Test::More 'no_plan';

BEGIN { use FindBin;
        require "$FindBin::Bin/lib/inc.pl";
        use_ok 'MyApp::Controller::Root';
}

my $req = POST '/login', [ user => $User, pass => $Passwd ];
ok( $req,            "Testing match: " . $req->uri );
```

Here's the exciting new feature of Catalyst::Test. As well as an HTTP::Response object, we can obtain a context object (i.e., ref($c) eq 'MyApp'), which makes it much easier to inspect the internal state of our $c object at the end of each request than has been possible in the past.

```
my ($res,$c) = ctx_request( $req );
ok( $res,            "  Requested " . $req->uri );
ok( $res->is_success,
                     "  Request succeeded" );
ok( $c->stash->{message},
                     "       Diagnostic message recorded" );
ok( $c->stash->{result},
                     "       Stash filled" );
```

See Also

The documentation for Catalyst::Test and Test::WWW::Mechanize::Catalyst. Database Fixtures are useful for keeping production and testing data separate. An example application with some commentary is available at http://dev.catalyst.perl.org/wiki/DatabaseFixtures.

Workflow Testing with Test::WWW::Mechanize::Catalyst

When you run `catalyst.pl` to create an application, a couple of simple tests are created to get you started with your application. These use LWP (lib-www-perl), the World Wide Web library for Perl. This is great—many an industrial-strength web scraper has been built with LWP as its basis—but it is a bit low level, and there's a lot of detail to attend to. WWW::Mechanize is (sort of) to LWP what Catalyst is to CGI.pm: a higher-level abstraction of the common workflow patterns for requesting and getting data from a web server.

Let's quickly look at Catalyst::Test first. When you start a Catalyst application, with the `catalyst.pl` helper script, you end up with a test script in the `t/01app.t` file. This file contains the following two lines:

```
BEGIN { use_ok 'Catalyst::Test', 'MyApp' }
ok( request('/')->is_success, 'Request should succeed' );
```

This is not terribly useful, and a better coding style would suggest that the second line should be rewritten as follows:

```
my $req = request('/');
ok( $req->is_success, "Request succeeds");
```

Now we can access the content with `$req->content`. Given that we have a standard vanilla Catalyst application, we can test for the presence of the string "Welcome to the world of Catalyst":

```
like ($req->content, qr/Welcome to the world of Catalyst/,
        "Content contains hello world text");
```

Things become a bit more awkward if you want to deal with form submissions or other types of GET or POST data. Recall how we make POST requests:

```
use HTTP::Request::Common;
my $req = request POST '/page', [
    bar => 'baz',
    something => 'else'
];
like ($req->content, qr/Some expected content here/,
      "Content contains expected content after form submission");
```

It's verbose and fairly inconvenient for behavior testing. For the usual case where you're grabbing a form from a web page, putting values in the form, and submitting the form, it's much easier to use Test::WWW::Mechanize::Catalyst. This module is a combination of Test::WWW::Mechanize and Test::Catalyst. Test::WWW::Mechanize in turn is an adaptation of WWW::Mechanize with added functions to make testing more convenient. WWW::Mechanize itself is a set of convenience functions built on top of lower-level components from the LWP (lib-www-perl) library. Aside from the convenience of having the low-level stuff wrapped up in convenience functions, the documentation for the three important modules (WWW::Mechanize, Test::WWW::Mechanize, and Test::WWW::Mechanize::Catalyst) is a fair bit easier to understand than the LWP documentation.

Let's rewrite our first test using Test::WWW::Mechanize::Catalyst.

```
use Test::WWW::Mechanize::Catalyst;
my $mech = Test::WWW::Mechanize::Catalyst->new(catalyst_app => 'MyApp');
$mech->get('/');
$mech->content_contains("Welcome to the world of Catalyst",
                        "Content contains hello world text");
```

Say we had a form submission part of our application. WWW::Mechanize parses the HTML to find form names and submission details, so we need to provide this information so it knows what to submit to:

```
$mech->submit_form( form_number => 1,
                    fields      => {
                                    bar => 'baz',
                                    something => 'else'
                                   }
);
$mech->content_contains("Some expected content here",
        "Content contains expected content after form submission");
```

If no such form exists, then Test::WWW::Mechanize::Catalyst will die. Note that we could use form_name = 'name_of_form' instead of form_number instead, or if we were only interested in the first or only form in the page we can omit the form_number or form_name argument from our code.

See Also

As noted, the documentation for WWW::Mechanize, Test::WWW::Mechanize, and Test:: WWW::Mechanize::Catalyst is pretty good. For an example of a simple application that used Test::WWW::Mechanize::Catalyst extensively during development, look at the t/01app.t file in the My Personal Home Page application at http://github.com/singingfish/my-personal-home-page/tree/master.

Write a Minimal Test Case to Troubleshoot

It's fairly normal during software development to come across a bug in your software or another implementation problem that you're having trouble explaining. It often makes sense to make a minimal test case to try to expose the problem. Usually this shows you that there's an issue with some aspect of configuration of your application. This kind of thing frequently happens when you've been thinking about the programming design of your application but are having trouble decoupling the independent components in your mind. To that end, here's the shortest possible Catalyst application:

```
package MyTestApp;
use parent qw/Catalyst/;
__PACKAGE__->setup();
```

Obviously, this application doesn't actually do anything, but it's a starting point. Now we can use this to build a self-contained test script:

```perl
#!/usr/bin/perl
use warnings;
use strict;
use Test::More tests => 1;

{
    package MyTestApp;
    use parent qw/Catalyst/;
    __PACKAGE__->setup();
}
```

This minimal application is only really useful to test internal methods (e.g., to check the integrity of MyTestApp->config). The application has no controllers and no way of making a request so, for example, ok($req->is_success, "request succeeds") will fail as there is no default method and in fact no Catalyst::Controllers in the application at all. For a really simple application, we can do the following:

```perl
#!/usr/bin/perl
use warnings;
use strict;
use Test::More tests => 3;

{
 package MyTestApp;
 use parent qw/Catalyst/;
 use parent qw/Catalyst::Controller/;
 __PACKAGE__->setup();

 sub default :Path  {
     my ($self, $c) = @_;
     $c->res->body('default action');
   }

}

use_ok "Catalyst::Test", "MyTestApp";
my $req = request('/');
ok($req->is_success, 'request succeeds');
is($req->content, "default action", "expected content");
```

Eventually, declaring our application inline with the tests will become cumbersome, and we'll want the test application elsewhere. At this point, we can move our application into a lib directory and give it the name MyTestApp.pm. We place the code for our minimal application in that file, remembering the line of code at the end that just says 1; and replacing the inline application with the following code:

```
use FindBin qw/$Bin/;
use lib "$Bin/lib";
```

FindBin locates the directory of the currently running script (sample.t in this case) and exposes it through the $Bin variable, as instructed.

At this point, we have all the tools we need to write tiny test cases. As you can see, it's pretty straightforward to write your own Catalyst code for a test application or use the catalyst.pl and myapp_create.pl helper scripts to do the scaffolding for you. Writing a minimal test case, along with use of the debugger (see Chapter 3), or using Devel::REPL can assist you in identifying bugs in your code and help improve your understanding of your application's implementation in a quick and efficient manner.

See Also

Refer to the documentation for Test::More, the book *Perl Testing: A Developer's Notebook* by Ian Langworth (O'Reilly, 2005), Chapter 3 of this book, and the recipe titled "Alternative to perl -d: Devel::REPL and CatalystX::REPL."

Bash Aliases to Make Starting the Development Server Easier

Note Thanks to Jonathan Rockway for the basics of this recipe.

It's easy to get sick of typing (or auto_completing) the following code all the time:

```
script/myapp_server.pl
script/myapp_server.pl -d
CATALYST_DEBUG=0 script/myapp_server.pl
```

and so on. If you're on a Unix system using the Bash shell, then you can add this to the .bash_ profile file in your home directory:

```
alias cats='CATALYST_DEBUG=0 script/*server.pl'
alias catsd='script/*server.pl -d'
alias catsdd='CATALYST_DEBUG=0 perl -d script/*server.pl -d '
alias catsddd='CATALYST_DEBUG=1 perl -d script/*server.pl '
```

Once you're in the application's root directory, you can then issue the command cats to run the server without debugging switched on (note the use of the CATALYST_DEBUG environment variable to override the possible presence of the -Debug flag in the application setup) or catsd to run with the server debug output switched on. The last two are for use with the Perl debugger. catsdd will run with the internal debugging output switched on. This is usually undesirable due to the large volume of output it can produce, so we also make an alias for running without the debug output: catsddd. Now running the development server is as simple as this:

```
$ cats
You can connect to your server at http://localhost:3000
```

Equivalent techniques are available for other Unix shells, such as csh and ksh. Unfortunately, if you're developing on Windows, this is probably one of the many convenient Unix features that you're missing out on.

Alternative to perl -d: Devel::REPL and CatalystX::REPL

Devel::REPL is an interactive shell for Perl. REPL stands for *read, evaluate, print, loop.* It can be used with Catalyst as an alternative to the Perl debugger. However, because Catalyst does a lot of error trapping behind the scenes, we use the CPAN module CatalystX::REPL to make debugging our Catalyst application straightforward. First, we install CatalystX::REPL from CPAN. To make use of CatalystX::REPL, which is another Moose role, we need to modify the use parent 'Catalyst' line in MyApp.pm with the following:

```
use Moose;
extends 'Catalyst';
with 'CatalystX::REPL';
use namespace::autoclean;
```

To demonstrate the usage of Devel::REPL, we can then place a die statement in our code. We'll put this line after the my ($self, $c) = @_; line in the index sub in MyApp::Controller:: Root:

```
die "ERROR!";
```

Next, we run the development server with the CATALYST_REPL environment variable set to true:

```
$ CATALYST_REPL=1 script/myapp_server.pl
```

Now when we request http://localhost:3000, the page appears to load and then gets "stuck." Over in our shell, we get a rather long stack trace and a prompt. In the prompt, we can examine data. Devel::REPL just prints out data if we type it in. It will return either an exception for bits of data that don't exist or just an empty string.

Here's an example session from an application:

```
$ CATALYST_REPL=1 script/myapp_server.pl
[output snipped]
You can connect to your server at http://fenchurch.local:3000
```

Then we pop over to our browser and request the application home page, and in our terminal we get the following output:

```
Catalyst::run('MyApp', 3000, undef, 'HASH(0x801764)')
    called at script/myapp_server.pl line 57
$ ▐
```

It happens that while the Perl debugger has special commands like x $data, in Devel:: REPL to see the contents of some data, you just need to type the variable. Let's look at $c:

```
$ $c
$MyApp1 = MyApp=HASH(0xdf24f0);
$ ▐
```

Not that useful by itself. However, we can interrogate the $c object quite effectively:

```
$ $c->action
$Catalyst_Action1 = index;
```

To get a dump of the action, we need to write some Perl:

```
$ use YAML;
$ Dump $c->action

--- !!perl/hash:Catalyst::Action
attributes:
  Args:
    - 0
  Path:
    - ''
  class: MyApp::Controller::Root
  code: !!perl/code '{ "DUMMY" }'
  name: index
  namespace: ''
  reverse: index
```

Something REPL doesn't provide for you that the Perl debugger does is the ability to add breakpoints during a session. However, if we have code that throws an error, REPL will stop at the error. So we can replace our original die "Error! "; statement with the following:

```
$c->model('Wrong')->explode;
```

Now if we run the code with the CATALYST_REPL environment variable enabled, we'll drop to REPL until we either fix the syntax error or create the Catalyst model None with the method do_something.

See Also

Refer to the documentation for CatalystX::REPL, Carp::REPL (upon which CatalystX::REPL is based), and Devel::REPL.

For usage of the Perl debugger, see perldoc perldebug. For running Catalyst applications under the Perl debugger, the $DB::single=1 statement (documented in perldebug) is particularly useful.

Summary

This chapter presented a cookbook consisting of short recipes for Catalyst programming. We covered a wide range of programming techniques and tricks that don't really fit into other parts of the book.

The next and final chapter of the book covers the Reaction framework, which is an advanced framework built on top of Catalyst.

CHAPTER 12

∎∎∎

The Reaction Component UI Framework

By this point, you should be well acquainted with Catalyst, and you may have written a few applications. The more you work with Catalyst, the more you'll find yourself wishing you didn't have to rewrite all that browser-application validation for your forms, lists, and pretty much most of the user interface. You'll start noticing how a tag cloud is just a special case of your preexisting CRUD row, listing and how displaying row data is very similar to displaying an update form (just remove the buttons and input field tags around the data).

Of course, building an application from structured, flexible, and reusable components is not an easy task, but during the course of this chapter, we'll explore how the Reaction framework can bring you closer to reusing your code to quickly build elegant and consistent Catalyst applications. We'll start with an overview of Reaction, and then we'll move on to an example application that provides a form to send an e-mail.

Reaction Overview

Reaction is a framework built on Catalyst that is more flexible and abstract. While Catalyst applies the Model/View/Controller (MVC) design, Reaction takes this a step further and splits the model into two parts: the Domain Model and the Interface Model. The *Domain Model* is (for most purposes) a representation of the business of a part of your application. The *Interface Model* is the representation of the mode of interaction with the Domain Model.

Splitting up the extra model stage into MMVC (for Model/Model/View/Controller) is what provides Reaction's flexibility. While it is built on top of Catalyst, Reaction is a separate framework that provides you with a greater level of abstraction for your business rules. This in turn means that your application code can be used not only for the Web (although this is where Reaction development has concentrated to date), but also for other representations of the same workflow (e.g., command-line programs and traditional GUIs).

Now that you have a good idea of what Reaction *is*, we'd like to address what it *isn't*:

- *Just a form validator.* Although it's easy to validate your forms by using Reaction, this is only one of the many things Reaction can do for you.

- *An Ajax library.* While Ajax can be used in your application with no negative side effects, it is not remotely related to how Reaction functions.

- *A CRUD framework.* We presented code for performing create, review, update, and delete (CRUD) functions by hand in Chapter 6. Initially, Reaction was developed using CRUD as a proof of concept for code reuse merely because that is one of the most common and well-known use cases. It has since evolved to accommodate many other needs of a typical user interface. Throughout this chapter, we will build a CRUD application from Reaction's building blocks, and then we'll demonstrate how to customize and extend it.

The Reaction Arsenal

At this point, we're going to go quickly through the programming concepts that Reaction uses. There are quite a few, and it will take some effort to digest them all. Once you've read through this section once, you'll then want to look at the sample application. If you're still interested in Reaction after doing so, then you'll want to read this section at least one more time.

Besides the traditional Catalyst/DBIx::Class/TT rig, Reaction boosts your application by adding Moose's introspection features into the mix, which add powerful development resources to your bag of tricks.

Metaprogramming

Metaprogramming is a technique whereby code can manipulate its own data at either compile time or runtime. Although it has many advantages, the most useful feature by far provided by metaprogramming is *introspection*, which allows the definition of a business model core that can then be reflected into other components of the system. In practice, that means you can have an entire set of distinct and unrelated user interface elements based on the same class. Recall the Point example from Chapter 2:

```
class Point;

has 'x' => ( is => 'rw', isa => 'Int' );
has 'y' => ( is => 'rw', isa => 'Int' );
```

To many of us, Moose is simply a clean, maintainable way to do Perl OO, add accessors and validation, and abstract things we do commonly. But it is actually much more. Its introspection facilities allow us to give semantic meaning to attributes, classes, and methods. You can easily think of the preceding code represented as a database table:

```
CREATE TABLE point (
  x INTEGER,
  y INTEGER
);
```

Or how about using the metadata you have available so you never have to write a form again?

```
<form name="point">
  <input name="x" value="...">
  <input name="y" value="...">
</form>
```

Both the database table and the HTML from the form can be inferred by the class definition. These are very basic examples, and Reaction allows you to define very complex systems in this manner.

Infrastructure

In a Reaction application, the back end and front end are completely decoupled and unaware of specific implementation details because they communicate via Reaction's API. On every request, the front end triggers mutation on the back end by dispatching events, and the front end then updates itself by observing the resulting back-end state, thus reflecting any changes. The following is an outline of the individual components of the Reaction API.

- *Domain Model*: As we have tried to recommend throughout this book for ordinary Catalyst applications, the Domain Model in a Reaction application is not part of the framework—it contains only your business logic. A typical example would be your DBIx::Class schema. This will be used wherever your application needs to handle your domain. This might mean command-line scripts like cron jobs. The Domain Model will be exposed to your web application (and ideally all other user interface parts in your system) through the Interface Model.

- *Interface Model*: The Interface Model defines the API through which the front end of the application talks to the back end. It's the central joining piece for all the other elements of your application. Reaction provides basic Interface Model classes that work out of the box and can be extended for your own specific needs. This API layer is what gives the application's interface logic a consistent way of access, so things like reusable, extendable CRUD operations are made possible. For common tasks like building an Interface Model from a DBIx::Class schema that has all components required for record management (i.e., CRUD), Reaction provides reflectors that inflate an Interface Model from a specific Domain Model implementation.

- ViewPorts: A ViewPort is an abstraction that represents the application's UI logic. ViewPorts provide all the business logic and data needed to interact with the user and render a specific piece of the application UI. Every ViewPort has a "location"—a string that uniquely identifies the ViewPort and allows Reaction to find it in the ViewPort hierarchy.

- *Event system*: An *event* is a signal that notifies the application when any interaction occurs. It's handled by the ViewPort responsible for the region of the UI where the interaction took place. Reaction automatically maps events into ViewPort methods and parameters, and dispatches them to the correct ViewPort, based on its location.

- **Widgets:** A Widget contains rendering logic for a given ViewPort and provides a communication layer between the ViewPort and the templates. Widgets decide what bits of the templates and what data to render for each given ViewPort state.

- **Layouts:** A Layout is a template definition used by the Widget in order to render a piece of the ViewPort. Layouts are packaged in files called LayoutSets. LayoutSets can inherit from each other, which means you can override any given Layout in the set.

Basic Interface Model Components

Remember that the Interface Model exposes your Domain Model via an API that can be used by the view logic to build your user interfaces. These are the most basic components that make up the Interface Model infrastructure. Reaction already ships with some commonly used Interface Model components, and the number of these can be expected to grow in the future.

The Domain Models that are exposed by your Interface Model can vary in shape, size, and type. They can be records from your storage layer, objects that simply operate on data given to them, or even something as basic as your user's session.

The sections that follow briefly describe the basic Interface Model components.

Objects

These are the objects or entities your application's users will be provided with, such as images or profiles. The Object Interface Model is also the base class for collections.

Collections

Collections are a grouping of Interface Model objects. To Reaction, there is not much difference between an object and a collection in the Interface Model. While collections can be introspected the same way, Reaction already ships with many components that ease the use of collections.

Actions

Actions contain the programming logic to be performed on an object or a collection. Examples of shipped actions are DBIC actions for resultsets or rows, Login, ChangePassword, ResetPassword, and SetPassword. These actions represent the things your user can do in your domain.

Reflectors

Reaction introduces the concept of reflectors that inflate an Interface Model with all its basic components out of an introspectable Domain Model. The most typical example is an Interface Model exposing your storage layer by building collections, objects, and actions (such as create, update, and delete) by introspecting a DBIx::Class schema.

Basic UI Components

While the Interface Model defines the entities and the operations that can be performed on them, the UI parts of Reaction are just as flexible when it comes to building an actual user interface. We'll cover these components in the sections that follow.

ViewPorts, Layouts, Skins, and Widgets

In a traditional Catalyst application, the controller would take data from the model and prepare it so the view can process it in its templates.

In Reaction, the controller merely passes an Interface Model target (or many or even none, to be precise) to a ViewPort and pushes that on the *focus stack*. You can think of this stack as the contents of your page from the outside in. First you have the SiteLayout that wraps your whole page, defining headers, the title, and so on. Below that could be a ViewPort that shows objects in a collection, all represented by ViewPorts themselves.

All of these ViewPorts are held in a UI Window instance. Reaction will flush this instance when it is time to render the page, and the Window will then build the page out of the ViewPorts in its FocusStack.

Each ViewPort will determine the LayoutSet that is used to render it. These LayoutSets are snippets of template code called Layouts. The LayoutSet itself will also define what Widget will be involved in the render. The Widget carries the implementation to render the ViewPort with the Layouts in the LayoutSet.

So to summarize, the controller will tell Reaction of the structure and data for the interface to build via ViewPorts. A LayoutSet will determine how the ViewPort will look, and the Widget will provide the Perl implementation back end.

Finally, Reaction bundles LayoutSets (and static content for the Layout, of course) in skins, which can also adjust the Widgets that are defined in the LayoutSets in it. Skins, LayoutSets, and Widgets can be subclassed and extended like you would expect from a flexible framework.

While this might seem confusing at first, the LayoutSets keep the whole view logic separated, and it is reusable and extendable. If you want to change the headers of your HTML output, you can simply extend the SiteLayout LayoutSet alone for your application, using one of Reaction's default skins for the rest of your application.

These classes usually come in groups. You have a SiteLayout ViewPort carrying all the information and logic that is needed to render the outer frame of your page. The default LayoutSet and Widget can be found under the same name, with the Widget containing the implementation on how the fragments are rendered and the LayoutSet providing the markup.

Objects

Objects are used to render an Interface Model object, like a user profile, an image, or even something as simple as a form field.

Collections

There are many ways to display Interface Model collections in Reaction. Among the typical use cases are the plain listing components that are ideal to extend upon; there are grids to render rows of members with multiple fields, and of course everything to implement typical CRUD collection handling.

Actions

Actions are needed to transform your Interface Model actions into user interface components such as links and buttons, as well as complex forms and multiform wizards.

Example Reaction Application

In this section, we'll create a small and simple Reaction application to provide context for the chapter content to this point. The application will provide a simple form that sends an e-mail to a single e-mail address.

First, you'll need to install Reaction from CPAN. Depending on the modules that you've already installed, this could take some time.

Setup

We'll start off by creating a normal Catalyst application:

```
$catalyst.pl MailerExample::UI
[ snip lots of output ]
```

Next, we create some directories that are required by Reaction:

```
$ cd MailerExample
$ mkdir -p share/skin/mailer/layout
```

We'll use this later to store all the information about the user interface details.

Our Interface Model

The core of our application will be the Interface Model. Since our application will be fairly simple, we have only two parts: the mailer interface model and the send action. Let's take a look at the mailer:

```
package MailerExample::InterfaceModel::Mailer;
use Reaction::InterfaceModel::ObjectClass;

use Email::Stuff;
use aliased 'MailerExample::InterfaceModel::Mailer::Send';

use namespace::clean -except => 'meta';

sub send {
    my ($self, %args) = @_;

    Email::Stuff->new
        ->using('SMTP', Host => 'smtp.example.com')
        ->from($args{sender})
        ->to('you@example.com')
        ->subject($args{subject})
        ->text_body($args{message})
        ->send or die "Unable to send mail with error: $!";
}
```

```
sub send_action {
    my ($self) = @_;
    return Send->new(target_model => $self);
}

1;
```

Tip If you want to see this application working, replace you@example.com with your e-mail address and smtp.example.com with your Internet service provider's SMTP server. If you want to use another option (e.g., Sendmail or an authenticating SMTP server), you'll want to read the documentation for Email::Stuff and Email::Send.

The Reaction::InterfaceModel::Object import will set up this class as an Interface Model object and provide us with Moose's syntactic sugar. We use Email::Stuff here to do the actual e-mail sending. All in all, it is a typical Perl class except for the send_action method. This method will return an instance of the Mailer::Send Interface Model action having the mailer as a target_model. You can think of the target_model as "the object the action is performed on."

Here is what this action should look like:

```
package MailerExample::InterfaceModel::Mailer::Send;
use Reaction::Class;

use MooseX::Types::Moose    qw( Str );
use Reaction::Types::Core   qw( NonEmptySimpleStr );
use Reaction::Types::Email  qw( EmailAddress );

use namespace::clean -except => 'meta';
extends 'Reaction::InterfaceModel::Action';

has sender => (
    is         => 'rw',
    isa        => EmailAddress,
    required   => 1,
    lazy_fail  => 1,
);

has subject => (
    is         => 'rw',
    isa        => NonEmptySimpleStr,
    required   => 1,
    lazy_fail  => 1,
);
```

```perl
has message => (
    is          => 'rw',
    isa         => Str,
    required    => 1,
    lazy_fail   => 1,
);

sub do_apply {
    my ($self) = @_;

    my $mailer = $self->target_model;
    $mailer->send(map { ($_ => $self->$_) } qw( sender subject message ));

    return 1;
}


1;
```

This is, again, just a Moose class initialized when using Reaction::Class. We use MooseX::Types libraries to import the Str, NonEmptySimpleStr, and EmailAddress types that we use to declare our attributes. These types tell Reaction how to handle the fields. These are either standard Moose types or user-defined types provided by Reaction. The types in the MailerExample::InterfaceModel::Mailer::Send class are as follows:

- Str: A normal string like Perl knows them. This is a Moose core type, and for us it means the message field will be rendered as a simple textarea.

- EmailAddress: This type is used to declare that the sender is in form of a valid e-mail address. This is what we want, since we pass this value to our mailer's send method. This will be rendered as a normal input field and the form field will automatically be validated against this.

- NonEmptySimpleStr: Like Str, but it's only valid when not it's not empty and doesn't contain newlines. Since the input can be only one line, Reaction knows that it can use a normal text input form field to manipulate or request that value.

These types are used to determine the rendered output of each field as well as its validation. There are many more types available, including advanced behaviors that come in handy when you use this facility to build CRUD applications out of Moose-based database schema descriptions.

The do_apply method does the real work. It fetches the mailer out of the (inherited) target_model attribute and calls send with its attributes as arguments. It returns 1 to suggest success. For a production application, this method would be where you would check for errors during the sending of mail.

The View

Returning to our UI application, we will need a view. Since Reaction's rendering infrastructure is component based, the view is implemented a bit differently from the standard Catalyst view style. That's why Reaction ships with its own View base class that you can just extend:

```
package MailerExample::UI::View::Site;
use Reaction::Class;

use namespace::clean -except => 'meta';

extends 'Reaction::UI::View::TT';

1;
```

Remember the share/skin/mailer/layout directory we created during the setup of our environment? That's the place where all skin-specific files will go. We need to tell our view which skin it should use, so it will be able to find our files. For this, we edit the mailerexample_ui.conf file and add the following:

```
<View Site>
    skin_name mailer
</View>
```

The Skin

Our skin will be very simple, so it makes sense to let Reaction do the heavy lifting and go forward from there with our own additions and modifications. To tell Reaction that our skin named mailer extends the skin called default, we create a file named share/skin/mailer/skin.conf containing only this:

```
extends /Reaction/default
```

That's all we need to set up our own skin.

Tying the Interface Model to the Application

We first need to hook up our Interface Model with our application so we can access it. It is a straightforward Moose class, so we can just use Catalyst::Model::Adaptor:

```
package MailerExample::UI::Model::Mail;
use strict;
use warnings;
use parent qw( Catalyst::Model::Adaptor );
use aliased 'MailerExample::InterfaceModel::Mailer';

__PACKAGE__->config(class => Mailer, args => {});

1;
```

This is all we need to provide our simple Interface Model to our application.

The Root Controller

As this is a simple application, we can put the functionality in the Root controller. Reaction provides a special base class for this. If we wanted to make a non–Root controller chaining to our Root, we'd use the Reaction::UI::Controller base class or one of its specialized forms (mostly for CRUD) as our parent instead. This is what your Root should look like:

```
package MailerExample::UI::Controller::Root;
use parent 'Reaction::UI::Controller::Root';
use Reaction::Class;

use aliased 'Reaction::UI::ViewPort::SiteLayout';
use aliased 'Reaction::UI::ViewPort::Action';
use aliased 'Reaction::UI::ViewPort';

use namespace::clean -except => 'meta';

__PACKAGE__->config(
    namespace => '',
    view_name => 'Site',
);

has site_title => (
    is         => 'rw',
    isa        => 'Str',
    required   => 1,
    default    => 'Reaction MailerExample',
);

sub base: Chained PathPart('') CaptureArgs(0) {
    my ($self, $ctx) = @_;

    $self->push_viewport(SiteLayout,
        static_base_uri => $ctx->uri_for('/static')->as_string,
        title           => $self->site_title,
    );
}

sub form: Chained('base') PathPart('') Args(0) {
    my ($self, $ctx) = @_;

    $self->push_viewport(Action,
        model => $ctx->model('Mail')->send_action,
        field_order => [qw( sender subject message )],
        apply_label => 'Send',
        on_apply_callback => sub {
            $ctx->res->redirect($ctx->uri_for($self->action_for('sent')));
        },
    );
}
```

```
sub sent: Chained('base') PathPart('sent') Args(0) {
    my ($self, $ctx) = @_;

    $self->push_viewport(ViewPort, layout => 'sent');
}

1;
```

The first thing you will notice as being different from the usual Catalyst controllers is that this is obviously a Moose class. We added a site_title attribute to allow the user of the application to configure the title of the rendered page.

We set the corresponding view for this controller to the Site view we created earlier. A base action is provided that our other actions will chain off from. Then we have a form action showing the form asking for the e-mail details and a sent action that will be shown when the e-mail has been sent.

The body of the actions does not look like the usual Catalyst controller action code. There is no stashing of values for the template; instead, we push ViewPorts. The base action will push a SiteLayout containing the framework of the page, the head, the body, and the title that we specify from our configurable attribute.

Inside the SiteLayout's body, we want to render a form. So we push an Action ViewPort in the form action that chains to base. This means (semantically) that the Action ViewPort is inside the SiteLayout one.

As arguments to the Action ViewPort, we're passing our mailer's send action, which we get by accessing the Mail model defined earlier.

The field_order and apply_label arguments are self-explanatory. With on_apply_ callback, we tell Reaction what it should do after our send action's do_apply method returns a true value to indicate success. We tell it to redirect to the sent action in the same controller.

The sent action is very simple. We just want to display a message, so we don't need any special logic and simply use the basic ViewPort.

Here we need to pass in a layout option with the name of the LayoutSet to use.

The LayoutSet

The LayoutSet tells Reaction how this region of the page should be rendered. For our simple purposes, we create a file named share/skin/mailer/layout/sent.tt containing the following:

```
=widget Sent

=for layout widget

Email sent!

=cut
```

The LayoutSet is built of fragments and set up using POD directives. We see a layout fragment named widget, which is always the root fragment, that contains our very simple "Email sent!" message. The =widget directive tells Reaction which Widget is required to render this LayoutSet. Since this Widget doesn't yet exist, we need to create it.

The Widget

To render our message, we need only the most basic Widget functionality. This can be as simple as the following:

```
package MailerExample::UI::Widget::Sent;
use Reaction::UI::WidgetClass;

use namespace::clean -except => 'meta';

1;
```

We can also provide implementation details for the layout fragments, defining their order and providing them with prepared data.

Reaction doesn't yet know about the MailerExample::UI::Widget namespace, so we need to tell it by creating share/skin/defaults.conf with these contents:

```
widget_search_path MailerExample::UI::Widget
widget_search_path Reaction::UI::Widget
```

Now Reaction will first look for every Widget in our namespace before checking its own. This also means that we can easily extend existing Widgets by subclassing them and putting them under the same name in our namespace.

Running the Application

And that's it. You can run script/mailerexample_ui_server.pl to try out the application and you will be presented with a (still rather unstyled, as we didn't concern ourselves with CSS) form with sender, subject, and message fields as well as a Send button.

Summary

This chapter presented a complete Reaction application from beginning to end. We built an Interface Model that is abstracted from our UI and can be used anywhere else (e.g., in non-Web GUI applications), and we created our own skin and provided our own additional Widget.

Reaction comes with many prewritten components such as ViewPorts, Widgets, base skins with all the common LayoutSets, and reflectors to turn your DBIx::Class schemas into Interface Models including objects, collections, and actions.

APPENDIX A

■ ■ ■

Compiling Your Own Perl

Compiling Perl on a Unix-like system is simple. First, obtain the source for Perl from CPAN (http://cpan.perl.org/src/README.html). Then input the following sequence of commands:

```
$ tar zxvf perl-5.8.8.tar.gz
$ cd perl-5.8.8
$ sh Configure -des
$ make
$ make test
$ sudo make install
```

On most Unix systems, this code will result in your perl being installed into the /usr/local/ directory tree. If you want it installed elsewhere—for example, in the local directory in your home directory—then replace sh Configure -de with the following:

```
$ sh Configure -des -Dprefix=~/local/
```

which should enable you to install Perl on your computer without root access.

Note that the -des flag uses all the default options for compiling Perl. If you know that you want nonstandard configuration, just use the flag -de instead to be prompted for your requirements.

Be aware that the source for Perl 5.10.0 requires a patch to work properly with Catalyst. This is fixed in subsequent versions of Perl 5.10.

If you need to test code guaranteed to run on a wide range of systems, you should consider using Perl version 5.8.7. Perl versions greater than 5.8.7 contain features that were not available in earlier versions of Perl, so Perl 5.8.7 is feature complete for all versions of Perl that Catalyst will run on (version 5.8.1 and later). Put another way, versions 5.8.8 and later have new features that you can't rely on in earlier releases. This should only be important to you if you're going to be programming libraries for CPAN that will be used very heavily, and you're having to pay very close attention to Perl's internals.

Further details for installation of Perl are available in the INSTALL file in the Perl distribution. If you are on a non-Unix system and you want to compile Perl, you will want to look at INSTALL.*yourplatform* (e.g., INSTALL.w32 for Windows) as well. However, for Windows we recommend Strawberry Perl (http://strawberryperl.com).

Once you've compiled Perl, you need to make sure that your PATH environment variable is set. Assuming you installed Perl into /local, you need to put /local/bin in your path. The best way of doing this (assuming that your shell is Bash) is to put the following in your .bashrc:

```
export PATH=$HOME/local/bin:$PATH
export MANPATH=$HOME/local/man:$MANPATH
```

Issue the command echo $SHELL and ensure that the output is /bin/bash or at that it at least ends in /bash to make sure that you're using the Bash shell.

Once you've done this, you need to either log off and then log in again or issue the following command from the shell:

```
$ source .bashrc
```

Patching Perl 5.10.0 to Work (Properly) with Catalyst

Details on how to fix this issue are described here: http://www.nntp.perl.org/group/perl. perl5.changes/2008/02/msg21106.html.

Condensing the instructions from this bug report, you should download Perl 5.10 (http:// www.cpan.org/src/perl-5.10.0.tar.gz). Prior to following the instructions in the main part of this appendix, modify the file toke.c (toplevel) on line 692 as follows (presented in diff format):

```
#else
    parser->nexttoke = 0;
#endif
+    parser->error_count = oparser ? oparser->error_count : 0;
    parser->copline = NOLINE;
    parser->lex_state = LEX_NORMAL;
    parser->expect = XSTATE;
```

APPENDIX B

■ ■ ■

Making Your Own CPAN Mirror with CPAN::Mini or minicpan.sh

Catalyst is very heavy on CPAN dependencies, so it can be useful to have your own CPAN mirror on your local machine or local network. Using CPAN::Mini, especially on a slow network, speeds downloading of CPAN modules dramatically and is recommended for anyone doing a lot of Perl development.

CPAN::Mini is available by installing it from CPAN. An alternative is minicpan.sh, which is available from http://trout.me.uk/perl/mirror.sh.txt. We'll describe using CPAN::Mini here. The advantage of the minicpan.sh script is that you can uncomment a single line and get a full CPAN mirror. minicpan.sh is also a good bit faster than CPAN::Mini.

First, install CPAN::Mini from the shell:

```
$ cpan CPAN::Mini
```

Next, create a .minicpanrc file in your home directory with the following content:

```
local:  /path/to/your/cpan/mirror
remote: http://your.closest.cpan.mirror
exact_mirror: 1
```

Then you can run the minicpan command from your shell:

```
$ minicpan
```

The first command installs CPAN::Mini, and the second makes a mirror of the fairly complete contents of the most relevant parts of the CPAN archive.

Once this is done, you can configure CPAN to use your local mirror:

```
$ cpan
cpan> o conf set urllist file:///home/kd/minicpan/
cpan> o conf commit
```

Note that you need to use the absolute path to the `minicpan` directory in your home directory as just shown.

You can update your mirror at any time by reissuing the `minicpan` command. As noted, it's best to have this as an automated job running daily.

Browsing Your minicpan on the Web

You can install the module CPAN::Mini::Webserver from CPAN to provide a web interface to browse your current `minicpan`. Once the module is installed, you just run the command `minicpan_webserver` from the shell, and then point your browser to `http://localhost:2963` (although the port is configurable). From here, you can make your `minicpan` and web server accessible over the local network so that small groups can use the local mirror.

Index

■XYZ

CPSIA information can be obtained at www.ICGtesting.com
Printed in the USA
LVOW050033191011

251050LV00002B/13/P

9 781430 223658